Dodgers Vs. Yankees

Dodgers *vs.* Yankees

THE LONG-STANDING RIVALRY BETWEEN
TWO OF BASEBALL'S GREATEST TEAMS

MICHAEL SCHIAVONE

SPORTS
PUBLISHING

Sports Publishing books may be purchased in bulk at special discounts for sales promotion, corporate gifts, fund-raising, or educational purposes. Special editions can also be created to specifications. For details, contact the Special Sales Department, Sports Publishing, 307 West 36th Street, 11th Floor, New York, NY 10018 or sportspubbooks@skyhorsepublishing.com.

Sports Publishing® is a registered trademark of Skyhorse Publishing, Inc.®, a Delaware corporation.

Visit our website at www.sportspubbooks.com.

10 9 8 7 6 5 4 3 2

Library of Congress Cataloging-in-Publication Data is available on file.

Cover design by 5mediadesign
Cover photo credit: Getty Images

Print ISBN: 978-1-68358-314-1
Ebook ISBN: 978-1-68358-315-8

Printed in China

For Su Lan and Valentina

CONTENTS

PREFACE

THE **LOS ANGELES** Dodgers and the New York Yankees are two of the storied and most popular teams in not only baseball, but all of sport. Their rivalry began in New York and continued even with the Dodgers leaving Brooklyn and moving to Los Angeles. The Dodgers and Yankees have met each other a record eleven times in the World Series. For a long time, the Dodgers-Yankees rivalry was *the* marquee matchup in baseball.

This is common knowledge to almost all baseball fans in New York and Los Angeles and any baseball aficionado. Yet I have a confession to make. For a long time I knew little about the teams' intertwined history. I have another confession: I like the New York Yankees. As a Los Angeles Dodgers fan, I am meant to hate the so-called "Evil Empire," but I never could. As I noted in *The Dodgers: 60 Years in Los Angeles*, I became a Dodgers fan while watching Game One of the 1988 World Series. However, growing up in Australia meant there was very little baseball on television. At most, there were the occasional highlights on television once the playoffs began, and if we were lucky, World Series games would be shown, albeit on delay. I had to rely on the local library. Every week I would go to the library to read the "latest" *Sports Illustrated*; by latest I mean at least two months out of date. Ah, the joys of being an American sports fan in Australia back in the 1980s and early 1990s. I read about the Yankees' struggles and how the once-proud franchise was on its knees. Despite their afterthought status, the Yankees became my second-favorite team. It was only later (this was in the pre-Internet era and when baseball books in Australia were in very short supply) that I realized that the Dodgers and Yankees were fierce rivals with the Bronx Bombers almost always being victorious. This should have led me to adopt another team as my second favorite, but I never could. Even when the Yankees were riding roughshod over baseball, I still was cheering them on, especially as the Dodgers were going through their own horrible period. Reading about the Yankees, Dodgers, and baseball in general in *Sports Illustrated* brought me immense joy.

Beginning with the 2005 season, I could finally begin to watch baseball regularly on television as cable television was becoming more widespread in Australia. A dedicated sports channel showed live baseball games a few times a week. Not surprisingly, considering their worldwide popularity, the majority of games shown were ones involving the Yankees. Likewise, when I moved to China, if there was a baseball game on, it almost always involved the Yankees. Even though I would have preferred to be regularly watching the Dodgers (something I could finally do in 2009 when I moved to the United Kingdom and finally had fast enough Internet speed to watch games on MLB.TV), I loved watching Yankees baseball. Their history and tradition made it incredibly enjoyable to me. However, the Yankees' domination over the Dodgers always intrigued me. Were the Yankees so much better than the Dodgers? Were the Dodgers "chokers" when it mattered most? Or was it simply the case that the baseball gods were actually malevolent and favored the team that would be later known to its detractors as the Evil Empire over the boys in blue? In the following pages I will provide a history of the Dodgers-Yankees rivalry and try to answer the question that has mystified me for so many years.

1

THE DODGERS AND
YANKEES BEFORE 1941

THE BROOKLYN GRAYS BECOME
THE BROOKLYN DODGERS

In 1883, the Brooklyn Grays played in the Interstate Association of Professional Baseball Clubs, before joining the American Association the following year. The team won the American Association championship in 1889 before losing to the New York Giants in a version of the World Series. The World Series—a matchup between the National League and American League champions—did not begin until 1903. In 1890, the team left the American Association and joined the National League. Even though the team had the less-than-flattering nickname of the Bridegrooms, they managed to win the National League pennant, compiling an 86–43 record well ahead of the Chicago Colts and the Philadelphia Phillies. The Bridegrooms moniker allegedly was used because seven members of the team got married in 1888. The Bridegrooms went on to tie the American Association champions, the Louisville Colonels, in the World Series. Both teams won three games, and there was one tie. During the Series the weather conditions continually worsened. This led to the managers agreeing that Game Seven, which Louisville won to tie the Series, would be the last game. While a deciding game was meant to be played the following year, it never occurred because of the respective leagues being at loggerheads due to the formation of the Players' League.

During the 1890s and into the new century, the Brooklyn side had other informal monikers such as Ward's Wonders (based on John Montgomery Ward, the skipper from 1891 to 1892), Foutz's Fillies (based on Dave Foutz, the skipper from 1893 to 1896), and Hanlon's Superbas (based on Ned Hanlon, the skipper from 1899 to 1905). Another moniker was attached to the Brooklyn side in the 1890s—Trolley Dodgers.

The term *Trolley Dodgers* first appeared in print in May 1895 and was picked up by other publications throughout the season. In the 1800s, when the city had a number of trolleys, they were initially pulled by horses. Brooklyn residents did not bother to look when they crossed the street because they knew without an ounce of doubt that horses would not run over them. However, when horse trolleys were replaced by electric ones, a number of Brooklyn residents still did not bother to look when they crossed a street. As such, they often had to jump out of the way to prevent from being hit. Many were not quick enough; eight people were killed in 1892, 51 in 1893, and in 1894 34 people were killed by the electric trolleys.

The Trolley Dodgers moniker was frequently used by the media throughout 1896. Eventually "Trolley" was dropped from the name, and the local baseball team simply was known as the Dodgers. However, it was still an informal nickname. From 1899 to 1910, the team was the Superbas. In 1911 and 1912, they were known as the Dodgers, but the following year the team was once again known as the Superbas. From 1914 to 1931, they were known as the Robins (based on Wilbert Robinson, who was then the team's skipper). In 1932, the team was once again the Dodgers. It was not until 1933 that the nickname became permanent, with the Dodgers name being put on the team's jerseys.

While they were a long way from being the powerhouse the Yankees were, the Brooklyn franchise did have some successful seasons. Indeed, they won the National League pennant in 1890, 1899, 1900, 1916, and 1920.

In 1916, the Brooklyn Robins lost in the World Series four games to one to the Boston Red Sox. In Game One, the Red Sox led, 6–1, heading into the top of the ninth. The Robins staged a dramatic comeback, scoring four times and loading the bases with two outs. Unfortunately for Brooklyn fans, Jake Daubert grounded out to short to end the rally. Game Two was a long drawn-out affair with Boston winning, 2–1, with pinch-hitter Del Gainer singling home the winning run for the Red Sox in the bottom of the 14th. Babe Ruth was the winning pitcher, going all 14 innings; for the Robins, Sherry Smith was the unlucky loser despite only giving up two runs in 13 1/3 innings. It would be the longest World Series game until Game Three of the 2005 World Series. The Robins won Game Three, 4–3, with Jack Coombs picking up the victory for Brooklyn as shortstop Ivy Olson drove in two runs. The Robins carried the momentum into the start of Game Four as they took a 2–0 lead after the first inning. However, the Red Sox scored three in the top of the second and were never headed, winning, 6–2. And in Game Five, Ernie Shore pitched a complete game only giving up one run on three hits as the Red Sox beat the Robins, 4–1, and captured the World Series by the same margin.

In 1920, Brooklyn lost, five games to two, to the Cleveland Indians in a best-of-nine series. The Indians took Game One, 3–1, at Ebbets Field in Brooklyn. The opener was played at a very brisk pace and only took one hour and 41 minutes. Future Hall of Fame inductee Stan Coveleski pitched a complete game for the Indians. Ebbets Field was named after Dodgers owner Charles Ebbets. When construction began on the new stadium, Ebbets was planning on calling it Washington Park after the Dodgers' old stadium. In response, the *Brooklyn Times*'s Len Wooster responded, "Washington Park, hell. That name wouldn't mean anything out here. Why don't you call it Ebbets Field? It was your idea and nobody else's, and you've put yourself in hock to build it. It's going to be your monument, whether you like to think about it that way or not." And the rest is history.

The Robins came back and tied the Series with a 3–0 victory in Game Two, and they followed that up with a tight 2–1 triumph in Game Three. Cleveland was never headed in Game Four winning, 5–1, with Coveleski once again throwing a complete game. Game Five had a number of firsts. The first World Series grand slam (courtesy of Indian right fielder Elmer Smith), the first triple play (and unassisted at that, turned by Cleveland second baseman Bill Wambsganss), and the first World Series home run by a pitcher (Cleveland's Jim Bagby). Cleveland ran out winners, 8–1. Game Six was the proverbial pitchers' duel with Sherry Smith giving up only one run over eight innings for the Robins. Once again, Smith was an unlucky loser in a World Series game, as the Robins' anemic offense could not capitalize on three Indians errors as Cleveland won, 1–0, thanks to a run in the sixth and a three-hit shutout by Duster Mails. And facing Coveleski in Game Seven, the Robins did not stand a chance. Coveleski was once again at his brilliant best, as he threw a five-hit shutout as the Indians won, 3–0, and captured their first World Series.

Rather than build on two World Series appearances in five years, Brooklyn instead became a very mediocre team for almost two decades. The best they could manage between 1921 and 1940 were two second-place finishes. In 1924, the Brooklyn Robins finished 1 1/2 games out of first. The team had numerous opportunities to win the pennant down the stretch but could never win when it mattered most. In 1940, the Brooklyn Dodgers finished 12 games behind the Cincinnati Reds but never truly contended for the National League (NL) pennant from mid-July on. Brooklyn (both as the Robins and later as the Dodgers) was just a very average ballclub, usually finishing in the lower half of the eight-team NL.

Indeed, there was another informal nickname bestowed upon the Dodgers in the mid-1930s. The Dodgers of this era were not exactly a model of perfection. The players were seemingly sorely lacking in the basic fundamentals of the game. The team continually committed basic errors, and defeat was more common than victory. Sports cartoonist Willard Mullin heard a cab driver ask, "So how did those bums do today?" and drew a cartoon based on circus clown Emmett Kelly with the heading "Dem Bums."

Rather than take offense at the cartoon, fans loved it, and as such, the Dodgers were dubbed "Dem Bums" by the Brooklyn faithful. Nobody berated and abused the Dodgers more than the Brooklyn fans, but at the same time nobody loved their baseball team more than they did. The Dodgers were a part of Brooklyn, and the borough was a part of them. However, another part of New York City loved a different team: the New York Yankees.

THE NEW YORK HIGHLANDERS BECOME THE NEW YORK YANKEES

Frank Farrell and Bill Devery bought the Baltimore Orioles in January 1903 for the princely sum of $18,000 and moved the franchise to New York. In March, the team was admitted to the American League (AL) and became known as the Highlanders because their home park was at 168th Street and Broadway, one of the highest points topographically on Manhattan island. The New York team was known as the Highlanders until the 1913 season, when their moniker was changed to Yankees following the team's full-time move to the Polo Grounds. The Yankees shared the stadium with the NL's New York Giants. The Yankees would have to wait until 1921 to play in their first World Series, their opponents being the Giants. The Giants captured their fourth World Series crown, beating the Yankees five games to three in the best-of-nine contest. The two teams squared off in the following year's World Series with the Giants once again victorious, winning the title in five games (four victories and a tie in Game Two). The two teams faced each other for the third time in a row in 1923. By then they no longer shared a home ground, as the Yankees moved to the original

Yankee Stadium at the start of the season. In 1920, Giants owner Charles Stoneham attempted to remove the Yankees as co-tenants of the Polo Grounds. While the move was unsuccessful, the Yankees were told that they needed a new home ballpark following the 1922 season. Led by Babe Ruth (an on-base percentage [OBP] of .556 and a slugging percentage [SLG] of 1.000), whom the Yankees acquired from the Red Sox in 1920 in one of the most infamous lopsided trades in baseball history, and pitcher Bullet Joe Bush (who also had a great series with the bat), the Yankees captured their first World Series crown, four games to two. The Yankees finished second in the AL in 1924 and a very disappointing seventh (out of eight teams) in 1925. They recaptured the AL pennant in 1926 before going to losing the World Series, four games to three, to the St. Louis Cardinals. The loss was all the more disheartening considering that Games Six and Seven were played at Yankee Stadium. Ruth was caught stealing to end the Series. Nevertheless, utter domination the likes of which the game has never seen was looming.

The 1927 Yankees were led by the Murderers' Row at the heart of the lineup: Earle Combs, Mark Koenig, Babe Ruth, Lou Gehrig, Bob Meusel, and Tony Lazzeri. There is a debate on how the term Murderers' Row originated. John Thorn, the official historian of Major League Baseball, notes, "The usual etymology for this term is plausible—that it derives from a row of cells in New York's prison popularly termed The Tombs, an area that was reserved for the most dastardly of criminals. . . . The Yankees' deadly lineup may owe its name to a row of entombed villains but the New York City history of the phrase dates to an actual row in what was regarded as a dangerous neighborhood.

Otter's Alley—always spelled in the singular form, never in the plural—which . . . [was] identified as one and the same as Murderers' Row, is mentioned not only in an 1827 book but also in an 1822 city directory. That volume provides a likely explanation for the name of the row, as it was the residence of a mason named James Otter."

The Yankees' Murderers' Row was (pun intended) deadly at the plate; Combs hit .356, with an OPS of .925. Ruth hit 60 home runs (a new single-season record) and drove in 164, with an OPS of 1.258. Gehrig had an OPS of 1.240, hit 47 home runs, and had 175 RBIs on the way to winning the AL MVP award. Meusel hit .337 with an OPS of .902 with 103 RBIs, while Lazzeri hit 18 home runs (third best on the team), with 102 RBIs. The '27 Yankees finished with a record of 110–44 and won the pennant by 19 games over the Philadelphia Athletics. The Yankees swept the Pittsburgh Pirates in four to capture another World Series crown.

The 1928 Yankees were spectacular; they finished with a record of 101–53 on the way to the AL pennant and a four-game sweep of the Cardinals en route to the World Series title. However, the 1929–31 Yankees were never really in contention and finished well behind the Philadelphia Athletics. Nevertheless, the mountaintop once again beckoned, as the 1932 Yankees dominated, going 107–47, winning the AL pennant by 13 games over the Athletics, and sweeping the Cubs in the World Series. That World Series is most remembered for Ruth calling his shot. In Game Three at Chicago in the top of the fifth, the score was tied at 4 with Ruth at the plate and Charlie Root pitching for the Cubs. The Cubs' bench and fans heckled Ruth, a not-uncommon occurrence during the Series.

With the count at 0-1, legend has it that Ruth pointed to center field. Ruth then proceeded to take the next pitch for a strike. He once again pointed to center field. On the next pitch, Ruth hit a massive home run to the deepest part of center field. And the legend of the called shot was born. Just like many things that are legends, there is debate about what actually happened, namely, whether Ruth was pointing to center field or at Root or at the Cubs' bench. For what it is worth, Root claims that Ruth never pointed to center field and if Ruth did such a thing he would have thrown the next pitch high and tight. Indeed, Ruth initially claimed that he was pointing to the Cubs' bench but later changed his story to state that he did call his shot. Whatever the truth, the reality is that the Yankees won the World Series and the called shot is now part of popular American folklore.

After a few "down" years, where they finished runner-up in the AL, the Yankees returned to the summit in 1936, helped in no small part by rookie Joe DiMaggio. The twenty-one-year-old led the team in hits and doubles and was second in home runs and RBI. Gehrig had another outstanding season, winning the AL MVP award while hitting 49 home runs and driving in 152. The '36 Yankees finished with a record of 102–51 and defeated the Giants in the World Series, four games to two. The '37 Yankees were equally fine on the way to defeating the Giants once again in the World Series, this time by a margin of four games to one. The '38 Yankees won 99 games, but it was enough to capture the AL pennant, and they easily swept the Cubs in the World Series. Led by DiMaggio, who captured his first of an eventual three AL MVP awards, the 1939 Yankees were better. They won 106 games, winning the AL pennant by 17 games over the Red Sox and sweeping the Cincinnati Reds in the World Series. Yet as great as the '39 Yankees were, the season will always be remembered for being the last season of Gehrig's Hall of Fame career. He only appeared in eight games and was not his usual self. He was eventually diagnosed with Amyotrophic Lateral Sclerosis (ALS) or, as it eventually became known, Lou Gehrig's disease. Gehrig died on June 2, 1941; he was only thirty-seven.

Perhaps stung by Gehrig's declining health, the 1940 team, while still good, was a shadow of its previous self, winning 88 games and finishing third in the AL (although only two games out of first). And this takes us to the 1941 Yankees and the first-ever meeting with their crosstown rivals, the Brooklyn Dodgers.

2

1941: BEGINNING OF
YANKEES DOMINATION

THE YANKEES AND the Dodgers entered the 1941 season with entirely different mind-sets; this was evident not to everyone involved in the respective organizations, but to the public in New York and across the United States. The Yankees were seven-time World Series champions, a powerhouse in the American League, and, while coming off a relatively poor year in 1940, still had all the attributes of a very successful ballclub. The Dodgers, despite their second-place finish the previous year in the NL (a whopping 12 games behind the Reds), were still seeking their first World Series triumph and were mired in mediocrity. In New York, at least, the Yankees were the proverbial ruling class, the Dodgers were the "lesser," and this can easily be viewed by the Dodgers fans embracing the Dem Bums nickname.

DODGERS VS. YANKEES

The epoch in the baseball world beginning with Murderers' Row and carrying on into the 1940s and 1950s was that of the Yankees. Other teams would challenge the power of the Yankees, but the boys from the Bronx were almost always the team to beat. It would be wrong to view the previous success of the Yankees and the Dodgers' mediocrity in strictly material terms; money matters, but as we shall see, the Yankees' dominance over the Dodgers was due to a number of other factors. However, the idea that the Yankees were *the* dominant team and the Dodgers also-rans was widely accepted. New York's dominance was, of course, widely embraced within their organization and by their fans. While those within Brooklyn's organization would deny that the Yankees were better than they, the idea that the Yankees were the proverbial ruling class, the intellectual force, riding roughshod over baseball had to take root, and the Dem Bums nickname clearly signifies that Dodger fans accepted and even somewhat embraced subjection. That there was a vast difference between the Yankees and Dodgers and their respective fans was perfectly captured by Marty Appel, a former Yankees public relations director, in *Pinstripe Empire*. He states, "Dodger fans were the little guys, the underdogs, the working stiffs from the borough of churches whose players lived in the neighborhood and seemed like regular guys. The Yankees fans were the Wall Street business crowd, better dressed, cockier, and not expecting to really meet any of the players on the street. Their ballpark was staid, proud, awe-inspiring. Ebbets Field was a place you snuck into after five innings, maybe wearing a T-shirt." In a capitalist system, it is the bourgeoisie who dominant and subject the proletariat to their system and ideas. Without necessarily meaning to, Appel clearly laid out the class divide in Marxian terms between the two teams and their fans. The Yankees were the bourgeoisie, the capitalists, the ruling class. The Dodgers and their fans were the proletariat, the working class.

Nevertheless, the 1941 World Series was a chance for the Dodgers to shake up and to overthrow the existing order. Instead, it was the beginning of a rivalry and the domination of the Yankees over the Dodgers.

THE YANKEES' 1941 SEASON

The Yankees were coming off a season where they could only manage third place in the AL. The Yankees faithful were not used to such mediocrity. Indeed, following a doubleheader loss to the Detroit Tigers on July 21, the crowd at Yankee Stadium engaged in unruly acts of petty vandalism as well as throwing food at the umpire. It was not just the fans taking the disappointing season badly, but also journalists. Writing in the *Daily News*, Jimmy Powers had the audacity to question whether some players had contracted polio. The implication was that the players were ill due to interaction with Gehrig. Gehrig was furious and sued Powers and the *Daily News*. The newspaper defensed itself by claiming that the Mayo Clinic (where Gehrig was treated) and the Yankees initially claimed that Gehrig had poliomyelitis, a disease that can be spread through contact. The *Daily News* stated it was only after the story was written and Gehrig sued that they found out that Gehrig did not have a form of polio, but Amyotrophic Lateral Sclerosis. The case never went to trial, with the sides agreeing to a $17,500 settlement.

The 1941 Yankees lineup was largely unchanged compared to the previous year, the main addition being rookie and future

Hall of Famer Phil Rizzuto at shortstop. Rizzuto had a very fine debut season, hitting .307 and finishing 20th in MVP voting. The Yankees had a solid April, going 10–6, but a below-average May, when they went 13–13, which was very disheartening for their fans. Indeed, on May 25, they were seven games out of first. However, a strong last few days of May saw the team only four games out at the start of June. The team went 19–7 for the month and never looked back.

Nevertheless, June 1941 will always be a sad month in Yankees history due to the death of Gehrig. The following month, the Yankees erected a monument in Gehrig's honor at Yankee Stadium. The monument states, "A man, a gentleman and a great ball player whose amazing record of 2,130 consecutive games should stand for all time." The record stood for 56 years before it was surpassed by Baltimore Oriole Cal Ripken Jr., who eventually appeared in an astonishing 2,632 straight games.

In a sad note, Babe Ruth and his wife showed up the worse for wear to the viewing of Gehrig's body. Gehrig's friend, the song-writer Fred Fisher, stated to the *New York Times* that Gehrig's wife, "Eleanor was very composed, having been prepared for the shock. But she became very angry when Ruth and his wife came in very intoxicated. He certainly wasn't wanted by the Gehrigs, as there was friction between them for years." Two of the greatest players in Yankees and baseball history, while they initially respected and admired each other, had fallen out prior to Gehrig's death. While relations between the two had grown frosty over the years, Ruth's public criticism of Gehrig's consecutive-game streak was the proverbial straw that broke the camel's back. Ruth claimed that "This Iron Horse stuff is just a lot of baloney. I think he's making one of the worst mistakes a player can make. He ought to learn to sit on the bench and rest. They're not going to pay off on how many games he's played in a row." While as fans we hope that all teammates are friends off the field, the reality is often painfully different.

On the field, the Yankees became all-conquering. The team went 25–4 in July and increased their lead atop the AL from 1/2 games at the end of June to 12 games just one month later. The Yankees cruised the rest of the year, winning the AL pennant by 17 games and finishing with a record of 101–53. Considering the team's below-average April and May, that they finished with more than 100 victories is nothing short of astonishing.

DiMaggio had a large role in the Yankees' stellar season. He hit .357 with 30 home runs, 43 doubles, and 125 RBIs. He was an All-Star and a worthy AL MVP. There is debate whether he should have won the MVP award considering that Boston Red Sox outfielder Ted Williams hit .406 (the last time a player hit above .400), with 37 home runs, 120 RBIs, 147 walks (DiMaggio had 76), and an OPS of 1.287 to lead the AL (DiMaggio's was 1.083). Undoubtedly the reason DiMaggio won the MVP award was that the Yankees won the pennant and his 56-game hitting streak, a record that still stands today. The previous record belonged to Wee Willie Keeler, who hit in 44 consecutive games in 1897. DiMaggio was no stranger to long hitting streaks; he hit in 61 straight games in the minor leagues in 1933 (the minor league record is 66).

On May 15, DiMaggio came into the game against the Chicago White Sox having a fine season, but he was hitless in his last two games. The Yankees were demolished, 13–1, but in his first at-bat DiMaggio singled in New York's only run. He failed to record a hit in his remaining three at-bats. DiMaggio then proceeded to hit in another 55 games in a row (the All-Star Game occurred during the streak, and while not officially counted toward the record, DiMaggio did manage a hit). The beginning of the streak was unnoticed at first; the *New York Times* first referenced it on June 3: "DiMaggio, incidentally, has hit safely in nineteen straight games." The streak, however, could easily have ended at 35 games. On June 24, DiMaggio was hitless in his first three at-bats against the St. Louis Browns when he came to the plate in the bottom of the eighth with the Yankees leading, 4–0, and nobody on base. Browns manager Luke Sewell told pitcher Bob Muncrief to walk DiMaggio. However, Muncrief refused to do such a thing. And after a heated discussion, Muncrief pitched to DiMaggio and gave up a single. The streak finally ended against the Cleveland Indians on July 17, when DiMaggio went 0-for-3 with a walk. That he failed to register a hit was costly for DiMaggio. If he had hit in 57 straight, he would have earned a cool $10,000 endorsing the Heinz 57 range of products. This aside, the hit streak is very unlikely to be broken (never say never) and was the exclamation point in the Yankees' regular season.

THE DODGERS' 1941 SEASON

Coming off the third-place finish in 1939 and second-place finish in 1940, there were increasing expectations that the Dodgers were becoming a force to be reckoned with in the NL. Yet the Dodgers finished 12 1/2 games out of first in 1939 and 12 games behind in 1940. In neither season did they truly contend for the pennant. However, considering their prior history, such seasons were to be relished. A large part of their turning around their fortunes was due to the hiring of Larry MacPhail as executive vice president. MacPhail introduced night baseball to Ebbets Field, hired manager Leo Durocher, and rejuvenated the Dodgers through a series of trades.

The most (in)famous signing was rookie Pete Reiser from St. Louis. MLB Commissioner Kenesaw Mountain Landis deemed the Cardinals farm system a monopoly. Landis broke up the system, making many players free agents; Reiser was one of them. In 1938, Branch Rickey asked MacPhail to sign Reiser from the St. Louis minor leagues and keep him out of sight in the Dodgers minor-league system until 1940, when they would trade him back to St. Louis. There was just one problem with the plan: Durocher was allegedly unaware of it, and when Reiser began to light it up in spring training in 1940, Durocher began to play him in exhibition games. Reiser reached safely in 12 straight games, hit three home runs, and the baseball world took notice. Ralph Berger, in his Society for American Baseball Research biography of MacPhail, notes, "MacPhail sent a wire to Durocher, 'DO NOT PLAY REISER AGAIN.' When Durocher inserted Reiser into the lineup in a game in Macon, Georgia, MacPhail called him to his hotel room, cursed him, and fired him. The angry Durocher shoved MacPhail, who fell over the bed in a somersault, got up, and, as if by magic, had a change of heart. He put his arm around Leo and told him he was still the manager, then calmly went on to say that Reiser should be optioned to Elmira [Dodgers' minor league team] so that he could further develop his talent."

Reiser was eventually called up to the majors by the Dodgers in July and had a solid rookie year. In 1941, Reiser became a superstar; he led the NL in batting average, OPS, runs, doubles, and triples. He was an All-Star and finished second in MVP voting. Brooklyn had the top three in the MVP race: pitcher Whit Wyatt finished third (he led the NL with 22 wins and seven shutouts, to go along with an ERA of 2.34). The MVP was Dodgers first baseman Dolph Camilli, who led the league in home runs (34) and RBIs (120). While Camilli had a great season, it is fair to say that either Wyatt or Reiser could have won the award.

Reiser was an exceptional talent; he followed up his great 1941 season with another superb outing in the first half of the 1942 season. Unfortunately, injury would cripple his career. Reiser had already had two head-related injuries due to being beaned by fastballs. On July 19, 1942, in the second game of a doubleheader in St. Louis, Reiser almost made a spectacular catch running full speed toward the center-field wall; the sickening crash against the wall jarred the ball loose, and the Cardinals walked it off in the 11th with an inside-the-park home run. Reiser fractured his skull and suffered another concussion. Reiser should not have played the rest of the season. However, he was back in the Dodgers lineup a few days later. Reiser wanted to play, but the Dodgers should have protected the player. He played most of the remaining games and, while serviceable, was not the same player he was before. When the United States joined World War II, Reiser enlisted in the military and missed the next three seasons. He rejoined the Dodgers in 1946 and had two good years. But he was no longer a superstar. Following a poor 1948 campaign in which he appeared in only 64 games, Reiser was traded to the Boston Braves. He eventually retired following the 1952 season. Over the course of his career, Reiser suffered five skull fractures, seven concussions, and was taken from the field eleven times on a stretcher due to outfield collisions. Durocher wrote, "There will never be a ballplayer as good as Willie Mays, but Reiser was every bit as good, and he might have been better. Pete Reiser might have been the best ballplayer I ever saw. He had more power that Willie. He could throw as good as Willie. Mays was fast, but Reiser was faster. Name whoever you want to, and Pete Reiser was faster. Willie Mays had everything. Pete Reiser had everything but luck." Unfortunately, injury, World War II, and that the Dodgers (including Durocher) did not protect Reiser from himself derailing his career.

As for the 1941 season, the Dodgers had a superb April, going 13–4. Their fine play continued at the start of May as they won nine of eleven games, including six straight. Then Dem Bums returned, and the Dodgers lost six straight. And the Jekyll and Hyde routine continued as the Dodgers then proceeded to win nine in a row. Even with those long win streaks, the Dodgers could never get a comfortable lead in the NL; the Cardinals were always slightly behind or ahead of Dem Bums; for example, the nine-game win streak only resulted in the Dodgers gaining two games in the standings. From July 16 on, there were never more than three games separating the teams. It came down to the final month of the season, and the Dodgers were a little bit better, going 18–8, including taking two out of three in St. Louis, while the Cardinals went 16–11. The Dodgers finished with a record of 100–54, winning the NL pennant over the Cardinals by 2 1/2 games. Dem Bums had won the pennant! Now all they had to do was beat the Yankees in the World Series and shake up the existing order.

THE 1941 WORLD SERIES

Before the start of the World Series, an idea was floated that all games should be held at Yankee Stadium as it had a larger capacity than Ebbets Field. Not surprisingly, the Dodgers were aghast and voiced their displeasure. MLB wisely did not press that matter further. Game One was set for Yankee Stadium, and apart from the Bronx Bombers fans, the rest of baseball was cheering on the Dodgers. People love to support the underdog, including the elite of society. New York mayor Fiorello La Guardia publicly backed the Dodgers, as did singer Kate Smith, best known for her rendition of "God Bless America." Of course, many of the people jumping on the Dodgers bandwagon cursed the team for the rest of their lives when the team left Brooklyn for the sunny skies and palm trees of Los Angeles. That was still to come, however.

Game One of the World Series saw the attendance record shatter as 68,540 packed into Yankee Stadium. Taking the mound for New York was future Hall of Famer Red Ruffing, a six-time All-Star. And for the Dodgers, somewhat bizarrely, their third- or fourth-best pitcher, veteran Curt Davis. Davis had only started 16 games during the regular season. Durocher thought that if the Dodgers won the opening game with Davis pitching, it would put them in a great position for the rest of the Series. That would be true *if* Brooklyn won the opening game. If they lost: ah, the best-laid plans of mice and men. And to use another old adage, "Those who cannot remember the past are condemned to repeat it." In the opening games of both the 1916 and 1920 World Series, Rube Marquard started for the Brooklyn Robins. While a very good pitcher and member of the Hall of Fame, Marquard was not the Robins' ace in either season. Brooklyn lost both openers and eventually the World Series. And history repeated itself in 1941.

New York second baseman Joe Gordon opened the scoring in the bottom of the second with a home run to left field. Bill Dickey doubled the lead with an RBI double in the fourth. While the Dodgers got one back in the fifth through a Mickey Owen triple, the Yankees scored again in the sixth. The Dodgers came back again in the seventh, scoring once, but a baserunning gaffe by Pee Wee Reese in trying to take third following the second out stifled their momentum. The Yankees got out of the inning with no more damage and held on to win the opener, 3–2.

With the NL wins leader Whitlow Wyatt taking the mound for the Dodgers in Game Two, Brooklyn was confident of leveling the series. However, Wyatt let nerves get the better of him and gave up two early runs. The Dodgers came back in the top of the fifth to load the bases with no outs. A Reese groundout plated one, as did an Owen single. A double play, though, would end the inning. A throwing error by Gordon in the top of the sixth let Dixie Walker reach to open the inning, and he was eventually driven home by Dolph Camilli to give Brooklyn the lead. And despite a few shaky moments, Wyatt pitched a complete game as Brooklyn held on to win, 3–2.

It was another nail-biter in Game Three at Ebbets Field, with Freddie Fitzsimmons pitching a great seven innings for the home side without giving up a run and Marius Russo doing likewise for the Yankees. However, in the seventh, Russo hit a ball back at Fitzsimmons that caromed off his knee and straight into Reese's glove. It was a fortuitous out, but it had lasting repercussions. Fitzsimmons was unable to continue and went to the hospital, where he was diagnosed with a chipped kneecap. In addition to being out of the game, his season was over. Fitzsimmons would only appear in one game the following season and nine the next before he retired at the end of the 1943 campaign. Whether it was luck involved, devil magic, or just an unfortunate occurrence, the Bronx Bombers capitalized on the injury to the Brooklyn starter. Hugh Casey replaced Fitzsimmons on the mound for Brooklyn in the eighth and with one out gave up four consecutive singles as the Yankees took a 2–0 lead. The Dodgers continued to fight and got one back in the eighth but went quietly in the ninth as New York won the game, 2–1, with Russo pitching a complete game. That takes us to Game Four and the proverbial "what could have been."

New York got off to a great start, scoring one in the first and two in the fourth to take a 3–0 lead. Once again, the Dodgers fought back. Brooklyn scored two in the bottom of the fourth and two in the fifth thanks to a Reiser home run. The score remained 4–3 heading into the top of the ninth. Casey, after pitching a scoreless eighth, remained in the game. He quickly got the first two Yankees out. That brought Tommy Henrich to the plate. He worked the count full. Henrich later recounted what happened next to *Sports Illustrated*: "I knew that Casey had a very good high curve, and that's a pitch that always gave me trouble. Couldn't hit it for the life of me. And so here I am with two strikes on me, and here it comes. It was a beauty, one of the best and craziest curveballs I've ever seen. It was definitely not a spitter, as some people have claimed. I thought it was going to be a strike, so I started my swing. And then that pitch broke sharply down. I tried to hold up, but it was too late. I'd committed myself. The funny thing is that even in that instant, while I was swinging, I thought to myself that if I'm having this much trouble with the pitch, maybe [Dodger catcher] Mickey Owen is, too. So I looked around behind me after I missed the ball."

On what should have been the game-ending pitch, Owen allowed Henrich to reach first on a strike-three passed ball. Dodgers first baseman Dolph Camilli woefully noted, "I couldn't believe it. Mickey Owen was a great catcher who hardly ever made an error. It looked to me as if he just took his eye off the ball. All he had to do was knock the darn thing down and throw it to me. But it didn't happen." Brooklyn still only needed one out, but seemingly rattled, Casey imploded. DiMaggio walked, Charlie Keller doubled, scoring two, Bill Dickey walked, Gordon doubled, scoring another two, Phil Rizzuto walked, and only then did Casey manage to get the final out. The Dodgers were lifeless in the bottom of the inning, going down in order as the Yankees won the game, 7–4, leaving them only one win away from another World Series crown. After the game, Owen simply said, "It was all my fault. I should have had it."

Yes, he should have. And that play doomed the Dodgers' hopes. It is almost impossible to recover from a loss like that. Just ask the Boston Red Sox about the 1986 World Series. Nevertheless, if Owen had caught the pitch, it would have only leveled the series. New York could still could have gone on to win it all. But by allowing a passed ball, Owen condemned Brooklyn and allowed the Yankees to start riding roughshod over the Dodgers. Any hope of challenging the existing order would have to be put on hold for several years.

The Yankees captured the title in Game Five at Ebbets Field. The Yankees, as was the norm, scored early; this time, two runs in the second courtesy of a wild pitch and an RBI single by Gordon. The Dodgers' offense was lifeless, managing only four measly hits the entire game off New York starter Tiny Bonham. Bonham threw a complete game as the Yankees won, 3–1, and the Series, 4–1. The Yankees were once again on top of the mountain for the ninth time. And once again, the Dodgers were simply not good enough when it mattered most, still searching for their first World Series. The existing order in baseball remained the same. The Yankees were dominant, and the Dodgers were Dem Bums when it mattered most. Following the game, the *Brooklyn Eagle* newspaper had an optimistic headline, "Wait 'til Next Year." Next year for the Dodgers ended up being over a decade away.

3

1947: STILL WAITING
FOR NEXT YEAR

THE YANKEES FOLLOWED up their World Series
triumph with another outstanding season, winning 103
games and making it back to the fall classic. Unfortunately for
them and their fans, the Cardinals were even better. St. Louis
won the 1942 World Series, four games to one. The roles were
reversed the following year as the Yankees defeated the Cardinals in the World Series by the same margin. Then New York
went into a period of decline; in 1944, they only won 83 games
(fewest since 1925) and finished third in the AL. In 1945, New
York was even worse as they won 81 games and finished fourth.
In 1946, the Yankees improved and won 87 games but were
an astonishing 17 games out of first (worst since 1929) as the
Red Sox ran away with the pennant, winning 104 games. The
Yankees were in danger of permanently losing their throne and
becoming just another baseball team.

The 1942 Dodgers were spectacular, winning 104 games. On August 5, they led the NL by 10 games. On September 3, the Dodgers still led the NL by 4 1/2 games. But five straight losses in the middle of the month basically handed the Cardinals the pennant. Of course, St. Louis winning an astonishing 43 out of their final 51 games had some say in the matter. Nevertheless, considering the Yankees were not as good as they were the previous years, Brooklyn fans still wondered what might have been, a common occurrence in Dodgers history. Brooklyn then reverted to its usual self: in 1943, they finished third in the NL with 81 wins, 23 1/2 games out of first. In 1944, Dem Bums were in full force as Brooklyn won a paltry 63 games, finishing seventh, which was a massive 42 games from the NL summit. The Dodgers then started to improve: 1945 saw the team finish third while winning 87 games. They continued to improve in 1946, winning 96 games, and finished the regular season tied with the Cardinals. The first-ever NL playoff, a best-of-three series between the teams, would decide who would advance to the World Series. Another common occurrence in Dodger history is that the Cardinals, just like the Yankees, were almost always better the Dodgers when there was everything to play for. In Game One in St. Louis, the Cardinals beat the Dodgers, 4–2. And back in Brooklyn, the home fans mourned as St. Louis won Game Two, 8–4. Once again, the Dodgers were oh so close. A similar refrain would be heard following the 1947 season.

THE YANKEES' 1947 SEASON

While having no impact on the success or otherwise of the 1947 team, the Yankees held the first Old-Timers' Day. Larry

MacPhail, now part-owner and team president of New York, stated that the 1947 Old-Timers' Day was the second in what would become an annual event, the first being the 1939 Lou Gehrig Appreciation Day. It has been held every year since 1947. The Yankees understand that it is important to appreciate and honor the ballclub's history. After all, those who cannot remember the past are condemned to repeat it: just look at Durocher using the Dodgers' fourth-best pitcher to start Game One of the 1941 World Series. A flawed tactic that had already failed twice previously.

The Yankees were progressive in honoring history, but not when it came to breaking the color barrier. The 1947 season saw no black players in the Yankee organization, unlike the Dodgers. New York, though, did unearth another future All-Star, MVP and Hall of Famer— Lawrence Peter "Yogi" Berra.

Yogi Berra would have preferred to play for the Cardinals. However, St. Louis offered Berra less than his one-time neighbor Joe Garagiola. This bothered Berra, so he signed with the Yankees instead. After having a good 1946 season with the Yankees' Triple-A affiliate in Newark, as well as a cup of coffee in the bigs at the end of the season *and* a solid preseason in left field with New York, Berra became a mainstay. Due to an injury to regular catcher Aaron Robinson, Berra moved back behind the plate. Berra had a good first full season in 1947, hitting .280 with 11 home runs, finishing 15th in MVP voting. To say that Berra had an amazing career would be an understatement. He was an 18-time All-Star, won three MVP awards, appeared in 10 World Series, and is a member of the Hall of Fame. Berra became a part of pop culture, and his Yogi-isms are known throughout the world. Here are a few: "When you come to a fork in the road, take it"; "It ain't over till it's over"; "It's like déjà vu all over again"; "Baseball is 90 percent mental, and the other half is physical"; and my favorite, "I never said most of the things I said." As is often the case, though, the public image of Berra does not necessarily line up exactly with the real Berra. In his 1969 book, *The Jocks*, Leonard Shecter, in a less-than-flattering portrayal, writes, "other ball players always complained that Yogi Berra would stand naked at the clubhouse buffet and scratch his genitals over the cold cuts."

In addition to Berra becoming a semi-regular, the 1947 team was also improved with the signing of thirty-seven-year-old first baseman George McQuinn, who had previously played for the Reds, St. Louis Browns, and Philadelphia Athletics. He was a decent-to-good player but was clearly on the downside of his career. However, playing for the Yankees revitalized McQuinn. He hit .304, was an All-Star, and finished sixth in MVP voting. And then there was DiMaggio. After having a below average (for him) 1942 season, DiMaggio did not play in the majors the following three years due to military service during World War II. His 1946 season was once again All-Star worthy but not up to his amazing standards. The 1947 season saw the old Yankee Clipper begin to return. DiMaggio led the Yankees in hits, home runs, RBIs, batting average, OBP, slugging, and was second on the team in doubles and triples. DiMaggio was an All-Star and captured his third (and final) AL MVP award.

The New York starting pitchers led the AL in wins and ERA. Both Allie Reynolds (19–8, 3.20 ERA) and rookie Spec Shea (14–5, 3.07 ERA, third in Rookie of the Year voting, and an All-Star) had fine seasons. Both though were overshadowed by reliever Joe Page. Page led the league in games finished as well as "saves" (saves were not an official MLB statistic until 1969). Page had a record of 14–8, with an ERA of 2.48. He was an All-Star and finished fourth in MVP voting. Page had started the 1947 season quite badly. He was scored upon in four of his first six appearances (all New York losses), and his ERA was a whopping 7.11. On May 26, facing the Red Sox at Yankee Stadium, Page's career was at a crossroads. With the Red Sox leading the Yankees, 3–1, Page replaced Shea on the mound with runners on first and second and nobody out in the third inning. The legendary Ted Williams reached on an error to load the bases. Page then proceeded to throw three straight balls to Rudy York. New York manager Bucky Harris later admitted that Page would have been demoted to the minors if he did not get York out. Page would battle back to strike out York and then got the next two outs to emerge from the inning unscathed. He would complete the game striking out eight, with the Yankees winning, 9–3. If York had reached base, Page would have been demoted, and who knows how that would have changed history.

Page was an extrovert on and off the field. He was also almost immaculately dressed. Writing in *Pinstripe Empire,* Marty Appel recounts, "Page's entrances to games became rituals. He'd hurdle the right-field bullpen fence and, jacket over shoulder, walk to the mound, glancing over his shoulder to get the game situation from the new auxiliary scoreboard, tossing the jacket to the waiting batboy and taking his warm-ups. There was no musical accompaniment, but the fans loved the show." Baseball back then, as it still is today, was about entertainment.

Indeed, in addition to the Old-Timers' Day, the Yankees held another entertainment spectacle that season. Baseball Commissioner Albert "Happy" Chandler deemed April 27 "Babe Ruth

Day." As the *New York Times* reported, "Just before he spoke, Ruth started to cough and it appeared that he might break down because of the thunderous cheers that came his way. But once he started to talk, he was all right, still the champion. It was the many men who surrounded him on the field, players, newspaper and radio persons, who choked up." It was one of the last times that Ruth appeared at Yankee Stadium. It was not that Ruth's speech was anything special, but the sentiment behind the words choked people up: "Thank you very much, ladies and gentlemen. You know how bad my voice sounds—well it feels just as bad. You know this baseball game of ours comes up from the youth. That means the boys. And after you're a boy and grow up to know how to play ball, then you come to the boys you see representing themselves today in your national pastime, the only real game—I think—in the world, baseball. As a rule, some people think if you give them a football, or a baseball, or something like that—naturally they're athletes right away. But you can't do that in baseball. You've gotta start from way down [at] the bottom, when you're six or seven years of age. You can't wait until you're fifteen or sixteen. You gotta let it grow up with you. And if you're successful, and you try hard enough, you're bound to come out on top—just like these boys [the current Yankees team] have come to the top now. There's been so many lovely things said about me, and I'm glad that I've had the opportunity to thank everybody. Thank you."

Regarding the 1947 season, the Red Sox failed to recapture their pennant-winning form, and the AL flag was there for the taking. The Yankees started out somewhat slowly, going 7–5 in April and 13–12 in May. But as they were only 3 1/2 games out of first, there was no reason to be alarmed (well, except baseball fans, since the game was first invented, tend to overreact). Indeed, after going 21–9 in June, the Yankees led the league by 5 1/2 games. And as much as a team could cruise for the final three months of the season, the Yankees did just that. New York eventually won the pennant by 12 games over the Detroit Tigers with a record of 97–57. And awaiting the Yankees in the World Series was . . .

THE DODGERS' 1947 SEASON

Coming off the NL playoff loss to the Cardinals the previous season, Brooklyn was determined to win the pennant. As such, management was willing to do everything necessary to give Dem Bums the best shot to do so. In this regard, the Brooklyn Dodgers did something shocking: they became the first major-league team to promote a black player to its roster. Prior to 1947, African Americans could go to war to defend the freedom of the United States, but heaven help us all if they wanted to play baseball in the majors. African Americans could get shot, maimed, and killed while defending the flag, but they could not swing the bat or throw a baseball for any of the sixteen major-league teams. Such a disgrace began to slowly unravel beginning with the 1947 season, when Jack Roosevelt Robinson broke the color barrier in baseball.

Branch Rickey, general manager and president of the Dodgers, laid the groundwork for the eventual integration of baseball. In 1945, Rickey signed Jackie Robinson to play for the Montreal Royals (Dodgers' farm team) the following season. Later that year, he also signed Don Newcombe and told Roy Campanella not to sign with any other team, as the Dodgers would eventually secure his services. Not surprisingly, Robinson had a great season for the Royals. He led the Triple-A International League in batting average and runs. Robinson enjoyed his time in Montreal, even though Royals manager Clay Hooper, to put it mildly, did not necessarily want Robinson. During spring training, he asked Rickey, "Do you really think that a [racial epithet] is a human being?"

While Rickey and the Dodgers were visionaries in this regard, other teams were not. In August 1945, the owners voted by a margin of 15–1 (the Dodgers being the lone dissenters) in favor of the MacPhail report that recommended major-league teams not sign any black players because in part it would lead to a decline in attendance and that African American players were substandard.

Robinson excelled for the Royals and in 1947 made the Dodgers' Opening-Day roster. Unfortunately, a substantial minority (or even a majority) of players was against integration. Cardinals players were allegedly planning a sit-down strike when Brooklyn went to St. Louis. There is still much debate about whether such action was planned, but NL President Ford Frick threatened lifetime bans for any players who undertook such action. Frick wrote to the Cardinals stating, "If you do strike, you will be suspended from the League. You will find that you will be outcasts. I do not care if half the league strikes. Those who do will encounter quick retribution." Several Philadelphia players and even its manager, Ben Chapman, directed disgraceful tirades against Robinson. In another despicable act, Cardinals outfielder Enos Slaughter deliberately spiked Robinson in the leg on what was a routine groundout to first. Robinson was forced to endure much abuse but was constantly told by Dodgers management not to retaliate. The prevailing wisdom was that Robinson needed to demonstrate that black players were mature, calm professionals and not hotheaded, as this would help pave the way for more African Americans in the majors. And what is also somewhat forgotten, a number of Dodgers players did not want to play with a black teammate. Dodgers player representative Dixie Walker, Bobby Bragan, Eddie Stanky, Carl Furillo, Hugh Casey, and Ed Head were against any black player suiting up for Brooklyn. In addition, Walker attempted to organize a wildcat strike across the National League on Opening Day once Robinson stepped onto the field. The Cubs, Pirates, and Phillies players agreed to strike. Nonetheless, the strike failed to materialize once Brooklyn management came down hard on its dissenting players. So dismayed that Robinson was on the team, Walker asked to be traded. If Pete Reiser had not been perennially injured, Walker's wish would most likely have been granted, and even with Reiser's injuries the Dodgers still tried to trade Walker in early May. However, a deal with the Pirates didn't come to fruition until after the season. In some cases, racism was the driving factor of not wanting black players in the majors. In other cases, it was simple economics. There were only a finite number of roster places; allowing black players on the team would squeeze out less-talented players. In Walker's case, following Robinson's outstanding season, he called Jackie a fine teammate and a gentleman.

Robinson had a mighty fine rookie campaign: he hit .297, led the Dodgers with 175 hits, had 31 doubles (tied with Walker), led the NL with 29 steals, finished fifth in MVP voting, and won the NL Rookie of the Year award. Likewise, Walker was an All-Star with a .306/.415/.427 slash line. On the pitching front, twenty-one-year-old Ralph Branca had a breakout season. He went 21–12 with a team-best 2.67 ERA and led the league in starts, while finishing 11th in MVP voting.

And in one of the last good years of his injury-riddled career, Reiser went .309/.415/.418. Unfortunately, another collision with a concrete outfield wall that rendered him unconscious was one collision too many. While Reiser had a few more seasons left in him and at times played well, he was never the same player. He turned to alcohol and was out of the majors following the 1952 season with Cleveland, during which he batted a paltry .136. Reiser became a manager in the lower leagues, and his final managerial stint was with St Petersburg. Reiser was fired because of his drinking. As recounted by Roger Kahn, in Reiser's fare-well meeting with the players, he told them, "I jes got one thing to tell you guys. None of you sonsabitches is ever gonna make the major leagues." Reiser died in 1981 at the age of sixty-four.

In addition to Robinson, there was another major change to Dodgers personnel prior to the start of the season. Brooklyn manager Leo Durocher and Larry MacPhail were at odds due to MacPhail hiring two Dodgers coaches. The two then leveled accusations against each other that they allowed gamblers and other assorted lowlifes into their respective clubhouses (Durocher was already warned to stay away from some of his friends). Durocher was also accused of rigging a craps game that led to a player (rumored to be Detroit's Dizzy Trout) losing a substantial amount of money. Baseball Commissioner Chandler, who was friends with MacPhail, suspended Durocher for the 1947 season. In his place stepped Dodgers scout Burt Shotton.

Even with the late managerial change, the Dodgers had the talent to make another run for the pennant, and things started off well in April with them going 8–3, but they had a horrid May with a record of 12–14. Yet the NL teams were not exactly grabbing the bull by the horns, and Brooklyn was only two games out of first coming into June. A five-game losing streak in the first half of the month meant the Dodgers were 27–25, but just three games out of first. It was at this point Brooklyn finally put things together. The team won nine out of the next ten games to take over first place. Apart from early August, when their 10-game lead was whittled away in the space of eleven days, Brooklyn cruised to the NL pennant, finishing with a record of 94–60, five games ahead of the Cardinals. It was time for another Yankees-Dodgers World Series. Could Brooklyn learn from history or were they doomed to repeat it? According to Karl Marx, history does repeat itself. The first time is a tragedy, the second time a farce. Whatever one may think of his political theory, for Brooklyn fans Marx was unfortunately a visionary.

THE 1947 WORLD SERIES

The 1947 World Series was the first fall classic to be televised. Any fears that this would lead to soft ticket sales were unfounded. Game One at Yankee Stadium saw 73,365 fans in attendance. With high ticket prices, the media complained that it was not "real" baseball fans in the stands, but rich people enjoying the spectacle of a subway series. As such, the ballpark was supposedly more subdued than usual. In other words, it is not just today that people bemoan that "real" fans are being priced out of high-profile sporting events and the elite are ruining the atmosphere at stadiums.

Finally learning from history, Shotton did not start Brooklyn's fourth-best pitcher in Game One of the Series, but their ace, Ralph Branca. Spec Shea took the mound for New York. After retiring the first batter, Shea gave up a walk to Robinson. Trying to make a statement early on, Robinson stole second. He pushed the envelope too far by trying to take third on a Reiser groundout, but he avoided being tagged out long enough for Reiser to make it to second. Walker then singled Reiser home, and Brooklyn had a great start to the World Series. And Branca did his part by being perfect through four innings. Brimming with confidence, he took the mound in the fifth with Brooklyn still clinging to a one-run lead. Branca then proceeded to give up a single to DiMaggio, a walk to George McQuinn, and he hit Billy Johnson to load the bases. Johnny Lindell doubled in two, followed by Branca walking Phil Rizzuto. Mercifully, Shotton had seen enough and pulled Branca. Hank Behrman took over and was little better, giving up a walk and a hit that plated three more. Page took over from Shea to start the sixth, and Brooklyn managed to score in the inning and plate another one in the seventh. But the fifth inning doomed the Dodgers as the Yankees held on to win the opener, 5–3.

Staying with youth, Shotton decided that twenty-four-year-old left-hander Vic Lombardi would start for Brooklyn. While possessing a mediocre 12–11 record for the season, his ERA was second-best amongst Dodger starters at 2.99. For New York, veteran Allie Reynolds, who was in his first season for the Yankees after being acquired from the Cleveland Indians, was looking forward to appearing in his first World Series game.

The Yankees struck first, scoring once in the opening inning on a Lindell double. Brooklyn leveled the score in the third thanks to Robinson's RBI double. The Yankees came right back in the bottom of the inning with Lindell tripling in Snuffy Stirnweiss (who tripled himself). But Walker led off the fourth with a home run to once again tie up the game. Not to be outdone, in the bottom of the inning Johnson scored on a Rizzuto double to give the Yankees the lead once again. A Tommy Henrich home run to start the fifth spelled the end for Lombardi and the Dodgers' hopes of winning the game. New York eventually won, 10–3, with Reynolds throwing a complete game.

With the Series then traveling across the city to Ebbets Field there was another high-scoring affair in Game Three. Thirty-nine-year-old veteran Bobo Newsom, who began his playing career in 1929 with the Dodgers, was back at his old home ground, this time starting for the Yankees. And he was horrible. The Dodgers ran themselves out of the first inning with Robinson and Reiser both being caught stealing. Newsom was not as fortunate in the second. He gave up five runs as Brooklyn took a 6–0 lead. Dodgers starter Joe Hatten was not much better, lasting 4 1/3 innings while giving up six. Luckily for Hatten, the Dodgers offense was on fire and had plated nine runs after four innings. The offense then slowed to a crawl, while the Yankees chipped away. New York scored two in the fifth and one each in the sixth and seventh (Berra hit the first pinch-hit home run in World Series history) to only trail by a single run. In the top of the eighth, with Hugh Casey pitching for Brooklyn, Henrich walked to start the inning, and Lindell (who was well on his way to having a monster World Series) singled. That brought DiMaggio to the plate. Unfortunately for Yankees fans, DiMaggio grounded into a double play. Casey then got McQuinn to ground out to end the inning. Still clinging to a one-run lead, Casey was perfect in the ninth, and Brooklyn somehow managed to hang on, winning, 9–8. Game Three was a slugfest; this would not be the case the following day.

Game Four began ominously for Brooklyn, as rookie pitcher Harry Taylor could not record one out to open the game. After two singles and an error, a bases-loaded walk to DiMaggio brought in a run for New York. Hal Gregg replaced Taylor and got McQuinn to pop up and Johnson to ground into a double play. The Yankees got another one in the top of the fourth thanks to a triple by Johnson, who was brought home on a Lindell double. The Dodgers got one back in the bottom of the fifth after a couple of walks, a bunt to move the runners over, and an RBI groundout. In the bottom of the ninth, with the Yankees leading 2–1, starter Bill Bevens was looking to secure the win for New York and a complete game. In his fourth year in pinstripes, Bevens was a good pitcher (as one has to be to be a major-league player) but was nothing special. He had a record of 7–13 for the year, but a lot of that was due to a lack of run support, as his ERA was only 3.82. Bevens was a long way from his best, as he had walked eight, but miraculously he had not allowed a hit. Looking for the first no-hitter in World Series history, Bevens got the first out before allowing a walk to Carl Furillo. Spider Jorgensen fouled out to first: two out. Bevens was one out from a World Series no-hitter. With Reiser pinch- hitting for Brooklyn despite having a broken ankle he sustained in Game Three, pinch-runner Al Gionfriddo stole second. On a 3-1 count, New York manager Bucky Harris then told Bevens to intentionally walk Reiser, Bevens's tenth walk allowed. As such, Harris defied all baseball wisdom by putting the winning run on base. Shotton replaced Reiser with the speedier Eddie Miksis and brought in

pinch-hitter Cookie Lavagetto. The thirty-four-year-old Lavagetto had only 69 plate appearances all year, collecting 18 hits.
Bevens was still one out from World Series immortality. Instead,
on a 1-1 count, Bevens followed the scouting report and threw
Lavagetto a heater high and away. There was just one problem.
Lavagetto liked pitches in that area; it was hard and tight stuff
that bothered him. Lavagetto hit a fly ball to right field that kept
going, landing well out of the reach of Tommy Henrich. With
the men on base running on contact, Gionfriddo scored, as did
Miksis from first. Rather than immortality, and the Dodgers'
lone hit destroyed Bevens's no-hitter, and the Dodgers won,
3–2. The Ebbets Field faithful witnessed a Dodgers miracle; the
World Series was tied at two games apiece. The following day,
Bevens noted that he "felt like a guy who had dropped ten stories
in an elevator. My heart and my brains and everything was right
down by my spikes." Bevens would appear in only one more
major-league game, Game Seven of the '47 Series. As for Lavagetto, he never had another hit in the majors.

Game Five was pivotal. Stepping on the mound for the
pinstripes was Shea, an excellent choice. For Dem Bums, both
Branca and Lombardi were hoping to start; either one would
have been fine choices. Instead, Shotton decided on Rex Barney.
Barney was used mainly in relief throughout the season, only
making eight starts and having an ERA of 4.75. Barney did
not have great command. For the year, he struck out 36, while
walking 59. To say the decision to start Barney was an odd one
is a massive understatement, and it may have cost the Dodgers
a World Series. Not surprisingly, Barney did not have a good
outing in Game Five, but the Yankees could not get a hit when
it mattered most. But they did just enough. It was left to Shea

to single in the first run of the day in the fourth after Barney walked two. DiMaggio hit a solo homer in the fifth to increase the lead. Barney went 4 2/3 innings, only allowing three hits but walking nine. Astonishingly, when he left the game, the Dodgers still had a chance. And they came back in the sixth as a result of two walks and an RBI single by Robinson to cut the lead to one. But in the end, the Dodgers could never get a crucial hit. In the bottom of the ninth, with a runner on second and two outs, Lavagetto had the chance to be the hero again, but it was not to be. Shea struck him out. New York won, 2–1, and were one win away from another World Series championship. Shea was magnificent, throwing a complete game while only allowing four hits, five walks, and striking out seven.

With the Series going back to Yankee Stadium, the pitchers' duels of the previous two games gave way to a slugfest. The Dodgers took an early 4–0 lead in the third. With Lombardi on the mound, Dem Bums had to be confident in forcing a deciding Game Seven. However, New York came roaring back in the bottom of the inning with Lombardi exiting after giving up two runs and with runners at first and second. As it was a must-win game, Branca was brought in but proceeded to give up singles to Billy Johnson and Bobby Brown to tie the game. And a Berra single in the next inning to score Henrich gave New York the lead. The Yankees had their own pitching woes: Reynolds did not make it out of the third inning, while Page could not hold onto the lead. He lasted just an inning while allowing four runs. The Dodgers were back in command. And the combination of Hatten and Casey secured the victory for Brooklyn, 8–6 being the final score. The result may have well been different if not for one of the greatest catches ever by Al Gionfriddo. With the Yankees trailing, 8–5, in the bottom of the sixth with two on and two out, DiMaggio hit a long drive to left field. Gionfriddo made a spectacular one-handed catch to rob the Yankee Clipper. DiMaggio responded by kicking the dirt in frustration.

The Yankees were frustrated; the Dodgers were hungry for their first championship *and* to end New York's dominance. Unfortunately for the Brooklyn faithful, history did repeat itself, and the second time was well and truly a farce. It was a farce because of Shotton's use of the pitching staff throughout the Series and Brooklyn starters being incapable of lasting even five innings.

Coming into the biggest game of the season, Game Seven of the World Series, Dodgers pitchers were running on fumes. Not one starter could go deep into a game; some of that was on the players, some of that was on Shotton being too quick with the hook. The three best Dodgers pitchers, Branca, Hatten, and Lombardi, pitched in the previous game and were largely unavailable (although Hatten ended up throwing a third of an inning). And Casey had bruised ribs and was overworked, as he had already appeared in five of the six games. Thus, Shotton turned to Hal Gregg, who started only 16 games during the regular season and had a whopping 5.87 ERA. As for New York, rather than start Bevens, Bucky Harris went with Shea. Shea, though, had nothing left in the tank.

He was fortunate in the top of the first as both Eddie Stanky and Pee Wee Reese were thrown out trying to steal. Shea was lucky, but he also had Harris to thank, as rather than starting Berra, against whom the Dodgers had little trouble stealing, he went with Aaron Robinson at catcher. And that could have been the difference. Gregg was good in the first inning as New York went down in order. And to the delight and anticipation of Dodgers fans everywhere, Brooklyn took a 1–0 lead in the second thanks to a triple and an RBI single by catcher Bruce Edwards. Furillo then singled, moving Edwards to second. Harris had seen enough and brought in Bevens. Spider Jorgensen then greeted him with a double to bring home another run. However, another baserunning mistake, this time by Furillo trying to score on a Gregg groundout with only one out, aided Bevens. Three outs on the basepaths in two innings hurt the Dodgers. Indeed, the Yankees came back in the bottom of the inning to cut the lead in half on Rizzuto's two-out RBI single.

This time, rather than having a quick hook, Shotton left Gregg in for too long, although to be fair, his options were limited. In the bottom of the fourth with two outs and a runner on first, pinch-hitter Bobby Brown (batting for Bevens, who went 2 2/3 innings and did allow a run in what turned out to be his final major-league game) doubled to left field, bringing home Rizzuto. Shotton than went to his bullpen, bringing in Hank Behrman, whose regular-season ERA was 5.48. Behrman walked Snuffy Stirnweiss before Henrich singled home Rizzuto. Behrman then retired the next batter, but the damage was done. New York led, 3–2, and into the game came Page. And he was *dominant.* Page went the final five innings, giving up only one hit. The Yankees, meanwhile, added single runs in the sixth and seventh. And in the top of the ninth, with a runner on first and one out, Page got Edwards to ground into a double play. New York won, 5–2, Page was credited with the win, and the New York Yankees were once again World Series champions. And the Brooklyn Dodgers were once again afterthoughts.

Quite simply, the Yankees were the better team. When it mattered, New York players got the crucial hit, and their starting pitchers could last deep into games (thus resting other starters and the bullpen). New York pitchers were used to going deep; they threw 73 complete games during the regular season. By contrast, Dodgers pitchers only threw 47 complete games. There was one other reason New York won: Harris outmanaged Shotton. Starting Robinson behind the plate in Game Seven and having faith in the pitching staff made a world of difference. Despite all of this, if one of the Dodger starters had gone even seven or eight innings, it is entirely possible Brooklyn would have been celebrating World Series glory. But that is playing the what-if game, which is always a futile exercise. All that mattered is the baseball hierarchy remained intact with the Yankees being the ruling class and the Dodgers being the upstarts incapable of toppling the existing order. History had repeated itself.

In a dramatic postscript to the game, in the final inning MacPhail, who was partaking in a few alcoholic beverages, told reporters he was going to retire. Later that night at the Biltmore Hotel to celebrate the Yankees' triumph, MacPhail got into verbal and physical altercations with at least one and maybe three people—John McDonald (former Dodgers traveling secretary), George Weiss (Yankees GM), and Dan Topping (Yankees coowner). According to *The Sporting News*'s J. G. Taylor Spink, MacPhail told Topping, "You're just a guy who was born with a silver spoon in your mouth and never made a dollar in your life." Topping replied, "Come here, you. . . . I have taken all of this I am going to take," and pushed MacPhail into the kitchen. The end result was that Topping and Yankee coowner Del Webb bought out MacPhail and rehired Weiss as GM. MacPhail was out of the Yankees and baseball.

4

1949: IS IT NEXT YEAR YET?

IN 1948, NEW York had another solid season. They went 94–60, but this was only good enough for third place, two games out. The Yankees were in contention all season, but losses to the Boston Red Sox on the final two days on the season led to the Cleveland Indians winning the pennant, following a one-game playoff with the Red Sox, and eventually the World Series. Whether fair or not, the decline of Joe Page was blamed for New York failing to reach the mountaintop. Page led all AL pitchers in appearances and games finished. All well and good if he was the same pitcher he was the previous season, but in 1948 Page ended up with a record of 7–8 with an ERA of 4.26. By contrast, he went 14–8 in 1947 with an ERA of 2.48. Because the Yankees failed to win the pennant and he was viewed as a MacPhail boy, Harris was let go following the season. In his place stepped former Dodgers player and manager Casey Stengel. And a dynasty was born.

Irrespective of the results on the field, 1948 was always going to be a sad year for the Bronx Bombers. On June 13, to celebrate the twenty-fifth year of Yankee Stadium, New York retired Babe Ruth's number. Ruth, ravaged by cancer, dressed in a Yankees uniform. He told the crowd, "Ladies and gentlemen, I just want to say one thing. I am proud I hit the first home run here against Boston in 1923. . . . It is marvelous to see these 13 or 14 players who were my teammates going back 25 years. I'm telling you it makes me proud and happy to be here. Thank you." Ruth died on August 16. He was fifty-three.

The 1948 Dodgers had Leo Durocher returning as manager following his one-year suspension. This did not give Brooklyn a boost; rather, the team did not play good baseball. They went 5–5 in April and had losing records in both May and June. At the All-Star break, the Dodgers were 35–37, and the ownership had had enough. Durocher was out, and Shotton was back at the helm. The managerial change revitalized Dem Bums, and after a win on September 1, they were in a tie for first. And then it all fell apart: Brooklyn, lost nine out of eleven games, and their season was effectively over. The Dodgers finished third with a record of 84–70, 7 1/2 games behind the Boston Braves.

THE YANKEES' 1949 SEASON

After a disappointing 1948 season, when they won 94 games and finished third (while other teams may consider that a successful season, it *was* a disappointing season for the Yankees), the major change for New York was Casey Stengel becoming manager. Like Berra, Stengel was very quotable; the media dubbed his quips "Stengelese." My personal favorite Stengel sayings are "There comes a time in every man's life, and I've had plenty of them" and "You have to go broke three times to learn how to make a living." Stengel was born to parade around a baseball field. *Houston Chronicle* journalist Mickey Herskowitz wrote, "It is fashionable to say that successful people, in any field, could have been whatever they wanted, but you could not picture Casey Stengel being anything else but what he was, the greatest showman baseball ever knew." Because Stengel was a showman and not a particularly successful manager, it was a shock that the Yankees hired him. Stengel was considered in some circles as a bit of a joke. Stengel later told Roger Kahn that at the press conference announcing him as Yankee manager, he said, "I know writers and I kept hearing a hum from writers in the room. And the writers were looking at me, damn near sixty years old, and they're saying, in this hum: 'That old bum managed nine years before in the major leagues and he never once got out of the second division.'" Stengel would prove the Yankees were right to hire him and that everyone who considered him a joke was sorely mistaken.

Stengel was ahead of his time in that he set the lineup in response to who was pitching for the opposition; he platooned players. He was not the first manger to employ such tactics, but he revived it. Indeed, Stengel himself had been a platoon player. While he was not necessarily a fan of such tactics as a player, he realized the success it could bring. Stengel also liked players who could play multiple positions. Stengel said, "I was gonna platoon right from the start. George Weiss knew that and I gotta say he left me alone to do that. We had differences . . . but he left me to do whichever lineups I commenced to choose. We had some great ball players, which was getting old, and whatever they felt about it, could not play in a hundred fifty-four games with the old bodies which they had." Stengel was a modern-day manager back in the 1940s. Remember that the next time someone tells you that the "nerds" and their constant lineup changes are ruining baseball. Stengel, though, was far from perfect. He often criticized his players in the press (this became more pronounced as he became more successful) as well as seemingly deliberately mispronouncing their names. For example, Stengel called Tommy Henrich "Handricks."

Despite employing a manager ahead of his time, the Yankees with Weiss at the helm were still not willing to integrate the ballclub. The team signed black players in 1948 and 1949, with Frank Austin and Luis Marquez briefly playing for the Yankees' Newark affiliate in 1949. However, Weiss allegedly told journalists, "I will never allow a black man to wear a Yankee uniform. Box-holders from Westchester don't want that sort of crowd. They would be offended to have to sit with niggers." As successful as the Yankees were, they *would* have been even better with black players on their team. Indeed, New York had ample opportunity to sign Willie Mays before he eventually signed with their crosstown rivals, the Giants. Just imagine a Yankees team with Willie Mays! The Yankees most likely did not sign Mays because he was black, and a laughable scouting report said Mays could not hit a curveball. As Campanella exclaimed to Kahn, "Willie couldn't hit the curve! He was eighteen years old. No way an eighteen-year-old kid is ever gonna be a good curve ball hitter. That takes time. Mickey [Mantle] and Duke [Snider], great as they were, they did not hit good curve balls when they were eighteen." Even with all the plaudits going to the Dodgers for integrating their ballclub, they were not interested in Mays. Kahn notes that Rickey said, "It would not have been prudent . . . to have had too many Negroes on any one club."

Nevertheless, a dynasty was about to begin with twelve Yankees on the 1949 roster who would be there for all five straight world championships—Hank Bauer, Yogi Berra, Bobby Brown, Jerry Coleman, Joe Collins (appeared in only seven games in 1949), Eddie Lopat, Johnny Mize (joined team in August 1949), Vic Raschi, Phil Rizzuto, Allie Reynolds, Charlie Silvera, and Gene Woodling.

One legend's career, though, was winding down, but he was not done yet. In 1949, DiMaggio and Boston's Ted Williams became the first AL players to command a $100,000 salary. Williams's 1949 season was beyond worldly. On the way to his second MVP crown, he slashed .318/.464/.556. He led the AL in OBP, slugging, runs (150), doubles (39), home runs (43), RBIs (159), and walks (162). It was a truly remarkable year. As for DiMaggio, injury kept him out of the Yankees lineup until late June. In addition to having an issue with his heel, DiMaggio was struggling mentally. He said, "I guess I was . . . a mental case. . . . The team kept sending me checks. Whenever one came, I told myself, 'You've certainly done a swell job of earning this money.' . . . I had trouble getting to sleep. . . . If my playing career was over, what was I going to do? Lying awake, sometimes until five in the morning, I figured out at least a half dozen careers. I must have been really upset, because right now I can't remember any of them."

The Yankees were such a powerhouse that they hardly seemed to miss DiMaggio. When he returned to the lineup on June 28 against the Red Sox, New York had a comfortable 4 1/2 game lead. In his return, DiMaggio made sure to remind the baseball public that he was every bit as good as Williams. In his first game back, he went 2-for-3 with a walk, a home run, and two RBIs. On June 29, DiMaggio hit two home runs. And on June 30, he hit another home run. To make the series even better, the Yankees swept the Red Sox in Boston and opened a 5 1/2 game lead in the AL to close out the month. In 76 games that year, the thirty-four-year-old DiMaggio hit .346/.459/.596 with 14 doubles and an equal number of home runs.

In addition to DiMaggio, Henrich had another great year with an OBP of .416 with 24 home runs. Yet apart from Berra (.802) and DiMaggio, no other Yankees starter had an OPS above .800. Rizzuto had a below-average year, hitting .275 but only slugging .358. His OPS was a paltry .711. Rizzuto, though, did have a good year defensively. However, in a case of voters being blinded by the position he played and the team he played for, Rizzuto actually finished second in MVP voting, and five deluded journalists placed Rizzuto first on their ballots. Rizzuto was not even the second-best Yankee that year, let alone the second-best player in the AL. Less onerous, but still bewildering, three journalists gave their first-place vote to Joe Page, who ended up finishing third. Page had an excellent rebound season, finishing with a record of 13–8, and led all pitchers in the league in appearances (60), games finished (48), and saves (27). Nevertheless, that actual journalists gave their first-place vote to Page instead of Williams is laughable. Apart from Page, Raschi had a mighty fine season. He went 21–10 with an ERA of 3.34 to cap off an All-Star season. Likewise, fellow starter Reynolds was an All-Star with his 17–6 record. Reynolds was helped out by the offense, as his ERA was 4.00 (highest of his career).

New York played good ball all year but could never open a commanding lead. They started the month of September with a two-game lead but by the end of the month, and with only two more games remaining, trailed the Red Sox by a game. As fate would have it, the final two games would pit New York against Boston at Yankee Stadium. And after three innings in the first game, it seemed that the Red Sox would be heading to the World Series as they took a 4–0 lead. Reynolds lasted only 2 1/3 innings, and Page put fuel on the fire, walking the first two batters he faced, allowing two runs to score. Page then settled down and pitched the remainder of the game, giving up just one hit and a walk. The Yankees' offense woke up in the fourth, plating two, and they tied the game an inning later. In the bottom of the eighth, with two out, Johnny Lindell homered to left field to give the Yankees the lead. Page made short work of the Red Sox in the ninth, and the AL was all tied up heading into the final day.

Raschi took the mound for the Yankees, while Ellis Kinder started for the Red Sox. And both were magnificent, with Kinder going seven. In the bottom of the first, Rizzuto led off with a triple before Henrich plated him with a groundout. The score remained 1–0 until the bottom of the eighth. Henrich led off with a home run, and later in the inning, with the bases loaded, Jerry Coleman cleared the bases to give the Yankees a 5–0 lead. There was pandemonium in the Bronx. However, a misplay by DiMaggio in center in the top of the ninth allowed two runs to score, and with two outs Boston plated another run. But, with Raschi still on the mound, he got Birdie Tebbetts to pop up in foul ground to end the game. The Bronx Bombers finished with a record of 97–57 (same as Brooklyn) and were once again headed to the World Series!

DODGERS' 1949 SEASON

While the Dodgers failed to win the 1948 NL pennant, the season was highlighted by a number of promising players who either debuted or got increased playing time. These included Roy Campanella, Gil Hodges, and Duke Snider. Added to this threesome was the debut of pitcher Don Newcombe in 1949. Brooklyn was in the process of creating a powerhouse.

Campanella had a fine rookie season, playing in 83 games. While he was only average with the bat (and that was going to change in subsequent seasons), he was magnificent behind the plate. He led the NL by gunning down 67 percent of all base stealers. *New York World-Telegram* journalist Tom Meany noted that "more than one observer has likened Campanella's quickness behind the plate to that of a cat. He can pounce on bunts placed far out in front of the plate and he gets his throws away with no wasted motion." Campanella was twenty-six when he debuted with Brooklyn; he should have been in the majors a lot sooner. Campanella's father was Italian. Nothing wrong with that; many Italian Americans were already in the majors. The reason why Campanella did not debut in 1948 was that his mother was African American. Due to the success of Jackie Robinson breaking the color barrier, other black players could slowly make their way to the majors. In 1949, with increased playing time, Campanella was an All-Star, slashing .287/.385/.498 with 22 home runs and stellar defense.

Nineteen-year-old Gil Hodges had played a single game for Brooklyn in 1943. In the final day of that season, he walked in three plate appearances, stole a base, but made two errors at third. Following the season, Hodges enlisted in the Marines. As a result, he did not play in either the 1944 or 1945 seasons. He finally made it back to the majors in 1947 for the proverbial cup of coffee, appearing in 28 games. In 1948, he played a full season but was disappointing, slashing .249/.311/.376. Hodges's 1949 campaign was anything but disappointing. He hit .285 with an OBP of .360 while hitting 23 home runs (tied with Snider for the team lead). Hodges finished 11th in MVP voting and was an All-Star. Despite a wonderful career, the best thing about Hodges was that he was an outstanding person. Teammate Clem Labine stated, "Not getting booed at Ebbets Field was an amazing thing. Those fans knew their baseball, and Gil was the only player I can remember whom the fans never, I mean never, booed." Arthur Daley wrote in the *New York Times* that Hodges "was such a noble character in so many respects that I believe Gil to have been one of the finest men I met in sports or out if it."

Edwin Donald "Duke" Snider made his major-league debut for Brooklyn in 1947 at the ripe old age of twenty. He appeared in 40 games but was a below-average player. His OBP was a dismal .276, and he did not hit even a single home run. The following season he played in 13 more games, with almost double the number of plate appearances. Nevertheless, the increase in playing time saw Duke become an average player. While his OBP was still below .300, he hit for more power with five home runs. Snider became the Dodgers' regular center fielder in 1949. And as with Campanella and Hodges, that season Snider put it all together. His OBP increased dramatically to .361, while his slugging percentage improved by almost 100 points. Snider tied Hodges for the team lead in home runs with 23 and was second on the team in doubles behind Robinson with 28. As Tommy Lasorda eloquently stated, "I was Duke's teammate and looked up to him with respect. Duke was not only a great player, but he was a great person, too. He loved his family and loved the Dodgers. He was the true Dodger and represented the Dodgers to the highest degree of class, dignity, and character."

The last, but certainly not least, member of this fearsome foursome was Don Newcombe. Newk was a pitching stud and one of the first African Americans to play in the majors at a young age; he was only twenty-two when he made his debut for the Dodgers on May 20, 1949. Newcombe should have been on the team the previous year, but even with the success of Robinson, the Dodgers did not want to rush African Americans onto the major-league team. Newcombe did not have a good debut; coming on in relief, he gave up three runs on four hits and lasted only a third of an inning. Two days later, Newk showed the baseball community what he was capable of. Starting for the first time, he threw a five-game shutout against the Cincinnati Reds. Newcombe finished the season with a 17–8 record and an ERA of 3.17, while leading the NL in shutouts (five). Newk finished eighth in MVP voting and was an All-Star and the NL Rookie of the Year.

The Dodgers also got fine contributions from right fielder Carl Furillo, who hit .322, had an OBP of .368 while slugging .506 with 18 home runs, 27 doubles, and 10 triples, and drove in 106 runs. He finished sixth in MVP voting and should have been an All-Star. On the pitching side, in addition to Newcombe the Dodgers were well served by Preacher Roe. Roe made his major-league debut with the Cardinals in 1938, playing in a single game. He did not appear again on the mound until 1944, this time with the Pirates. He joined the Dodgers in 1948 and had a very good first campaign with Brooklyn. He was arguably better in 1949, going 15–6 with an ERA of 2.79. He made the first of four straight All-Star teams.

The standout on the 1949 Dodgers, however, was Jackie Robinson. Robinson led the NL in hitting (.342) and stolen bases (37), had an OBP of .432, and slugged .528. Robinson also had 203 hits including 38 doubles and 12 triples, leading the Dodgers in all of these categories. He was an All-Star and captured his first, and only, NL MVP award.

Despite all these outstanding seasons, the Dodgers were in a dogfight with the Cardinals. Even a disappointing April, when Brooklyn went 6–6, only meant they were one game out of the NL summit. For the rest of the year, the Dodgers were at most four games out of first or three and a half games up. On September 25, the Dodgers were 1 1/2 games out of first. However, the Cardinals imploded and lost four straight. On the final day of the season, a Dodgers win against the Phillies in Philadelphia would secure the pennant. And the Dodgers did a mighty fine job of imploding themselves. Going into the bottom of the fourth, the Dodgers had a commanding 5–0 lead, and with Newk on the mound the Brooklyn faithful were already in party mode. However, the Phillies scored four runs in the inning. The Dodgers came back with two in the fifth, but the Phillies countered with one in the fifth and two in the sixth. That ended the scoring, and the game was tied after nine. In the top of the tenth, RBI singles by Snider and Luis Olmo gave the Dodgers a 9–7 lead. With Jack Banta on the mound, the Phillies could not muster another comeback. Banta was the star. Coming on in relief, he went 4 1/3 scoreless innings, giving up only two hits. Brooklyn had won the pennant. The only downside was who was waiting for them in the fall classic.

THE 1949 WORLD SERIES

The Dodgers were again pitted against the Yankees. Would the third time be the charm? Another chance for the boys from Brooklyn to overcome the image that they were T-shirt-wearing little guys, the underdogs, the working stiffs of society. Another chance to overthrow the Yankees. Another chance to prove that they were *the* team in New York, *the* Brooklyn Dodgers, and *not* Dem Bums. History may have already repeated itself for the Yankees and the Dodgers with the Bronx Bombers proving their superiority and that they were the ruling class of baseball, while for Brooklyn and their fans, the two World Series losses were a tragedy and a farce. Nevertheless, the 1949 Dodgers were already changing history with black superstars Campanella, Newcombe, and the soon-to-be NL MVP Robinson. They changed the ruling-class belief, which was championed by former Yankees owner MacPhail, that black players were ill-equipped to play in the major leagues. The Brooklyn Dodgers were changing history and society. There was just one thing left to do: would they be able to overthrow baseball's powerhouse, *the* New York Yankees?

The Dodgers entrusted rookie Newcombe with the ball for Game One, while Reynolds, now in his eighth season in the bigs, took the mound for the Yankees. A crowd of 66,224 fans packed into Yankee Stadium to watch the two maestros at work. Brooklyn had good scoring opportunities early. Spider Jorgensen doubled with one out in the first, but neither Snider nor Robinson could drive him in. Reynolds walked the first two batters in the second, but he got Hodges to ground into a double play and Campanella to fly out to right to end the threat. In the bottom of the third, Reynolds doubled, but Rizzuto and Henrich both popped out to end the inning. The Dodgers wasted another scoring opportunity in the fifth as they put runners on first and second with only one out. However, Shotton let Newcombe hit rather than enlisting a pinch-hitter. Considering Newcombe hit .229 for the season, it was not a bad decision, especially as Newk was rolling. However, Newcombe struck out, and Pee Wee Reese grounded out. Once again, Reynolds got out of trouble, something he did again in the top of the eighth. With one out, Reese singled and then stole second. This time, Jorgensen and Snider could not pick up the crucial hit. Likewise, in the bottom of the inning, Coleman doubled with one out for New York. Stengel allowed Reynolds to bat for himself. As with the decision to allow Newcombe to hit, Reynolds had a decent year with the bat, hitting .218, and did hit a double of Newk earlier in the game. Nevertheless, at such a late stage of the game, a pinch-hitter would have been a better option. And considering Reynolds struck out looking, the decision not to pinch-hit for him was looking very bad indeed. More so after Rizzuto flew out to center. The Yankees were 0-for-4 with runners in scoring position; the Dodgers a pathetic 0-for-8. Reynolds made short work of the Dodgers in the top of the ninth. He had given up only two hits and walked four while striking out nine. Henrich stepped up to the plate in the bottom of the inning. And he did something that had never been done before; with a powerful swing of the bat, Henrich launched the ball into right field. The first walk-off homer in World Series history. Once again, Henrich had tortured the hopes of the Brooklyn faithful.

Considering the heartbreaking loss, it was imperative the Dodgers bounce back in Game Two. Conversely, the Yankees were looking to drive the nail in the coffin and once again assert their dominance over the baseball world. And once again it would be an outstanding pitching duel, this time between Vic Raschi and Preacher Roe.

Robinson led off the top of the second with a double. Raschi then retired the next two Dodgers. However, then something miraculous happened: a hit with a runner in scoring position. Gil Hodges drove home Robinson with a single to left. Raschi then intentionally walked Campanella to bring up Roe. Considering that Roe only hit .114 for the year while striking out 28 times in 84 plate appearances, the result was predictable: Raschi struck out Roe to end the inning. Both teams would have numerous opportunities to score, but the Dodgers were hopeless with runners in scoring position, going 1-for-10. As for the Yankees, they were even worse. Their best opportunity came in the eighth with runners at first and second and two out. However, Dodger-killer Henrich flew out and Bauer grounded out: another opportunity wasted. In the bottom of the ninth, with Roe still on the mound, DiMaggio singled to lead off the inning. Shotton kept faith in Roe and was rewarded as he got out of the inning without DiMaggio moving another ninety feet. The Yankees ended up 0-for-6 with runners in scoring position as the Dodgers tied up the World Series with a 1–0 victory.

Roe was special, throwing a complete-game shutout while only allowing six hits. Raschi was not bad himself, allowing only one run in eight innings of work.

As in the 1941 World Series, after losing Game One at Yankee Stadium, the Dodgers battled back and won Game Two. History repeated itself in that regard, as it would for the rest of the Series.

Game Three would bring the Series to Ebbets Field with Branca on the mound for the home side and Tommy Byrne for New York. The Yankees struck first thanks to a Rizzuto sacrifice fly in the third inning. Reese led off the fourth inning with a solo homer to tie the game. Then, with one out, Furillo singled before Robinson and Hodges walked to load the bases. Stengel had seen enough and brought in Page. Brooklyn once again could not get a single crucial hit. Luis Olmo popped up in foul territory, and Snider grounded out to end the inning. Both pitchers cruised into the bottom of the eighth. Branca struck out looking to start the inning, but then Reese walked and Eddie Miksis singled. Yet again, though, the Dodgers were Dem Bums as Furillo and Robinson both flied out. The game was still tied heading into the top of the ninth, and Brooklyn's failure to get the big hit cost them. With Berra on first and two out, Branca was tiring. Brown singled and Woodling walked to load them up. Stengel inserted Mize, a left-handed hitter, into the game as a pinch hitter. Rather than go to the bullpen and get a lefty, not a Dodgers strong suit, Shotton stuck with Branca. It was not a good decision. Mize singled home two, and at that point Shotton pulled Branca. Unfortunately or fortunately, depending on your viewpoint, Coleman singled off reliever Jack Banta to bring home another run. That run was to be essential, as Olmo and Campanella hit solo homers off Page in the bottom of the ninth to cut the deficit to one run. With Page still on the mound, Bruce Edwards was the Dodgers' last hope. Page had enough left, though, to strike him out. The game was over; the Yankees won, 4–3, and took a 2–1 lead in the Series. The Dodgers' inability to hit with runners in scoring position cost them: they went 0-for-4 for the game and were an astonishingly awful 1-for-22 in the first three games. Things would get better in that regard for the Dodgers in Game Four, yet as often was the case when the Dodgers battled the Yankees, it would not be enough.

After the Game Three loss, Shotton panicked and decided to start Newcombe in Game Four on short rest. Starting a veteran on short rest diminishes the chance the team will be successful. Starting a rookie, even one as good as Newcombe, in the World Series on short rest was almost assuredly a strategy to end in tears. Meanwhile, Stengel stuck with his original plan to start Eddie Lopat. Newcombe did not even have close to his best stuff. In the first inning, he gave up two singles and a pair of walks, but thanks to a double-play ball and a lineout, he got out of the inning unscathed. Neither he nor the Dodgers would be so lucky in the fourth. With two men on and one out, Cliff Mapes doubled to clear the bases. Coleman flied out to bring up Lopat. Lopat had a stellar year, for him, with the bat, posting a fine .733 OPS, a career best. And he helped his and the Yankees' cause immensely with a double to left to bring home Mapes. Mercifully, Shotton finally had had enough and replaced Newcome with Joe Hatten, who got the final out of the inning but faltered in the fifth. Henrich walked, Berra singled, and an intentional walk to DiMaggio loaded the bases. Brown tripled, bringing home all three runners. New York had a 6–0 lead, and the Ebbets Field crowd was morose. Hatten got out of the inning without allowing Brown to score, but the game was well and truly over. Or was it? In the bottom of the sixth, Brooklyn mounted a comeback. Reese and Cox singled to open the inning, but Snider then grounded into a double play. Shockingly, the Dodgers then proceeded to hit with runners in scoring position. Robinson, Hodges, Olmo, Campanella, and Gene Hermanski all singled off Lopat to score four. It was only after the fifth hit with two outs did Stengel pull Lopat. Reynolds took the mound and struck out Jorgensen. Trailing by only two runs with three innings remaining, Brooklyn was still in the game. However, Reynolds was outstanding. Not one Dodger in the final three innings could reach base. Reynolds stuck out five in 3 1/3 innings. New York won the game, 6–4, and another World Series triumph was all but assured.

The Game Five starter for the Yankees was All-Star Vic Raschi. Starting for the Dodgers was their fifth-best starter, Rex Barney. Joe Hatten was due to the start but was pressed into service the previous day in trying to rescue Brooklyn's season following Newcombe's short outing. Thus, the decision to start Newcombe on short rest had the effect of forcing Shotton to start Barney, an average pitcher who went 9–8 for the year with an ERA of 4.41. Barney did not stand a chance against the New York bats. In the top of the first, he walked the first two men he faced, who then both moved up ninety feet on a botched pickoff attempt. DiMaggio scored one with a sacrifice fly before Brown singled to bring another run home. The game was over by the end of the third. Barney got the first two batters out but then loaded the bases on two walks and a single. Another single by Coleman brought two runners home. Jack Banta replaced Barney and gave up a hit to Raschi as the Yankees scored another. New York eventually ended up winning, 10–6, to capture another World Series crown, four games to one.

While the majority of the games were close, New York was better in all aspects. They got the crucial hit when it mattered. By contrast, the Brooklyn offense was horrible in the first three games. It was only due to some outstanding Brooklyn pitching that the Dodgers managed to win one of those games. And of course, when the offense managed to string hits together and even hit home runs, the pitching fell off a cliff. The Dodgers scored 13 runs over the final three games yet lost all three. The Yankees were a class act and performed under pressure. The Dodgers did not do that. Moreover, Stengel outmanaged Shotton. Stengel's decision to pinch-hit Mize in Game Three while Shotton did not bring a lefty but kept Branca on the mound was *the* turning point of the Series. The resultant New York victory led to the rash decision to start Newcombe on short rest, which doomed Game Four for Brooklyn and had major repercussions for Game Five. Once again, the Yankees won the World Series because they were simply a batter ballclub and were better managed.

New York finished the 1940s with four World Series crowns (one less than in the 1930s), while Brooklyn had three World Series losses. The Yankees were still the undisputed rulers of all of baseball. They were the ruling class. The Dodgers were still Dem Bums.

5

1952: A NEW DECADE,
THE SAME RESULT

THE NEW DECADE brought continued Yankee dominance. However, it seemed that New York would not make
it back to the World Series in 1950. On August 17, the Bronx
Bombers were 4 1/2 games out of first. It was not an insur-
mountable deficit, but it would be challenging. Well, a challenge to anyone but the Yankees. New York won thirteen out of
their next fifteen games, and by the end of the month the deficit
had been wiped away. In its place, a two-game lead in the AL.
And while they stumbled a bit in September, the Yankees won
the pennant by three games over the Detort Tigers.

By contrast, Brooklyn was decidedly average for most of the
season. So much so that on September 18 they were a whopping nine games out of first. The Phillies were cruising to
the NL title. However, the Phillies forgot how to win, while
the Dodgers went streaking. Philadelphia came to Brooklyn for

the final two games of the season clinging to a two-game lead. The Dodgers beat the Phillies in the penultimate game of the season. As such, the NL pennant came down to the final day. And it was a magnificent pitching duel between Newcombe and Robin Roberts. With the scored tied, 1–1, in the bottom of the ninth, Cal Abrams walked to begin the inning, and Reese followed with a single. Snider then singled, but rather than be conservative and load the bases with none out, third-base coach Milt Stock waved Abrams home. But he was promptly thrown out at the plate by center fielder Richie Ashburn. With first base open, the Phillies walked Robinson. A measly sacrifice fly would force a playoff for the NL crown. But Furillo could not get the job done, popping up to the first baseman, and Hodges flew out to right. The inning was over, and Newcombe went out to start the 10th. He gave up singles to the first two hitters, and a bunt moved the runners over before Dick Sisler launched a three-run home run. The Dodgers went quietly in the bottom of the inning. The Phillies were headed to the World Series, and the Dodgers could only think what could have been. If it was any consolation, while all games were close, the New York Yankees once again proved that under pressure they were the best damn team by sweeping the Phillies in the World Series.

And they were equally good in 1951. New York was in contention for the pennant for the entire season. On September 18, they were tied for first with the Cleveland Indians. The Indians faltered, while the Yankees played some of their best baseball for the season and ended up winning the AL pennant by five games. They should have met the Dodgers, but Brooklyn collapsed in dramatic fashion. On September 14, the Dodgers had a six-game lead. The Giants then went on a tear, while Brooklyn played average baseball. The two teams were tied at the end of the season; a three-game playoff would decide who would be the sacrificial slaughter for the Yankees. The Giants won Game One, 3–1, while the Dodgers dominated Game Two, winning, 10–0. The Dodgers led the decider, 4–1, heading into the bottom of the ninth with Newcombe on the mound looking for a complete game. Once again, though, the Dodgers' manager left Newcombe in for too long. This time the blame rested with Chuck Dressen, who replaced Shotton before the start of the season. The first two Giants reached. With one out, Whitey Lockman doubled to score one. It was only then that Dressen replaced Newcombe. In came Branca, who went eight innings in Game One, to face Bobby Thomson. And the end result was the "shot heard 'round the world." Thomson homered, and the Giants were headed to the World Series. Thus, the Dodgers not only collapsed in the regular season, they collapsed in the play-offs. Just a tale of woe. In part due to Branca giving up *the* shot, he was labeled weak when it mattered. *Daily News* journalist Dick Young wrote that some Dodgers players were chockers. He later told Kahn that "no one in his right mind would call Reese or Robinson a choker. I meant the pitchers. Specifically I meant Ralph Branca. The other players agreed with what I wrote. Quietly they agreed with me. Sometimes it looked like everybody on the Brooklyn club knew who the chokers were, everybody except the ball club manager."

Branca later revealed that he was told that the Giants were stealing signs. In his 2011 autobiography, Branca wrote that "to be called a goat, as I was, for half a century hurt like hell especially when I knew that the team that tagged me with that label had implemented an elaborate and outrageous system of cheating. I had learned about the cheating less than three years after it happened. Yet for many long decades I kept quiet. I was advised to capitalize on and expose the scheme. Go to the press. Write a book. Do something. But I refused. I didn't want to be seen as a whiner, a sore loser or a baby crying over spilt milk. Take it on the chin. Accept the blow. Move on with your life. Or, best of all, forget about it, which proved impossible."

Whether the Giants were stealing signs, Branca did not perform under pressure, or whatever, the reality is that they and not the Dodgers were World Series-bound. The Giants put up more of a fight than the Phillies did the previous year, including winning Game One at Yankee Stadium. But as was the norm, the New York Yankees dug deep, did all the little things right, and ended up winning the Series, four games to two. The clincher occurred on October 10.

That date is always remembered because in addition to another World Series going to the Bronx, it was the last time DiMaggio suited up for the Yankees in a competitive game. DiMaggio had a subpar year and knew it was time to hang up the pinstripes. In his final game, he had a double, two walks, and a run scored. He was an All-Star in each of his 13 seasons, had a career batting average of .325, was a three-time MVP, won the batting title twice, played on nine World Series-winning teams, was elected to the Hall of Fame, and was briefly married to Marilyn Monroe. The Yankee Clipper did it all.

THE YANKEES' 1952 SEASON

To be considered *the* dominant team in the hearts and minds of the public around the world, winning, while very important, is not good enough. A classic example in basketball of a successful team, but not really embraced, is the San Antonio Spurs from the late 1990s onward. A great and successful team, but not really taken to their hearts by the basketball public. By contrast, the Los Angeles Lakers during the Showtime era or the Chicago Bulls led by Michael Jordan will always be fondly remembered. A good example in baseball is the St. Louis Cardinals, a great team in many eras with many Hall of Famers, but outside of Missouri, it is fair to say that they are not universally loved or despised; every powerhouse is always hated by a large segment of the population. The Cardinals are just a baseball team.

The New York Yankees are disliked by many in the baseball public; they are despised because they often have the largest payroll and are usually that damn good. Yet even amongst this group, people instantly know the names of the great Yankees players throughout history such as Gehrig, Ruth, DiMaggio, Mantle, Berra, Derek Jeter, and Alex Rodriguez, just to name a few. Larger-than-life players that have transcended into the hearts and minds of the general public across the globe.

With DiMaggio retiring, the Yankees were losing that larger-than-life character. The team still had Berra and to a lesser extent Rizzuto, but they needed another superstar. Other teams losing an icon like DiMaggio could struggle to replace such an iconic player. As for the Yankees, they replaced DiMaggio with Mickey Mantle.

Scout Tom Greenwade discovered Mantle at a game in Coffeyville, Kansas. Mantle was a horrible shortstop, but oh could he hit. Greenwade was in awe and very fortuitously there was not another scout at the game. An eleven-hundred-dollar signing bonus convinced Mantle's father to allow his son to turn pro. It is possible that if the Dodgers had a better scouting network, Mantle could have been a Dodger. He told Kahn, "We didn't have a television but we had a radio and I used to listen to the broadcasts from St. Louis. The best games were National League, the Dodgers and the Cardinals. My two idols were Stan Musial and Pee Wee Reese. I wasn't that much turned on by the Yankees. But they were the only big league team that wanted me." Mantle made the Yankees out of spring training in 1951; the team wisely moved him from shortstop to the outfield. New York slotted him in right with DiMaggio in center. The Yankees had found DiMaggio's successor. While the team may have expected DiMaggio to mentor Mantle, this did not occur. For whatever reason, DiMaggio preferred Mantle to find his own way in the bigs.

Mantle had a good, but not spectacular, rookie season in 1951. He hit .267 while belting 13 home runs in 96 games. The following season, Mantle was ready to take on the world, batting .311 with 37 doubles and 23 home runs. He led the league in OPS (.924), but also in strikeouts (111). Just remember that when some talking head says that players of yesteryear had power and rarely struck out. Mantle was an All-Star and finished third in MVP voting. And equally important for the selling of the Yankees' image, the baseball public loved Mantle. He was the All-American kid. While Mantle may not have been as wholesome as the public thought, that did not matter; image was everything. Mantle was beloved. And with television being more prevalent, Mantle was not just a baseball star in New York, and not even a baseball star across America, he was a celebrity across the country. The perception and the reality that the New York Yankees were the best and most dominant baseball team with the biggest stars were beamed to homes through the power of television. Mantle was great for the Yankees, and playing for the New York Yankees was great for Mantle. If New York were an average ballclub, Mantle would never have become such a larger-than-life icon. But because he and the club were often dominant, Mantle is still an icon today many years after his death.

In addition to Mantle having a great second season with New York, Berra hit .273 and led the team with 30 home runs and 98 RBIs. Gene Woodling also had a very solid season, hitting .309 and leading all regulars with a .397 OBP. The pitching staff was led by Reynolds, who had another outstanding year with a 20–8 record and an AL-leading ERA of 2.06. He also led the league in strikeouts (160) and shutouts (six). Reynolds was an All-Star and finished second in MVP voting. He was ably supported by Raschi, who had an All-Star season with a record of 16–6 and a career-best 2.78 ERA.

As for the season, the Yankees started slowly, having a losing record in April, and while things improved in May, they were only 18–17 by the end of the month. Luckily for them, no other team played consistent baseball, and as such New York was only 3 1/2 games off the AL lead. And the Yankees took advantage, playing some great baseball in June, finishing the month with a 21–9 record and leading the AL by three games. With the exception of one day in August, the Yankees held onto the league lead for the rest of the season. The team played sub-optimal baseball in July and August but posted a 19–5 record in September and an overall record of 95–59, two games better than the Indians. Once again, New York was heading to the World Series.

THE DODGERS' 1952 SEASON

Following the great collapse of the previous season, one would have expected Brooklyn's front office to try to add a few pieces to the puzzle to not only increase their chances of winning the NL pennant, but, more important, capture the World Series crown. Anyone expecting that was sorely mistaken. The Dodgers' ownership was confident, many would say overconfident, going into the new season. The only major additions were starters Ben Wade and Billy Loes, plus twenty-eight-year-old rookie closer Joe Black.

After previously playing only two major-league games in 1948 with the Chicago Cubs, Wade made the Dodgers' opening-day roster and had a decent season. Wade appeared in 36 games and had a record of 11–9 with an ERA of 3.60. Loes made 10 appearances with Brooklyn in 1950, and his ERA was an astronomical 7.82. He did not play in 1951 due to military service. Loes was a much better pitcher in 1952. He compiled a 13–8 record and led all Brooklyn starters with an ERA of 2.69 while appearing in 39 games. Only Black had a better ERA and appeared in more games.

The reason why Black did not make the majors until he was in his late twenties is because he was African American. His daughter, Martha Jo Black, writes that as a high school player, Black could not understand why a scout would talk to his teammates but not him. Black confronted the scout, who told Black that he was a good player but "Colored guys . . . don't play in the big leagues." In his first and only great big-league season, in fifty-six games Black went 15–4 with an ERA of 2.15 while leading the league in games finished (41). Black easily won the NL Rookie of the Year award and finished third in MVP voting. Unfortunately, Black would never be the same pitcher; continued overuse by Dressen stifled what should have been a great career. Black appeared in 31 more games than any other Dodgers reliever while pitching 142 1/3 innings, 45 more than the next highest reliever. Despite his baseball career never reaching the same heights as his 1952 season, Black's daughter notes that "my father went to every PTA meeting. He'd tell my teachers, 'Hi, I'm Joe Black, I'm Martha Jo's father. If there's any problem, you call me.' My dad was very instrumental in everything that I did. I loved my mother, but my father was a great parent." And that is better than any World Series triumph.

Of course, World Series triumphs means so much to baseball fans, players, and management; and with the additions of Wade and Black, the Dodgers would have been a better team than the previous season. However, Newcombe would not suit up for the Dodgers after being called up by the military. And worse was to follow in spring training, as Branca fell off a chair and landed on a Coke bottle. Branca did not experience any pain but later noticed blood on his clothing. He went to Brooklyn's trainer, who confirmed there was a cut but nothing else was wrong. But something was indeed wrong. When Branca fell, the bottle hit the base of his spine, putting his alignment out of whack. Branca notes in his autobiography that the Dodgers' trainer never checked for any alignment issue; as a result, months later when Branca went to an osteopath, the physician noted a serious problem. Branca writes, "A thorough examination showed that my left side was an inch and a half higher than my right. My left side was bunched up and my right side elongated. In short, I was seriously out of alignment." And because it was months after the injury, the osteopath told Branca that his alignment would always be an issue and forever affect his pitching. The osteopath was unfortunately proven right: Branca was never the same pitcher. He appeared in only 16 games in 1952 and seven games in 1953 before he was traded to the Tigers during the 1953 season. He was out of the majors for good after the 1956 season; the one game was with Brooklyn. Falling on a bottle destroyed Branca's career.

While the Dodgers were weakened through the loss of Newcombe and Branca, they were fortunate that the Giants also had their own ill fortune. Future Hall of Famer Monte Irvin was limited to only 46 games through injury, while Willie Mays, after a great Rookie of the Year campaign the previous year, suffered a sophomore slump at the beginning of the season. By May 28, Mays was only hitting .236. Mays did not have time to recapture the magic of his rookie season; he was drafted and joined the Army. These two key losses hampered the Giants' season. And the 1952 NL pennant was always going to be a battle between the Dodgers and the Giants.

The difference between the two teams was that the Dodgers' offense was potent. Robinson had a slash line of .308/.440/.465 with 24 steals. Hodges hit just .254, but when he connected, he connected with power. He led the team with a slugging percentage of .500 with 27 doubles and 32 home runs. Hodges also led the team with 107 walks. Likewise, Campanella hit 22 long balls, while Snider hit for average (.303) and power (25 doubles and 21 home runs).

While the Dodgers pitchers were not out of this world, one of them had a game to remember. On June 19 against the Cubs at Ebbets Field on a cloudy day in front of a paltry crowd of

7,732, Carl Erskine had electrifying stuff. After being perfect through 2 2/3 innings, Erskine walked Willie Ramsdell on four straight fastballs. That was his only mistake. Despite him only striking out one Chicago batter, the Cubs batters could not do anything against Erskine. In the top of the ninth and with two out, Erskine faced Eddie Miksis. On a 3-2 count, Miksis grounded out to short. The Dodgers won, 5–0, and Erskine had pitched a no-hitter. He was rewarded with a $500 bonus from Brooklyn owner Walter O'Malley. Reflecting on his performance on the sixty-second anniversary of his no-hitter in 2014, Erskine recalled that "I used to ride the subway in Brooklyn with Pee Wee Reese and Duke Snider. I was just a tagalong, and nobody recognized me. When I pitched the no-hitter, I was suddenly recognized on the Brooklyn subway." Erskine went on to have a career year with a record of 14–6 and an ERA of 2.70.

With their powerful offense and decent-to-good pitching, Brooklyn was cruising. During August, the Dodgers had a 10 1/2 game lead. By the end of the month, they still had a nine-game lead. Dem Bums then decided to live up to their unofficial nickname and lost six of seven; their NL lead was down to four games. By September 15, the lead was down to three games. However, unlike the previous disastrous season, the Dodgers rallied while the Giants faltered. Brooklyn ended up winning the NL pennant by 4 1/2 games (the half game due to the Dodgers tying their final game of the regular season with the Boston Braves: the score was deadlocked at 5 at the end of 12 innings). The Dodgers were once again heading to the World Series and had another chance to break the Yankees' domination of baseball.

THE 1952 WORLD SERIES

Despite having home-field advantage for the first time, the Dodgers went into the World Series as decided underdogs. The Yankees were the unstoppable force that won the AL pennant against many a worthy foe, while the Dodgers were the best of a weaker NL. Dressen realized that luck would have to be on Brooklyn's side if the team was going to overcome New York. As such, he sprang somewhat of a surprise by starting Black in Game One. It was not a total surprise, because Black started the final two games he pitched in the regular season. On September 21, Black pitched a complete-game shutout against the Braves, allowing only three hits. His next start, also against the Braves, did not go as well. Black was scorched as he allowed five runs in five innings of work. These was the only two starts Black made in the majors all year. Pitching for New York was 20-game winner Allie Reynolds.

Both teams went quietly in the first, but Robinson led off the bottom of the second with a home run to left field. The lead did not last long, as Gil McDougald led off the top of the third with a carbon copy of Robinson's shot, also to left field. With both pitchers at the top of their game, neither offense could get going. That all changed in the bottom of the sixth. With two out, Reese singled, and with Snider at the plate a wild pitch moved him to second. Snider then proceeded to do something that he was great at for the majority of his career, namely, hit one out of the park. A two-run shot to right field gave Brooklyn the lead. And while Bauer got one back in the top of the eighth thanks to a sacrifice fly after Woodling tripled to open the inning, Reese homered in the bottom of the inning to restore the Dodgers' two-run lead. Black made short work of the Yankees in the ninth, and the Dodgers had won the opener, 4–2. And Black was the first African American pitcher to win a World Series game. In another first, a Brooklyn manager's decision to spring a surprise starter in the World Series opener actually worked. Now Brooklyn needed to press home its advantage in Game Two, but the men in pinstripes had other ideas.

With Erskine on the mound, the Dodgers walked the tightrope in the first two innings. The Yankees ran themselves out of a huge inning in the first with two runners caught stealing. In the second, the first two men reached, but Erskine struck out the next two before getting Billy Martin to ground out. Vic Raschi walked the bases loaded in the bottom of the inning, but Erskine could not help his own cause, flying out to end the scoring threat. Brooklyn broke through in the third on an RBI single by Campanella. New York came right back with a Berra sacrifice fly with one out plating Mantle, who had led off the inning with a double. And New York captured the lead in the fifth. Gil McDougald walked, promptly stole second, and Martin brought him home with a single. Erskine was clearly laboring, but once again a Dodgers manager left his starting pitcher in for too long. New York capitalized in the sixth. The first three Yankees reached to load the bases. Dressen finally pulled Erskine and replaced him with Loes. Collins grounded out to plate one. And then the wheels fell off for the Dodgers. McDougald singled in another run, and this brought up Martin, who crushed a pitch to deep left field for a three-run shot. The Yankees led, 7–1, and that finished the scoring for the day. Considering New York was only 3-for-14 with runners in scoring position, the score could have been even more of a blowout. After his early struggle,

Raschi was superb. He pitched a complete game, and while he gave up five walks, he only allowed three hits.

With the Series going across town to Yankee Stadium and their utter domination of Game Two, one would assume that New York would run away with it. And they broke through in the second inning of Game Three with pitcher Lopat hitting an RBI single off of Preacher Roe to bring home Bauer. This time it was Brooklyn's turn to come right back, with Furillo scoring on Robinson's sacrifice fly. New York had a golden opportunity to break the game wide open in the fourth. Berra doubled to open the inning, and he moved to third on a sacrifice bunt. Roe struck out McDougald, but then walked Martin and Lopat to load the bases. Rizzuto grounded out, and the inning was over. The Yankees paid the price next inning as the Dodgers took the lead thanks to an RBI single from Reese. With Lopat still on the mound, Brooklyn scored again in the top of the eighth, but Berra homered off Roe in the bottom of the inning to cut the deficit to one. This time it was the Yankees' turn to fall apart. In the top of the ninth, with one out Reese and Robinson singled off Lopat. Stengel brought in Tom Gorman. Throwing caution to the wind, Reese and Robinson pulled off a double steal. Gorman then got Campanella to pop up. With two out and Andy Pafko at the plate, Gorman threw a fastball that somehow Berra could not hold onto. As a result, not only did Reese score from third, Robinson made it home from second. Two runs scored from a passed ball. Considering that Johnny Mize hit a solo shot in the bottom of the ninth to cut the margin to two, the runs scored from the passed ball ended up being the difference maker. The Dodgers ended up winning, 5–3, with Roe pitching a complete game. Yet all people cared about after the game was the passed ball. Stengel put the blame on Gorman, saying that Berra had been crossed up. To his credit, Berra refused to throw Gorman under the bus, taking full responsibility for the passed ball. Berra told reporters, "I called for a fast ball and I got it. . . . It was my fault that it got away. I knew what was coming." Berra went on to note that "the pitch hit the tip of mitt and smashed the finger. . . . There was such sharp pain, for a moment I was stunned." Berra said that he asked home-plate umpire Larry Goetz, "Where the hell is the ball, Larry? Where is it?" A costly and painful passed ball. For the first time in Yankees-Dodgers World Series history, Brooklyn was leading after three games.

The Dodgers were looking to continue their momentum in Game Four. In a rematch from Game One, Reynolds was on the mound for New York and Black for the Dodgers. Both teams had opportunities to score, but a vital hit with runners in scoring position eluded them; the Dodgers were 0-for-3 and the Yankees 0-for-7. Two hits and an ill-advised stolen-base attempt would decide the game. In the bottom of the fourth, veteran Dodger-killer Johnny Mize led off the inning with a home run to deep left field. Brooklyn had a wonderful opportunity to come right back in the fifth. Pafko singled to open the inning, followed by a Hodges walk. A sacrifice bunt, by Furillo moved the runners over. One can question why Dressen called for the bunt, as this brought Black to the plate. Black had hit a paltry .139 during the regular season while striking out more than a third of the time. Maybe sensing that Black would strike out, Pafko decided to steal home, but he was gunned down, and the Dodgers had lost a great scoring opportunity. This was even more true, as Black earned a walk. However, Billy Cox fouled out and with it foiled the Dodgers' best chance to score. New York doubled its lead in the eighth with Mantle hitting a triple to lead off the inning, and a throwing error allowed him to score. And in the ninth, Brooklyn went quietly; New York won, 2–0, and the Series was tied, 2–2. Reynolds was stunning, pitching a four-hit shutout.

Game Five saw Erskine back on the mound for Brooklyn, while Ewell Blackwell pitched for New York. Blackwell was a somewhat strange choice considering he had only started two games, while appearing in five, for the Yankees since being acquired from the Reds in August. Stengel was hoping that the side-armer Blackwell would mesmerize the Dodger hitters. Unfortunately, for the Yankees that was not the case. Brooklyn opened their account in the second thanks to a Pafko RBI single that drove in Robinson. And Brooklyn added to its advantage in the fifth. Hodges led off the inning with a walk, and Erskine sacrificed him over via a bunt. The Yankees tried to get Hodges at second, but he beat the throw. The Dodgers bunted again; this time the Yankees got Cox at first. Hodges would score on a sacrifice fly by Reese. And with Blackwell still on the mound, Snider followed with a home run to deep right, and the Dodgers led by four. With Erskine pitching well, a four-run lead should have been enough. But the Yankees were the best team in baseball and came right back in the bottom of the inning. The first two batters reached, and then pinch-hitter Irv Noren got one back with an RBI single. Gil McDougald then plated another run with a groundout. Rizzuto singled, which moved McDougald to third with one out, but Mantle popped up in foul ground. Erskine was clearly laboring, but Dressen left him in. It was a costly mistake, as Mize belted a ball to deep right for a three-run jack. The Yankees scored five in the inning and had taken the lead. The lead did not last long, however, as Snider tied the game in the seventh with an RBI single off Johnny Sain. Considering the horrid fifth, somehow Erskine was still in the game. One of the consequences of Black starting for the Dodgers is that their bullpen was devoid of reliable options. Thus, Dressen stuck with Erskine. And in this case, the pitcher did not let the manager down. Not a single Yankee reached base after the fifth. The score remained tied until the top of the 11th. With runners at first and second with one out, Snider doubled in a run. Erskine cut through the Yankees in the bottom of the inning as he went 11 innings while only giving up five hits and three walks. The Dodgers won, 6–5, and were one win away from their first World Series title.

Game Six was at Ebbets Field. Yet the ballpark was not packed. Rud Rennie of the *New York Herald Tribune* stated that "there were only 30,037 persons at Ebbets Field for this game . . . which would have had the effect of an A-bomb with noodles if the Dodgers had won. It was the smallest crowd of the Series, probably because many did not think they would be able to get tickets; or maybe because many people did not want to stand in line and preferred to stay at home and look at it on television." The small crowd was surely noted by O'Malley.

The Brooklyn fans in attendance were ecstatic when in the bottom of the sixth, Snider, who was having a hell of a World Series, led off the inning with a home run to right. With Loes pitching wonderfully well, surely 1952 would be *the* year. Unfortunately, the Yankees refused to follow the fairy-tale script. Berra led off the top of the seventh with a home run, and then Woodling reached on a single. Loes then balked the runner over. He came back to retire the next two Yankee batters. This brought up Raschi, who hit a comebacker straight at Loes. The Brooklyn pitcher seemingly did not see the ball, and it caromed off his leg, allowing Woodling to score. The Dodgers faithful were crestfallen. And there was more heartbreak in the eighth when Mantle took Loes deep to open the inning. There was renewed hope for Brooklyn in the bottom of the inning when Snider, who else, hit another home run to deep right to cut the margin to one. And Dodgers fans were at the edge of the seats later in the inning when George Shuba doubled with two outs. This brought Campanella to the plate. It was an all-hands-on-deck situation, so Stengel brought in Reynolds to pitch. And Reynolds did not let his manager down, striking out Campanella; crisis adverted or despair, depending on which jersey one cheered. Brooklyn had one final chance in the bottom of the ninth. With one out, Reynolds walked Furillo. But Pafko popped up and Cox grounded out. New York won, 3–2. The Series was tied at three games apiece, and in that situation, who would want to bet against *the* New York Yankees? Following the game, Loes's explanation that he lost Raschi's hit in the sun did not sit well. But it is the logical explanation. In the book *Bums,* Carl Erskine told author Peter Golenbock, "When Loes said he lost it in the sun everybody laughed, and the fact is, if you ever pitched in Ebbets Field, you know that's possible in October with a ball that's hit with a little bounce on it."

Whatever the reason, the reality was that Ebbets Field hosted Game Seven, which surely had to favor the Dodgers. A Game Seven that almost no one predicted would occur given that the Yankees were the overwhelming favorites heading into the Series. Brooklyn had the opportunity to overcome their nemesis and to show the baseball world that no matter how good the Yankees were, they were beatable. Taking the mound for New York was Lopat and for Brooklyn, a tired Black, who had started only two games in the entire regular season; Game Seven was his third World Series start. Both pitchers were efficient in the first three innings. The Yankees opened the scoring in the fourth with Mize singling home Rizzuto, who had led off the inning with a double. The Dodgers came right back in the bottom of the inning. Snider led off with a single, and then both Robinson and Campanella reached on bunt singles. This brought to the plate Hodges, who was looking for his first hit in the fall classic. Stengel had seen enough and brought in Reynolds. On a 2-0 count, Hodges lined a ball to left field to bring home Snider with a sacrifice fly, and Robinson advanced to third on an error. Reynolds then struck out Shuba, and Furillo grounded out to end the inning. The failure to capitalize was costly, as Woodling homered to lead off the top of the fifth. The Dodgers came right back in the bottom of the frame; with one out Cox doubled and Reese singled him home and advanced to second on an error. But once again, Brooklyn could not hit with runners in scoring position. This time it was Snider and Robinson who could not get the crucial hit. The score was tied at two, but it would not remain that way for long. With one out in the sixth, Mantle homered on a 3-1 count to restore New York's lead. Mize then singled, and only then did Dressen replace Black. With Black starting, the Dodgers had no reliable pitchers in their bullpen, and it cost them dearly. The Yankees increased their lead in the seventh. With one out, McDougald singled to right and advanced to second courtesy of a Rizzuto sacrifice bunt. This brought Mantle to the plate. And on the first pitch that he saw, he singled to left, scoring McDougald. The twenty-year-old Mantle was already a superstar and in the biggest game of the season came through in the clutch. This was not the case for the Dodgers. In the bottom of the inning, Brooklyn loaded the bases with one out. Stengel called on Bob Kuzava.

The journeyman left-hander was in his sixth major-league season that included previous stints with Cleveland, the White Sox, and the Washington Senators. Kuzava got the save in the deciding Game Six of the 1951 World Series in his only appearance of that year's fall classic. And in 1952, history would repeat itself. On a 3-2 count, Kuzava got Snider to pop up for an easy out. He then proceeded to get Robinson to do the same, but first baseman Joe Collins lost the ball in the sun. Just when the home crowd thought the ball would land for a hit, Billy Martin scampered in from second base and caught it just above his knees. The inning was over and with it the last real opportunity for Brooklyn to score. Kuzava stayed in the game and worked around a one-out error to retire the side in the eighth. In the ninth, he was equally as good, retiring the Dodgers in order. New York had defeated Brooklyn, 4–2. Kuzava earned the save for the New York Yankees, as once again they were World Series champions. And once again the Dodgers were the also-rans who were outmanaged and constantly failed to get a hit when it mattered most. Brooklyn had overperformed to push New York to a Game Seven, but in the end once again the Yankees were the better all-around team and proved it. New York's superstars performed, while the Dodgers players did not. Hodges went 0-for-21, and Robinson hit a paltry .174. Snider had a great Series, hitting .345 with two doubles and four home runs. However, in Game Seven he had two golden opportunities to plate runners but failed to do so. By contrast, Mantle burned the brightest in Game Seven, while also hitting .345 throughout the Series. The Yankees had proved once again that they were at the pinnacle of the sport.

6

1953: YANKEES 5, DODGERS 0

COMING INTO THE 1953 season, the Yankees' domination showed no signs of abating, while the Dodgers were wracked by "what if." Brooklyn had numerous chances in the prior three Yankees-Dodgers World Series to break the New York stranglehold. But they could not overcome failing to get a hit when it mattered most, Yankees managers out-thinking their Dodgers counterparts, or their pitchers being unable to go deep into games or left on the mound long past their expiration date. So many "what-ifs" across three World Series had to take a mental toll on fans, the players, Dressen, the front office, ownership, and the Dodgers organization as a whole. Brooklyn may now have been considered a powerhouse in the NL, but on the biggest stage of all, coming up short undoubtedly affected the Dodgers' psyche greatly. Dem Bums may have been a humorous nickname, yet at the same time it cut to the core what the team was. The Yankees' almost total domination of the Dodgers in the World Series reinforced the notion that New

York was the ruling class, the aristocrats; Brooklyn were Dem Bums. Nevertheless, the 1953 season was another opportunity for the Dodgers to overcome their Yankee hoodoo. Instead, it just reinforced the baseball class structure.

THE YANKEES' 1953 SEASON

The Yankees were largely unchanged from the previous season and as such were favorites to once again capture the AL pennant and go on to be crowned World Series champions for the fifth straight season. The one major change was that Reynolds was being transitioned from a starter to a reliever. Even though Reynolds had a career-best and AL-leading ERA of 2.06 the previous season, Father Time was catching up to the thirty-six-year-old. Of course, Reynolds was not like mere mortals. In his 12th major league season, Reynolds still started 15 games and had a record of 13–7 with an ERA of 3.41. Most pitchers in their prime would be ecstatic with such numbers. With Reynolds moving to the pen, that left an opening for a starter. That slot was ably filled by Whitey Ford.

Edward Charles "Whitey" Ford was a thinking man's pitcher. He noted that when it comes to pitching, "You need arm, heart and head. Arm and heart are assets. Head is a necessity." Ford was a picture of calm on the mound. Mantle stated that "I don't care what the situation was, how high the stakes were—the bases could be loaded and the pennant riding on every pitch, it never bothered Whitey." Mantle was an unabashed fan of Ford. Indeed, Mantle said if the World Series was on the line, he would always choose Ford as the starting pitcher. Ford was a Yankees fan as a child with his favorite player being DiMaggio.

As fate would have it, the two would play together a year before DiMaggio's final season in pinstripes. The Yankees' recruitment of Ford demonstrates why the team was so great for so long. There was somewhat of a bidding war for Ford's services between the Red Sox, Giants, and Yankees. Even though the Yankees eventually offered Ford the highest dollar amount, because he was a Yankees fan, and successful teams almost always have the most fans, there was only one team that he wanted to play for. As the old adage goes, success breeds success.

Ford made his debut as a twenty year old during the 1950 season. The rookie was a phenomenon in the making. Ford went 9–1 with an ERA of 2.81 and finished second in Rookie of the Year voting. It was an impressive achievement considering Ford was less than stellar in his first few games. And to cap off the season, in the World Series clincher against the Phillies, Ford went 8 2/3 innings to pick up the win, giving up just two runs as a result of an error. Unfortunately, Ford did not play in 1951 or 1952 due to military service, but he was back with a vengeance for the 1953 season. In 1953, Ford appeared in 32 games, with 30 starts, 11 complete games, 18 wins (leading all Yankee starters in these categories) with an ERA of 3.00. Not bad for a twenty-four-year-old who had not appeared in the majors since 1951. Ford was ably supported by Vic Raschi in his final season in pinstripes. Raschi ended the season 13–6 with an ERA of 3.33. Another veteran who performed superbly was thirty-five-year-old Eddie Lopat, who went 16–4 with an AL-best ERA of 2.42.

In addition to the veterans, the Yankees' youngsters were also outstanding. Mantle had a slash line of .295/.398/.497 with 21 home runs and 92 RBIs. And it was because of Mantle that the term "tape-measure home run" entered the baseball lexicon. On April 17, the Yankees were playing the Senators. With two outs in the top off the fifth, Mantle hit a home run out of Griffith Stadium. Arthur "Red" Patterson, the publicity director of the Yankees, claimed that he left the stadium to track down the ball. He encountered a ten-year-old boy, Donald Dunaway, who had possession of the ball. Dunaway told Patterson where the ball had landed. Patterson then stated that he used a tape measure to determine how far the ball had traveled. Patterson marveled to the press that Mantle's home run was 565 feet. *New York Times* journalist Louis Effrat wrote that the home run traveled 460 feet to clear the stadium, and "it was estimated that the ball came to rest 105 farther back . . . and to get there, it could not have bounced in the street immediately outside the park. It is unlikely that the ball could have bounced high enough first to clear a two-story building, behind which it was picked up by a ten-year-old lad." The truth, as is often the case when it comes to legends, was something different. Decades later, Dunaway told author Jane Leavy that he was in the stadium and, seeing the ball fly out, ran outside and managed to retrieve it. On his way back into Griffith Stadium, an usher led him into the visitors' clubhouse. It was there that he first saw Patterson, not outside the stadium, as in Patterson's story. The reality is that while Mantle's home run was a monster, there is absolutely no way that it traveled 565 feet even with a strong tailwind. Nevertheless, the legend of Mantle's 565-foot tape-measure home run was born and is still somewhat believed even to this day.

Apart from Mantle, the other offensive powerhouses for New York were Berra and Woodling. Berra hit .296 with 27 home runs and 23 doubles, while driving in 108 runs. Woodling was something of an unsung hero for the Yankees. Always in the shadow of his more famous teammates, Woodling was a consistent performer for many championship teams. In 1953, he led the AL in OBP (.429) while hitting .306.

As for the Yankees' season, they lost on Opening Day to the Philadelphia Athletics, 5–0. Was the sky falling? Were the Yankees finally descending from the heavens and becoming mere mortals? Not quite. New York then won nine out of their next ten games and led the AL by two games. Even for great teams, it is often the case that capturing the pennant is a season-long struggle. This was not the case for the 1953 Yankees. New York took over first place on April 21 and did not surrender their lead for the rest of the season, eventually winning the AL crown in a canter by 8 1/2 games with a record of 101–50. Yet the consensus was that they were not even playing to their maximum capacity. The Yankees did enough to assert their dominance without overpowering the league. Quite simply, the Yankees' dominance over the AL was not seriously challenged even with them losing nine straight at one stage. After that horror run, New York still had a five-game lead. It was the season for long streaks. Apart from that losing streak, New York also set a franchise record with an 18-game winning streak. The men in pinstripes were seemingly unstoppable. And facing them in the World Series was their crosstown punching bag.

THE DODGERS' 1953 SEASON

Coming off yet another heartbreaking season, one would have expected Brooklyn management to go all out to secure the elusive first World Series title. Such a thought would be rational unless you knew the history of the Dodgers. Once again, there were some minor changes, with the team largely being unchanged from the previous season.

One move was to transfer Robinson to the outfield to allow rookie Jim Gilliam to slot into second. Gilliam was an exciting prospect for the Cubs after playing in the Negro Leagues and the Puerto Rican Professional Baseball League. Cubs scout Harry Postove stated Gilliam was "the best young prospect in the Negro American League" and that he was "a clean-cut youngster with an accurate, snap throw, a good eye, a hustler with the knack for punching the ball to all fields." At the time it was incredibly difficult for a black player who was not "clean-cut" to make the majors. Gilliam was assigned to the Cubs' Triple-A affiliate in Springfield, Massachusetts, but he did not play well and was demoted to Single A, where once again he failed to perform. The reasons given for Gilliam's lackluster play were that he could not hit good pitching and/or the Cubs had a better second-base prospect in Triple A. Dodgers reliever Joe Black, who was Gilliam's roommate and teammate in Montreal, claimed that Gilliam, who was naturally shy and quiet, was not used to playing with and against white players. Whatever the reason, Gilliam was released by the Cubs at the end of the 1950 season and picked up by the Dodgers, who sent him to Montreal. Gilliam starred in Montreal with his breakout season occurring in 1952. Gilliam was ready for the majors, except that Robinson was entrenched at second for the big-league club. Dressen decided to move Robinson to third or put him in the outfield, and Gilliam would be the everyday second baseman. The result was that Gilliam had a good first year with Brooklyn. He led the NL in plate appearances (710) and triples (17) but also led the league in caught stealing (14). Gilliam also set an NL rookie record for walks (100). He was rewarded for his fine season by being named NL Rookie of the Year. Although, truth be told, the award should have gone to Cardinals pitcher Harvey Haddix, who went 20–9 with an ERA of 3.06 and led the NL in shutouts with six while also slashing .289/.337/.412 in 107 plate appearances. Nevertheless, in the record books it is Gilliam who is listed as the 1953 NL Rookie of the Year.

Of course, if Robinson had a down year, moving him from second would have been a mistake. Instead, Robinson was his usual classy self with a slash line of .329/.425/.502. The Dodgers were an offensive powerhouse. Snider led the NL in slugging (.627), OPS (1.046), total bases (370), and runs (132), while hitting 42 long balls. Likewise, Campanella was superb on the way to winning his second NL MVP trophy. Campanella hit .312/.395/.611 with 41 home runs while leading the NL with 142 RBIs. Apart from Snider, Campanella, and Robinson, Carl Furillo (.973) and Gil Hodges (.943) also had an OPS above .900.

That the Brooklyn offense was a juggernaut masked that the pitching side was not as good as in the previous season. Things started to go off the rails in spring training when Dressen, in his infinite wisdom, wanted to make Black a starter. To say Dressen was in love with Black's pitching stuff would be an understatement. One just had to look at Dressen's (over)use of Black during the regular season and in the World Series to see what the Brooklyn manager thought about Black. Now, Black could have been a very good and even a great starter. But Dressen thought that Black needed to add another pitch to his arsenal. Specifically, Dressen wanted Black to throw a curveball. There was just one problem: Black suffered from finger tendinitis, which made it almost impossible for him to throw a good curveball. Nevertheless, Dressen insisted that Black incorporate the pitch. The end result was that throwing the curveball threw off Black's mechanics and destroyed his confidence. These were on top of his being overused the previous season, which affected his performance. Black was never the same, and in 1953, he appeared in 34 games and posted an ERA of 5.33.

The only pitching bright spot was Carl Erskine, who had a record of 20–6 with a 3.54 ERA. But even then, his ERA increased from 2.70 during the previous campaign. No other Dodgers starter posted an ERA below 4.00. Russ Meyer, acquired from the Phillies, went 15–5 with an ERA of 4.56. Billy Loes's ERA was 4.54, but he still won 14 games. Preacher Roe had a great won-lost record of 11–3 even with his ERA being 4.36. In 1952, the Dodgers' team ERA was 3.53 (league average 3.73), second in the NL. Brooklyn gave up 603 runs. In 1953, they slipped to third best with an ERA of 4.10 (league average 4.29), conceding 689 runs. Quite simply, the Dodgers' offense masked the weakness on the pitching side. And the Dodgers' offense was simply out of this world. In 1952, Brooklyn scored 775 runs. In 1953, they scored 955 runs, which led all of baseball. To show how dominant they were, the Yankees were second best in the majors; they scored 801 times. The Dodgers had a killer offense and an average pitching staff. What would this mean across the season as a whole?

The Dodgers, as was (and still is) often the case, had a relatively slow start. The team went 9–5 in April and 18–9 in May. May was looking like a particularly bad month, but Brooklyn finished the month with a 10-game winning streak. In both months, the calendar turned over with Brooklyn a half-game off the league lead. June was another lackluster month for Brooklyn, as they could not find any rhythm to their play. The team was often hurt by their lack of frontline pitching. Indeed, they lost one game despite scoring eight runs and lost another two despite scoring nine runs! After going 15–12 for the month, the Dodgers were once again a half-game out of first. Brooklyn was a very good team, but one that had yet to put it all together. That changed from July. In that month, Dem Bums went 23–8 and had an eight-game lead. They were even better in August, finishing with a 25–6 record and a ten-game lead in the NL. The team eased off in September with a 15–9 record, but their lead following the final day of the season was a mammoth 13 games. The 1953 Brooklyn Dodgers set a then-franchise record with 105 wins. Would 1953 finally be their year, or would their crosstown rivals once again crush the Brooklyn faithful's dreams?

THE 1953 WORLD SERIES

Understandably, Brooklyn went into the World Series brimming with confidence coming off their record-breaking season. Yet at the same time, New York won the AL pennant by 8 1/2 games, were a much more well-rounded team, and played in undoubtedly a tougher league. Quite simply, if the Dodgers were going to break their World Series hoodoo, they would need their pitching staff to bring their A game.

Game One of the World Series would pit Allie Reynolds against Carl Erskine. Brooklyn had a runner in scoring position with two outs in the top of the first, but once again the Dodgers could not get the crucial hit, as Robinson grounded out. This was Erskine's sixth World Series game, so one would have assumed that he would be up to the task. But he was horrendous. After retiring the first Yankee, he walked Joe Collins, and then Bauer tripled, scoring Collins. Berra then proceeded to strike out. The Dodgers could have gotten out of the inning without major damage, but Erskine then walked Mantle and Woodling to load the bases. Up to the plate stepped Billy Martin, who then cleared the bases with a triple to left-center. Rizzuto grounded out to end the inning with New York holding a 4–0 lead. That was all for Erskine, who was pinch-hit for in the top of the second with runners at second and third and two out. But in the Dodgers way, Wayne Belardi struck out, and Dem Bums had once again stranded runners in scoring position. Brooklyn finally got on the board in the top of the fifth thanks to a solo shot from Gilliam, but Berra hit one of his own in the bottom of the inning. Brooklyn's offense was the best in the majors, and they came storming back. Hodges led off the sixth with a home run. And with a runner on, pinch-hitter George Shuba homered to deep right. The deficit was a single run. Johnny Sain replaced Reynolds and walked Reese with two out. Snider then singled, moving Reese to third. However, the Dodgers once again failed with runners on, Robinson grounding out to third. In the top of the seventh, following singles by Campanella and Hodges, the Dodgers finally got a hit with a runner in scoring position. Furillo singled home Campanella, and the score was tied, 5–5, and there was still nobody out. Billy Cox bunted, but the Yankees got the lead runner at third. This brought up the pitcher's spot. Rather than pinch-hit for Clem Labine, who had thrown a scoreless sixth, Dressen allowed him to bat. Labine had two hits all year and batted .071. He bunted, but once again the lead runner was cut down at third! Horrid baseball. Gilliam then fouled out, and the inning was over. Not surprisingly, the Yankees made the Dodgers pay: in the bottom of the inning, Collins hit a two-out solo shot, and the Yankees reclaimed the lead. They added three more in the eighth. Sain doubled home two (even Yankee pitchers could get a hit with runners in scoring position), and Collins singled him home. New York won, 9–5. Brooklyn needed their pitching staff to be at their best; instead, they were putrid. And despite scoring five times, the Dodgers were only 1-for-8 with runners in scoring position, and they left 12 men on base.

Things did not get any better for Brooklyn in Game Two. Eddie Lopat started for New York, while Preacher Roe was on the mound for Brooklyn. To show how mediocre the Dodgers pitching staff was and how dominant their hitters were, Roe had an ERA of 4.36 but had an 11–3 won-lost record. The Yankees opened the scoring in the bottom of the second through a Berra sacrifice fly. The Dodgers took the lead in the top of the fourth. With two out, Hodges and Furillo singled. And shockingly, Cox doubled home both runners. Shockingly, because after being horrible with runners in scoring position in Game One (1-for-8), the Dodgers were even worse in Game Two (1-for-10). Not surprisingly, an inability to hit in the clutch is a prelude for failure. Martin tied up the game with a solo shot in the seventh. In the eighth, Bauer singled with one out. Roe was used to going deep into games, but he was nearing the end of his career and was prone to giving up home runs; he led all Dodger pitchers in all home runs allowed. Martin had already homered off him, and with Berra and Mantle due up, a pitching change would have been the smart approach. Yet Dressen kept faith in Roe, perhaps mindful of how Dodgers relievers performed in Game One. Roe partly repaid his manager's faith by getting Berra to fly out. However, once again, a Dodgers manager and the team as a whole would be burned because the starting pitcher had a long leash. Once again, a Yankees manager outmanaged his Dodgers counterpart. Mantle was quickly ahead, 2-0. In something that was quite unusual at the time, Stengel put the "hit" sign on. Mantle then proceeded to slam a home run to left. The Yankees took a 4–2 lead, and that ended up being the final score with Lopat closing out the complete game, stranding two runners. Following the game, Stengel surmised, "One bad pitch can decide any game in this Series, and maybe the Series." Roe denied it was a bad pitch, instead giving credit to Mantle: "I thought it was a heck of a pitch. I don't see how he hit it. It was way below his knees. . . . He just got hold of it and slammed it out of the park, that's all. It was some hit." By contrast, Roe said that Martin's home run was because of a horrible pitch, a high curveball. Roe claimed the pitch "was the greatest mistake since they invented butter-milk." Whether buttermilk was an abomination or the second coming is debatable; what was beyond dispute is that Brooklyn was in real trouble.

And in the Dodgers tradition, in times of trouble the manager goes back to the proverbial well. This time it was Dressen starting Erskine in Game Three despite the pitcher's shellacking in Game One. Vic Raschi started for the pinstripes. Amazingly, Dressen's seemingly rash decision looked like a genius move after four innings, with both teams yet to score. Erskine was dealing and was a strikeout machine. But he got in trouble in the fifth. With runners at second and third and one out, Gil McDougald singled home a run. However, Erskine got out of the inning without further damage. Brooklyn tied it up in the bottom of the inning and took the lead an inning later with Robinson's single plating Hodges. Brooklyn kept the lead until the top of the eighth. With one out, Bauer singled, and Berra was hit by a pitch. With Mantle coming to the plate, now would have been a good time to bring in a reliever. Yet Dressen stuck with Erskine, and for once Mantle was not the hero, striking out. The next batter was Woodling, and he promptly singled home the tying run. Erskine got Martin to ground out to end the inning. The game did not remain tied for long. In the bottom of the eighth, with Raschi still on the mound and one out, up stepped Campanella, who was nursing a broken right hand after being hit by Reynolds in the second inning of Game One. But he refused to leave the game or get it checked out. The broken hand limited Campanella's power. The injury limited Campanella throughout the Series, but he had one power shot left in him, blasting a pitch to deep left to give Brooklyn back the lead. Erskine was still on the mound in the ninth to try to finish off New York. He struck out the first two batters before issuing a walk to Irv Noren. But he was not to be denied as Collins grounded out and the game was over. The Dodgers did just enough, winning, 3–2. Considering his horrid Game One, that Erskine could come back on short rest to throw a complete game while striking out a then-Series-record 14 Yankees was a tremendous performance. There was still life left in the World Series.

The Dodgers further picked themselves off the canvas in Game Four. Yankees starter Whitey Ford only lasted one inning, giving up three runs. Meanwhile, Billy Loes went a very strong eight innings, giving up three runs. New York would have had a chance if their bullpen had performed well, but it was their turn to cough up numerous runs. Gilliam doubled three times, driving in two runs; Snider doubled twice and homered while plating four runs; and even Loes got into the act, singling twice, and Brooklyn ran out easy winners, 7–3. After the first two games, it seemed the men in pinstripes would run away with the Series, but Brooklyn came back and had all the momentum coming into Game Five. In baseball and in life, momentum is often a fleeting thing. And all the Dodgers' momentum evaporated early in Game Five.

In another case of a Dodgers manager overthinking things, rather than start Russ Meyer, who was Brooklyn's second- or at worst third-best pitcher throughout the season, Dressen decided on rookie Johnny Podres. It was a curious decision considering that Podres had not started a game for more than a month and in his last start had only pitched two-thirds of an inning. And Podres got off to the worst possible start as Woodling homered to open the game. Podres then settled down to retire the next six Yankees in order. Going into the top of the third, the score was tied, 1–1, thanks to the Dodgers scoring an unearned run in the second. Unfortunately for Dodgers fans and fortunately for Yankees fans, Brooklyn then imploded. Rizzuto walked to lead off the inning, but Podres retired the next two batters. However, with Rizzuto now on second, an error by Hodges allowed Collins to reach and Rizzuto to score. The Dodgers should have been out of the inning; instead, carnage awaited. Bauer was hit by a pitch, and Berra walked to load the bases. With Mantle due up, Dressen pulled Podres and inserted Meyer. And on the first pitch, Mantle welcomed Meyer with a grand slam to left field. The Yankees had a five-run lead, and the game was well and truly over. The Yankees would win in a slugfest, 11–7. In addition to Woodling and Mantle, Martin and McDougald homered for the pinstripes, while Cox and Gilliam homered for Dem Bums. Once again, Dodgers pitching had faltered when it mattered most. And considering that Meyer was horrendous in relief, maybe starting Podres over him was the smart option. But Podres was decidedly average himself. The reality is that the Yankees' offense was only slightly inferior to the Dodgers', but their pitching was vastly superior, and the Yankees were better managed.

This was again proven in Game Six. Stengel placed his faith in Ford to redeem himself after his less-than-stellar Game Four. Considering he only pitched for one inning, Ford was fresh and hungry for redemption. Rather than go to Roe, Dressen decided to go with Erskine on short rest. Game Six was the third time New York saw Erskine in the Series, and the Brooklyn pitcher was anything but fresh after throwing a complete game only three days earlier. The Dodgers had a chance to score in the first, but with runners on first and second and two out, Hodges lined out to Joe Collins. Once again, the Dodgers failed to get a hit when it mattered most. That was not the case with the Yankees. In the bottom of the inning, with runners on first and second with only one out, Berra doubled home a run. Following an intentional walk to Mantle, Martin hit a groundball that Gilliam should have handled, but he misplayed it, and another run scored. There was further excitement for Yankees fans the next inning when the first two batters reached and a Woodling sacrifice fly scored another. The Yankees then proceeded to load the bases with one out, but Ford tried to score on Berra's fly ball and was thrown out at the plate. The Dodgers got one back in the sixth, but it seemed the fight was over. Ford pitched a strong seven innings, allowing only six hits, and Reynolds was brought in for the final two innings. He successfully navigated around a two-out single in the eighth and was looking to close out proceedings in the ninth. He got Hodges to fly out to open the inning before Snider walked. This bought the tying run to the plate in the form of Furillo. Furillo, who led the NL in batting average (.344) and also set a personal best with 21 home runs, shockingly tied the game with one swing of the bat. Yet the Yankees had a chance to win the game and the Series in the bottom of the inning. Clem Labine was on the mound for Brooklyn. It was his third appearance of the World Series. After being saddled with the loss in Game One after allowing a run in 1 1/3 innings, he pitched a scoreless frame in Game Four. In Game Six, Labine was perfect in the seventh but got into trouble in the eighth before wiggling his way out of it. He was not so fortunate in the ninth. Bauer drew a leadoff walk. With one out, Mantle reached on an infield single. Stepping up to the plate was Martin. Martin was having an amazing World Series. He was 11-for-23 with a double, two triples, and two home runs. And he was not done. A single up the middle scored Bauer. The Yankees won, 4–3, and were World Series champions for the fifth straight year. A walkoff to win it all is pretty sweet. Martin's twelve hits was a World Series record, and his .500 batting average tied the record. New York had outhit, outpitched, outfielded, and outmanaged Brooklyn. As in other years, the Yankees had beaten the Dodgers not because of money, magic, or malevolent (or benevolent) gods, but because they were simply the better team in all facets of the game. The Yankees were truly the ruling class, and the Dodgers, while dominating the NL, were simply not in the same stratosphere as the men in pinstripes.

7

1955: IT *IS* NEXT YEAR

THE 1954 SEASON was a disappointment for both teams. The Dodgers had a new manager, Walter Alston. Brooklyn ownership tired of Dressen taking credit when the team was playing well but blaming the players when the club was struggling. Following the 1953 season, Dressen asked for a two-year contract. However, Brooklyn owner Walter O'Malley only ever offered one-year deals. Dressen held firm in his belief he deserved some job security. O'Malley did not see it that way, and out went Dressen and in came Alston at a much lower salary. As for the season, once again both Dodgers ownership and management thought the team did not need any major changes. GM Buzzie Bavasi told reporters following the 1953 season that the Dodgers would win the 1954 World Series. His reasoning was that "the fact is that fellows like Allie Reynolds, Ed Lopat, Vic Raschi and Johnny Sain ain't exactly kids anymore." That meant there was no need for any great rush for personnel changes. Bavasi stated, "We'll be content to go with the same team." The offense was still a powerhouse and led the NL in OPS. However, it was not as good as the previous season. Brooklyn's OPS was .794; in 1953, it was .840. That proved costly, because the mediocre pitching of 1953 was even worse in its 1954 version. In 1953, team ERA was 4.10; in 1954, it was 4.31, which was fourth in the NL. The 1953 team overperformed. The 1954 team won 92 games, but the New York Giants with Willie Mays back after military service was simply better, finishing with a record of 97–57 and the NL pennant. Thus, while some Yankees were nearing the end of their careers, Brooklyn would not be appearing in the 1954 World Series.

As for the Yankees, their management started the year by selling Vic Raschi, a four-time All-Star who had gone 13–6 with an ERA of 3.33 in 1953, to the Cardinals. Yet the Yankees have always been about winning *and* making money. Management wanted Raschi to accept a 20 percent pay cut. When he refused, he was shipped out to St. Louis. In hindsight, it was a good move, as Raschi was dealing with injuries and had a poor 1954 season. He was traded during the 1955 season to the Kansas City Athletics and retired at the end of the year. Even without Raschi, the Yankees had another mighty fine season, winning 103 games. There was just one problem: Cleveland played some of the best baseball ever seen on the way to winning 111 games. Cleveland was overwhelming favorites heading into the World Series, but while the regular season determines the best team in baseball, the playoffs often showcase which team got hot at the right time. In 1954, Cleveland's bats seemingly were already hibernating for winter, and the Giants shockingly swept the Indians for their seventh World Series crown but first since 1933. The Giants' triumph was a particular bitter pill to swallow for Dodgers fans, who had yet to see their team crowned champions. Would next year ever come?

THE DODGERS' 1955 SEASON

As noted earlier, the big change for the Dodgers was not playing personnel—the front office and ownership were seemingly always content to go into a season with largely the same players—but with a new and cheaper manager at the helm. Growing up, Walter Emmons Alston loved baseball. In a 1955 profile in *Sports Illustrated,* he reminisced, "When the old man wasn't there to play catch with me, I was bouncing the ball around on the barn door. That's how I got my nickname 'Smokey,' 'cause I used to have a real fast fireball." Yet it was with the bat that Alston shined. On September 27, 1936, the final day of the season, Alston made his debut in the majors. Future Dodger-killer Johnny Mize was thrown out of the game, and in stepped Alston. It was not a good debut: Alston made an error and struck out on three straight pitches. Alston never played another major-league game. Luckily, he did not give up on baseball and became a player-manager for minor-league teams. After being let go by the Cardinals organization in 1944, he was picked up by the Dodgers in late July and became manager of the team's Class B Interstate League affiliate. Beginning in 1948, Alston was the Dodgers' Triple-A affiliate manager, first in St. Paul and then in Montreal. Alston was a success at the Triple-A level, but it was still a surprise that he replaced Dressen. The media generally had no idea who Alston was, and even though he managed several future Dodger players at Triple A, many players seemingly did not respect Alston. In particular, Robinson had issues with his new manager. Things came to a head following a game in Chicago in late September, 1954. Snider hit one over the fence, but it was only ruled a double. Robinson ran out of the dugout to protest. Alston was not happy with Robinson and later told reporters that it was just "Jackie's temper tantrum." Nor was Robinson happy with Alston. He made it abundantly clear after the game, saying, "The team might be moving somewhere if Alston had not been standing at third base like a wooden Indian."

Jackie's friend, the outspoken Billy Loes, was also a critic of Alston. Loes was his own man and hated how players were treated by teams. Loes's issue with Alston was that the manager and GM Buzzie Bavasi were viewed as O'Malley's mouthpieces. O'Malley always wanted to keep payroll down and to control everything that went on in the organization. That bothered Loes, who felt players should get a bigger cut of the pie and be treated as people rather than commodities. The Dodgers front office was also not happy that Loes, despite being a good, but not great, pitcher, had negotiated a $21,000 bonus when he signed with the team in 1949, straight out of high school. Loes was a damn fine negotiator. The largest signing bonus for a Dodger before Loes was $6,000. That Loes outnegotiated them and was not afraid to speak his mind annoyed some in the Dodger organization. As a result, there were people in Dodgers management who told reporters, without explicitly saying so, that Loes was not particularly bright. Alston also got into the act. In 1954, when Loes had a sore arm, Alston told reporters that Loes's shoulder hurt and his head also hurt. The description of Loes as a simpleton stuck, and even Loes's obituary in the *New York Times* notes he made strange comments and that "when the Dodgers faced the

Yankees in the 1952 World Series, Loes became a modern-day incarnation of the Dodgers' Daffiness Boys of the 1920s, when they once had three men on third base at the same time." The big crime that led the paper of record to imply Loes was not a genius was that he picked the Yankees over the Dodgers in the World Series (he was right), allowing a game-tying home run in Game Six, balking, and losing a ball in the sun that caromed off his leg, which allowed another run to score. Not exactly great baseball, but a long way from meaning Loes was stupid. The obituary also claimed that one of Loes's strange comments was that he had little desire to be a 20-game winner because if he achieved such a feat, the Dodgers would always expect him to be that good. In that regard, Loes was smart; win 20 games, hit 30 home runs, etc., and people will always expect you to do so from that point onward. Anything else would be a "disappointment." Baseball was not the be-all and end-all for Loes, and he had realistic expectations. Loes was not stupid, an idiot, or whatever. He was just a freethinker in an era when freethinking was looked down upon and as a result was made an example of. As Loes told the *New York Times* in 1957, "When they [reporters] asked me a question, I answered them honestly. . . . But most of them turned it around because they knew it would make better copy that way. It got to the point where I told a few writers, 'Go ahead, write what you want about me and say I said it. You've been doing it right along anyway.'"

While there was not exactly harmony within the team heading into the 1955 season, winning heals all wounds. And the 1955 Dodgers were winners. Brooklyn won their first ten games, were tied for first after their third game, and ran away with the pennant (doubleheaders prevented the Dodgers from being in first place every day throughout the season). Their offense once again led the NL: Hodges slashed .289/.377/.500 with 27 home runs and 102 RBIs, Furillo hit .314 with 26 long balls, Campanella had a slash line of .318/.395/.583 with 32 home runs and 107 RBIs, and Snider was amazing with .309/.418/.628 while hitting 42 homers and driving in 136. Campanella ended up being voted the NL MVP, but as good as he was, Snider was better. Campanella's WAR was 5.2, while Snider's was 8.6. It was the year of catchers being voted MVP despite not necessarily deserving the award, as will be discussed later. Based purely on WAR, the best in the NL was Willie Mays (9.1). Mays had a slash line of .319/.400/.659 with 51 home runs. Arguably the reason why Mays did not win the award is that the Dodgers had a dominant season and the Giants were also-rans.

On the pitching side, the Dodgers had a great year, leading the league in ERA. Newcombe returned to the Dodgers in 1954 after two years of military service but had a substandard year. He was back to his brilliant best in 1955, finishing with a record of 20–5 with an ERA of 3.20. By the end of July, Newcombe was 18–1, and his ERA was 2.95. But back and shoulder injuries slowed him down in the second half. Erskine went 11–8 with an ERA of 3.79, while Loes in his last full season with the Dodgers (he would be traded during the 1956 season) finished 10–4 with an ERA of 3.59.

The Dodgers' offense was still a powerhouse, and with vastly improved pitching it was not a surprise that Dem Bums cruised to the NL pennant, winning by a 13 1/2-game margin over the Milwaukee Braves, with the Giants in third place, a mammoth 23 1/2 games behind. That the Dodgers won the pennant by so many games and clinched the title on September 8 (the earliest a team has captured the pennant in NL history), yet "only" won 95 games, clearly demonstrates that the NL was not that great in 1955. Nevertheless, with the Giants winning it all the previous season, could Brooklyn finally break through for their first crown as well as NL teams winning back-to-back World Series titles for the first time since the Giants and the Cardinals in 1933–34?

THE YANKEES' 1955 SEASON

The Yankees entered the 1955 season following their second-place finish in the AL the previous year. For most teams, winning 103 games would be cause for celebration, but then again, most teams are not the New York Yankees. New York was so disappointed with their failure to win another World Series title that on the final weekend of the 1954 season, they gave fans at Yankee Stadium a brochure that included team photos and a "letter of apology" making clear that the team was not happy with second place. One could laugh at Yankees management for thinking they had to appease their fans over the disappointment of a 103-win season or realize that for the team, at the very least, a pennant is required for a successful season.

Helping the Yankees regain their dominance were the Philadelphia Athletics. In 1954, the Athletics were purchased by Arnold Johnson, who then, as some owners are wont to do, moved the team. The Athletics ended up in Kansas City. These things happen, but the important part of the story for our purposes is that Johnson also owned Yankee Stadium. Johnson was forced to sell the Stadium, which he did in 1955. Nevertheless, it seemed that Johnson had a soft spot for the Yankees. Marty Appel notes that in the five seasons that Johnson owned the Athletics, "the Yankees and Athletics would make sixteen trades involving fifty-nine players, with the Yankees basically giving up players who were no good to them and obtaining players who were. Observers hated this cushy arrangement and called the Athletics little more than a Yankee farm club. Over the years the Yankees obtained Art Ditmar, Bobby Shantz, Clete Boyer, Ryne Duren, Harry Simpson, Duke Maas, Virgil Trucks, Murry Dickson, Hector Lopez, Ralph Terry, and finally Roger Maris, all of whom contributed to pennant winners." Johnson died in 1960, and the Athletics were bought by Charles Finlely. Finlely was not happy that his team was seemingly a breeding ground for future Yankees and stopped the unequal trades between the teams.

Trades were the order of the day for the Yankees in the mid-1950s. On November 17, 1954, New York and Baltimore agreed on a seventeen-player trade. Out of the seventeen players, only Ted Del Guercio never made the majors. The big name going to the Orioles was Gene Woodling. Woodling, who won five straight World Series titles with the Yankees, would eventually retire in 1962 after 17 seasons in the majors. For New York, the major acquisitions were pitchers Bob Turley and Don Larsen. Turley had a productive first year in pinstripes, making the All-Star team and finishing with a record of 17–13 with an ERA of 3.06. His finest season came in 1958, when, in addition to being an All-Star, Turley won 21 games with 19 complete games, finished second in MVP voting, and won the Cy Young award. And to cap it off, he was the 1958 World Series MVP.

New York needed reinforcement to their pitching staff, because in addition to the trade of Raschi in 1954, Allie Reynolds retired at the end of the season. Reynolds, who broke Dodgers hearts throughout the years, finished with six World Series titles and was a six-time All-Star. New York also traded Eddie Lopat during the 1955 season to Baltimore. Lopat, who retired at the end of the season, won five World Series in pinstripes and criminally only made the All-Star team once.

Nineteen fifty-five was a time for change for the boys from the Bronx, and arguably there was no bigger change than when the first black player appeared in a regular-season game in pinstripes. As discussed earlier, certain sections of Yankees management were notorious for not wanting black players to appear for the team. Appel states that even as late as 1953, Bill McCorry, who when he was a scout infamously did not think much of Willie Mays due to Mays's skin color and was now the Yankees traveling secretary, did not want black players on the team. He said, "I don't care what he [Mays] did today or any other day. I got no use for him or any of them. I wouldn't want any of them on a club I was with. I wouldn't arrange a berth on the train for any of them." Despite the racism, New York was ready to promote a black player, Elston Howard, to the big-league club.

Howard was with the Negro League's Kansas City Monarchs when he was sold to the Yankees. He debuted for their Muskegon Class-A affiliate in 1950. Unfortunately, he was drafted and spent the next two seasons playing baseball for the military. In 1953, he returned to the Yankees' organization playing at the Triple-A level for the Kansas City Blues in the American Association. The following year with the Toronto Maple Leafs in the International League, Howard hit .330 with 21 doubles, 16 triples, and 22 home runs on the way to being named MVP. Howard was ready for the majors. It could be argued that the reason Howard was promoted to New York was their "failure" the previous season; in addition, Howard was well liked and was perceived to be the quiet type. *New York Times* reporter Arthur Daley wrote, "Howard doesn't carry a chip on his shoulder the way the aggressive Robinson does. Nor is he a hearty hail-fellow-well-met the way the popular Roy Campanella is. Elston is a nice, quiet lad of 25 whose reserved, gentlemanly demeanor has won him complete acceptance from every Yankee." In that day and age, in addition to being great players, almost all black players in the majors had to be shy, reserved types. Howard made the opening day roster, and in the second game of the year, following Irv Noren's ejection, the New York Yankees became the thirteenth major-league team have a black player appear in a game. In his first at-bat in pinstripes, with runners at first and second and one out, Howard singled to center, scoring Mantle. Howard had a decent rookie season. He hit .290 with 10 home runs and seven triples in 97 games. Howard was generally accepted on the team, and while certain sections of Yankees management and fans were not happy with a black player on the team, things were finally changing for the better.

One thing not changing was that New York had an unnerving habit of finding great players. In 1954, another one debuted for the pinstripes: first baseman Bill Skowron. Skowron appeared in 87 games and slashed a more-than-respectable .340/.392/.577. While not as good in the 1955 campaign, across 108 games he went .319/.369/.524. He would eventually win five World Series titles and be an eight-time All-Star.

In addition to Howard and Skowron, Berra had another great year. He had a slash line of .272/.349/.470 with 27 doubles and 20 home runs while driving in 108 runs, on the way to winning his third MVP Award. While Berra was superb as always, based on WAR, he was only the 11th-best player in the AL. As mentioned earlier, 1955 was the year of catchers winning, but not necessarily deserving, the MVP award. Just as Snider had a better season than Campanella, yet the catcher winning the award, there was a much better player on the Yankees.

Mickey Mantle had a stupendous season. He went .306/.431/.611. In addition to leading the AL in OBP and slugging, Mantle led all comers in triples (11), home runs (37), and walks (113). Looking at WAR, Berra's was 4.5; Mantle's was 9.6. Mantle was more than twice as good. WAR is not perfect, but even on traditional stats alone, Mantle had a much better season and was robbed of the MVP award.

Nevertheless, while the Yankees once again led the AL in OPS, that does not paint the full picture. The team was actually below average in batting average and OBP (fifth in both categories), but they hit for power (first in slugging). Even though the team did not hit many doubles (sixth in the AL), they led the AL in triples and home runs. The 1955 Yankees were in many ways the archetype of modern teams that certain sections of the media decry for their all-or-nothing approach.

While the offense was hitting for power, the pitching staff quietly went about being as dominant as always. Ford was spectacular. He went 18–7 with an ERA of 2.63 and 18 complete games. Turley had an even better second year in pinstripes, going 17–13 with an ERA of 3.06 while making the All-Star team. And Tommy Byrne, who made his major-league debut with the Yankees in 1943, had a renaissance year and his best season ever. The thirty-five-year-old finished with a record of 16–5 with an ERA of 3.15.

Since New York had the best offense and pitching, one would assume that they would have run away with the pennant, but that was not the case. New York had a mediocre April, going 9–6, but played solid ball in May and June and by July 1 led the AL by 6 1/2 games. In seasons past, with that type of lead, the Yankees would have cruised to the pennant. However, they had a wretched July (12–17), so much so that by the end of the month they had lost their lead. New York was much better in August, but they still entered September a half-game behind in the race. As late as September 13, New York trailed Cleveland by two games. Luckily for the men in pinstripes, they won seven in a row, while Cleveland lost five of their next six. The Yankees ended up winning 96 games and captured the AL pennant yet again, this time by three games over the Indians. Cleveland may have interrupted New York's dominance in the AL for one year, but it takes more than one season to overthrow a dynasty.

The Yankees' late burst to take the pennant was all the more remarkable because Mantle injured his hamstring and appeared in only three games (all as a pinch-hitter) after September 14. Thus, while New York was a heavy favorite heading into another Yankees-Dodgers World Series (what kind of insane person would place a wage on Dem Bums over New York?!), Mantle's injury was a glimmer of hope for long-suffering Brooklyn fans.

THE 1955 WORLD SERIES

While Mantle's injury caused concern for the Yankees (indeed, he did not play in the first two games), they had home-field advantage for the Series, and the fact that Dodgers ace Newcombe was ailing gave the team more than quiet optimism that their dominance over their crosstown rivals would continue. Game One saw Newcombe match up with Ford, a matchup that certainly favored the home team. Yet it was the visitors who led early. Furillo led off the top of the second with a home run. Then, with one out, Robinson tripled and was brought home by a Don Zimmer single. It was a great start by Brooklyn, but their joy would be fleeting. In the bottom of the inning, Collins walked with one out. And then in his first World Series at-bat, Howard homered to tie the score. The Yankees as a team were great at hitting the long ball, but so were the Dodgers. Snider led off the top of the third with a homer. The Dodgers were back in the lead, but once again the Yankees came back in the bottom of the inning. This time, some small ball tied the score: a walk and a single to open the inning, a groundout to move the runners over, and Irv Noren's groundout allowed Ford to score from third. New York did not rely on small ball too often and soon reverted to their all-or-nothing approach—well, in this case, *all*. Collins homered to lead off the fourth to give New York a 4–3 lead. And in the sixth, with Berra on first, Alston left Newcombe in to face Collins. It was not smart baseball. Collins homered again to bust the game wide open. Once again, a Dodgers manager left a starting pitcher in for too long and paid the price. Considering that Newcombe was hurting and would not appear in another game in the Series due to his ailments, it was utterly mind-boggling that Alston allowed Newcombe to pitch to Collins again. The decision arguably cost Brooklyn the game. In the top of the eighth, a Zimmer sacrifice fly with the bases loaded cut the deficit by one and allowed Robinson to move from second to third. With Ford still on the mound, Robinson then decided to do something audacious: he attempted to steal home. Robinson broke for the plate, but Ford made a precise throw to Berra who tagged Robinson, who slid feet first. It was a close play, and to the shock of Berra, home plate umpire Bill Summers called Robinson safe. Berra went absolutely ballistic and remonstrated with Summers. Not surprisingly, Summers did not change his call. Even now, people still debate whether Robinson was safe. Berra never wavered from his belief that Robinson was out. Robinson's steal of home is one of the most famous plays in baseball history; even former President Barack Obama made mention of it more than five decades after it happened. Yet what is often lost in discussion of the play is that Robinson's steal of home only cut the margin to one, and New York held on to win Game One, 6–5.

Also forgotten is that Robinson's steal of home was not the first attempt in the game. In the bottom of the sixth, Martin tripled. It was only then that Alston pulled Newcombe. With Don Bessent on the mound, Martin tried to steal home. Martin got a great jump, and it seemed he beat the tag from Campanella. Yet Summers called Martin out. Martin was shocked and boiling with anger and threw an elbow at Campanella. To his credit, Campanella did nothing. The Dodgers, though, were not happy. New York was not treating them with respect. This, combined with the constant World Series defeats by the Yankees and the disrespect from certain sections of the media who were calling Robinson a has-been, drove Robinson to steal home. In his autobiography, *I Never Had It Made*, Robinson wrote, "There was a saying in Brooklyn which everyone has heard about the Dodgers ('the bums'): 'Wait 'till next year.' Well, here we were in our seventh world series in fifty years and there was hope that this would be the year, but our fans were also ready to shrug their shoulders and say 'Wait 'till next year' if we lost. The way we were playing in that first game—down 6–4 in the eighth inning—it looked like we might have to wait. I was on third base and I knew I might not be playing next year. There were two men out, and I suddenly decided to shake things up. It was not the best baseball strategy to steal home with our team two runs behind, but I just took off and did it. I really didn't care whether I made it or not—I was just tired of waiting."

Yet the steal home did not result in Brooklyn winning Game One, and the team with the momentum heading into Game Two was New York. Stengel decided to go with the veteran Byrne, and while disliking him personally, Alston started Loes. Both pitchers got through three innings unscathed; that was not the case in the fourth. Once again, the Dodgers opened the scoring. Pee Wee Reese led off the inning with a double and scored on a Snider single, but Duke was thrown out trying to stretch the single into a double. It was aggressive baserunning by Snider, but his being thrown out on the basepaths allowed Byrne to regroup, and he got out of the inning without any more damage being inflicted. And in the bottom of the inning, the Yankees played small ball to effectively kill off the game. With two out, Berra singled, and Collins followed that up by walking. Howard then singled to left, scoring Berra. Martin followed by also singling to left, scoring Collins. Pinch-hitter Eddie Robinson was then hit by a pitch. Five straight Yankees had reached base, and as always, a Dodgers manager was too slow to pull a starting pitcher. Considering Byrne was now at the plate, maybe Alston thought that Loes could get one more batter. However, Byrne hit .205 in 1955 and was more than decent with a bat in his hand, as he proved here, by singling to

115

center to bring another run home. It was only then that Alston pulled Loes; too little too late. While the Dodgers got another run back in the fifth, that ended the scoring. The Yankees won, 4–2, and took a commanding 2–0 lead in the World Series. Byrne was magnificent, pitching a complete game while only allowing five hits. Brooklyn's bats had gone quiet, their starting pitching could not go deep into games, so what hope did they have to prevent another October heartbreak even with the next three games at Ebbets Field?

New York had to be feeling extra confident, as the pitching matchup saw Turley, coming off an All-Star season, against Johnny Podres. The Dodgers lefty was in his third major-league season and had posted a record of 9–10. One of the reasons for his losing record was lack of run support, but his ERA was still decidedly average at 3.95. Podres was pitching on his twenty-third birthday, while Turley was appearing in his first World Series game. Moreover, Mantle returned to the starting lineup, but it was clear that his troublesome hamstring still bothered him. Once again, it was Brooklyn taking the early lead. In the bottom of the first with a runner on, Campanella launched one, and Dem Bums were up by two. The script of the first two games continued as New York came right back when Mantle homered to lead off the second. And then with two outs and a runner on second, Rizzuto singled to left. Bill Skowron attempted to score and Sandy Amoros threw a strike to Campanella, but the Dodgers catcher dropped the ball after Skowron ran him over. Rizzuto made it to third on the play, and the game was tied. Luckily for Podres and the Dodgers, Turley was the next batter, and he grounded out to end the inning. This time, though, something surprising happened. The Dodgers bats remained hot, and

Podres regained his focus. In the bottom of the second, it was the Dodgers' turn to play small ball. With one out, Robinson walked, Amoros was hit by a pitch, and Podres bunted to move the runners over and also managed to beat the throw to first. The bases were loaded, and Robinson, the runner at third, got into Turley's head. Turley was so psyched out by Robinson dancing off the base that he walked Gilliam to force in a run, giving Brooklyn a 3–2 lead. Stengel then replaced Turley with Tom Morgan, but he walked Reese, and another Brooklyn run scored. While Morgan managed to get the next two batters, the damage was done. This time the Dodgers did not give up the lead. Brooklyn ran out winners, 8–3, with Podres throwing a complete game. It was a nice birthday present to himself.

Despite the loss, New York was still overwhelming favorites. And the start of Game Four seemed to prove their superiority. With Larsen on the mound for the Yankees and Erskine for the Dodgers, one could have expected runs. And it was runs that the fans got. This time it was New York who scored first. McDougald hit a solo homer in the opening inning. New York once again reverted to small ball to score a run in the second. A leadoff walk to Collins followed by a bunt and a groundout moved the runner to third. He was then cashed in by a Rizzuto single. Gilliam got a run back for Brooklyn with an RBI double in the third, but in the fourth the Yankees knocked Erskine out of the game by scoring another run through more small ball. The Yankees led, 3–1, and the team was undoubtedly thinking that they were about to take a stranglehold on the Series. However, the Dodgers were not ready to surrender. Campanella opened the bottom of the fourth with a solo shot to cut the margin to one. Furillo singled, and then Hodges, who had an awful 1952

World Series where he did not collect a hit before being great in the fall classic the following year, had one of the biggest hits of his career, a home run to right-center. The Dodgers were now in the lead, and it was to remain that way for the rest of the game. Brooklyn effectively ended the contest the next inning. With Larsen still on the mound, Gilliam walked and stole second. Stengel then replaced Larsen with Johnny Kucks. It turned out to be a mistake. Reese singled to send Gilliam to third. Up stepped Snider, and he homered to deep right. The Dodgers led, 7–3, and ended up winning, 8–5. The Series was now tied at two games apiece. Was it a mistake to remove Larsen? Probably not. Stengel was in a conundrum that all managers go through. Damned if you do, damned if you don't. It was a bad day for the Yankees all around: aside from losing, owner Del Webb was struck in the head by a foul ball hit by Larsen. In his autobiography, *The Perfect Yankee*, Larsen states that after Stengel pulled him from the game, he went to the dressing room where he saw Webb looking the worse for wear. Larsen jokingly notes that fearing that his Yankees career could have been over he "tiptoed out of the room before he saw me."

The Dodgers now had all the momentum, and it continued in Game Five. New York was dealt a blow when Mantle was unable to play due to his injured hamstring. Taking the mound was rookie Roger Craig. Craig made only 10 regular-season starts (in 21 appearances) after being called up in July. It was the latest in a line of World Series managerial pitching surprises by the Dodgers. One only has to read the previous pages to know how they usually turned out for Brooklyn. Bob Grim was Craig's opposite number. Grim debuted in 1954 and had a magnificent rookie campaign, winning 20 games with an

ERA of 3.26. He finished 11th in MVP voting and was the AL Rookie of the Year. His 1955 season was not as good, as his ERA ballooned to a decidedly average 4.19. Both pitchers lasted six innings in Game Five. The difference between the two was that the Dodgers offense continued to wreck Yankee pitching with long balls. Brooklyn opened the scoring in the bottom of the second. With a runner on first, left fielder Sandy Amoros homered to deep right. Dem Bums increased their lead to 3–0 when Snider homered to begin the third. New York got one back in the top of the fourth via a Martin RBI single. The defining moment of the game occurred in the bottom off the fifth. With one out and Snider coming up to the plate, Stengel decided to keep Grim in the game. Perhaps Stengel was thinking about the previous game, when he pulled Larsen and then Reese singled before Snider hit a three-run jack. Damned if you do, damned if you don't. This time Stengel was damned by doing nothing. Snider hit his second solo shot of the game; both homers came on two-strike pitches. Brooklyn increased their lead to 4–1 and ended up winning, 5–3. Brooklyn was now one win away from their first World Series title. Of course, it was the same scenario as 1952, when New York reigned supreme.

Stengel did not panic and started Ford. Perhaps buoyed by the success of his decision to start Craig in the previous game, Alston went with twenty-four-year-old Karl Spooner, a rookie who had first appeared in two games the previous year for the Dodgers late in September. In his major-league debut, he pitched a three-hit shutout while striking out 15 Giants. He was not as good in his next game; he only struck out 12 and allowed four hits on the way to another complete-game shutout. An arm injury during spring training delayed the start to his 1955 campaign. He eventually appeared in 29 games, with 10 starts. He was not the same pitcher but still had a serviceable ERA of 3.65. Spooner was a flamethrower with a fastball touching the mid-90s, but the injury took away his heater. In his last two starts of the year in mid-September, he only lasted 3 1/3 innings each time. Not exactly great preparation for the biggest start of his career. Spooner did pitch three innings in relief in Game Two and was dominant, only giving up a hit and a walk while striking out five. However, there is a difference between starting a World Series game and coming on in relief. Quite simply, the decision to start Spooner over Russ Meyer bordered on the bizarre. And it was soon proven how foolish it was. Rizzuto opened the bottom of the first with a walk and stole second. With one out, McDougald walked. Up stepped Berra, and he singled, scoring Rizzuto as McDougald moved to third. Spooner was not exactly helped by his second baseman, Gilliam, who was late getting to the bag on Rizzuto's steal and then allowed the ball to roll under his glove on Berra's hit. If Gilliam had performed better defensively, the inning could have been over. Instead, New York had a run, and then Bauer singled, scoring McDougald. Up stepped Bill Skowron to the plate. And the game was as good as over when Skowron homered to right. New York had a 5–0 lead, Alston pulled Spooner, and the once-promising career of the Dodgers lefty was over. Despite a September call-up in 1956, the last pitch Spooner ever threw in the majors was Skowron's three-run shot. Meyer entered the game and did not allow a run. New York won the game, 5–1, with Ford being everything Spooner was not. Spooner lasted a third of an inning; Ford pitched a complete game while striking out eight. To make matter worse, Snider stepped on a sprinkler head in the outfield and hurt his knee. He only made one plate appearance before being replaced by Zimmer. Snider was in doubt for the decider but did start, although he was clearly hampered by the injury. Similarly, Mantle was limited to pinch-hitting duties due to his injured hamstring. Following the game, the Dodgers were not exactly unified. Spooner lashed out stating, "when a runner goes down to steal somebody had better cover second. Maybe I should have struck out everybody." The flamethrower pre-injury Spooner could strike out the side; the 1955 incarnation of Spooner could not.

There was more tension within the Dodgers camp in the form of Zimmer. After he was not in the lineup for Game Three, Zimmer told reporters that he would only hear if he was in the lineup through reporters. He said, "If 1 can't play here, I want to play somewhere else." He further stated that he was "sick of sitting out a week, playing a week, and sitting out another week." This is not exactly the talk that should be aired publicly during the World Series, let alone by a second-year player who only appeared in 88 games during the regular season. Nevertheless, Alston did not hold the outburst against him, and Zimmer was in the lineup for Game Seven, but in the biggest game of the season, a Dodgers stalwart was not.

Following Game Six, Robinson noted that his Achilles was bothering him; he told reporters, "I can't tell right now whether I can play. It all depends on how the foot feels. It is up to Walt." And sure enough, Robinson was not listed in the starting lineup and did not even appear as a pinch-hitter. To this day, no one knows why Robinson did not play aside from Robinson and Alston, who took the reason why to their graves. At an event to mark the 50th anniversary of the World Series, Erskine claimed the reason why Robinson did not play was that "Jackie had chronic bad knees from his college football playing days." Jackie's widow Rachel said, "I don't know why Jack didn't play. I really don't know. That was 50 years ago, buddy." Interestingly, when the final out was recorded, Robinson did not slowly make his way onto the playing surface; instead, he ran onto the field with nary a limp to be seen.

Whatever the reason was why Robinson did not play, the fact of the matter is that the World Series had come down to the deciding Game Seven. Following his stellar performance in Game Two, Byrne was well rested and took the ball for the Yankees. Rather than repeat the matchup from Game Two, Alston bypassed Loes and gave the ball to Podres. Considering the multitudes of wrong pitching decisions by Dodgers managers through the years, Alston's decision was either going to be brilliant or mind-numbingly awful; there was no middle ground. Both pitchers started well, but Podres got into trouble in the bottom of the third. With two out, Rizzuto walked and moved to second following a Martin single. It was then that the baseball gods decided to shine lady luck on Brooklyn. McDougald hit a slow chopper to third that had base hit written all over it. The Dodgers' best chance was for third baseman Don Hoak to tag out Rizzuto. As Rizzuto slid feet first into third, the ball struck him. Rizzuto was out, the inning was over, and from the heavens, the baseball gods smiled (at least that is what Brooklyn fans tell themselves). The intervention by the gods was to prove decisive. In the top of the fourth with one out, Campanella hit a bullet to left field for a double. Furillo grounded out, moving Campanella to third. It was then that Stengel made a major blunder. Up to the plate stepped Hodges, who had a fine year and a very good World Series. An intentional walk to Hodges would have brought up Hoak. In his second year in the majors, Hoak only hit .240 for the year, and Game Seven was his first start in the World Series. The logical decision would have been to walk Hodges to face Hoak. Instead, Stengel told Byrne to pitch to Hodges. Despite being jammed by the pitch, Hodges muscled the ball into the outfield, scoring Campanella. New York had a great opportunity to tie or even take the lead in the bottom of the inning. Berra opened the inning with a routine fly ball, but a mix-up between Snider and Gilliam allowed the ball to drop, and Berra hustled to second. But none of the following three Yankee batters could bring the runner home, and when the inning was over, Berra was still rooted to second. While in World Series past it was Brooklyn's inability to hit with runners in scoring position, this time it was New York's undoing. In addition, lady luck was clearly on Brooklyn's side. Reese singled to open the top of the sixth. This brought up Snider. Alston told Snider, he with a slugging percentage of .628 with 42 home runs, to bunt. Snider had exactly four sacrifice bunts all year. Snider duly did his job, moving Reese over. Rather than jog to first to protect his injured leg, Snider hustled. While the New York infielders were shocked that Snider bunted, they still did the job: Byrne threw the ball to first baseman Skowron, who tagged Snider on the shoulder, but the ball popped out of his glove. Snider was safe. Alston also ordered Campanella to bunt. The runners moved over with Campanella out at first. Furillo was then walked to bring the double play into the equation. Stengel pulled Byrne and brought in Grim to face Hodges. Hodges powered a ball to the warning track, allowing Reese to score easily. A wild pitch allowed Snider to take third, and this led New York to intentionally walk Hoak to bring up Zimmer. Alston then pinch-hit George Shuba. While Shuba grounded out, this series of moves was to prove very fortuitous. Gilliam moved from left to second taking over from Zimmer, with Sandy Amoros taking over in left.

Martin led off the bottom of the sixth with a walk, and McDougald followed that by reaching on a bunt, moving Martin to second. To say that Podres was struggling would be an understatement, but Alston left him out there to face Berra. On a 1-0 count, Podres pitched outside to Berra, but being a smart hitter, Berra went with the pitch and drove it to deep left field. McDougald was sure it was going to fall in safely, so he broke for second, but Martin, to his credit, hesitated. Amoros was a good outfielder, and more important, he was lightning quick. And he got a great jump, which he had to do because he was positioned slightly toward center. Amoros sprinted and as he was nearing the wall held out his glove and the ball, as if guided by heat-seeking technology, landed perfectly in the outfielder's glove. Rather than settle for one out, Amoros instantly turned and threw a rocket to Reese, who in turn fired the ball to Hodges at first. McDougald could not get back in time and was doubled off. Amoros did everything perfectly. Anything less than that would have resulted in a hit and most likely a tied ballgame. Bauer then grounded out to end the inning. New York, though, would have other chances. In the bottom of the seventh with two outs, Howard singled to bring up the pitcher's spot. Stengel called upon Mantle, who had homered off Podres in Game Three. Once again, Alston had faith in his pitcher. And once again, the baseball gods were on Brooklyn's side. Mantle had a perfect pitch to drive out of the stadium, but he got slightly under it. Rather than a two-run homer, it was a simple pop fly. Crisis adverted for Brooklyn. New York had another scoring chance in the bottom of the eighth. Rizzuto singled to lead off the inning, and with one out, McDougald singled, moving Rizzuto to third. With Berra at the plate, there was no way that Alston would let Podres face him, right? But there was no one warming up in the bullpen, so it was up to Podres. He threw an inside pitch that Berra could only meekly hit to short right field. Rizzuto had to stay at third. Podres then struck out Bauer to end the inning, and Alston looked like a genius for having faith in his pitcher. In previous World Series, it was always the Yankees manager outperforming his Dodgers counterpart. In 1955, almost everything Alston did worked out. Likewise, in previous Dodger-Yankee matchups, it was New York who hit with runners in scoring position. This time around, while not great, the Dodgers got the crucial hit. In Game Seven, the Dodgers went 1-for-5 with runners in scoring position and also got a run on a sacrifice fly. The Yankees were 1-for-9 and could not score a run with a man on third with less than two outs.

Alston left Podres in to face the Yankees in the bottom of the ninth. Skowron hit the cover off the ball to lead off the inning, but miraculously (the baseball gods were undoubtedly still favoring Brooklyn), Podres stuck out his glove and the ball got lodged in it. Podres ran to first trying to get the ball out, which he finally did, and threw the ball to Hodges. One out. Cerv then hit a lazy fly ball to left. Two out. Howard was the last Yankees hope. On a 2-2 count, Howard kept fouling off fastballs. Campanella wanted more heat, but the twenty-three-year-old Podres shook Campanella off. It was time for a changeup; Campanella agreed. Howard hit a weak grounder to Reese. The Dodgers' captain, who was on the field when New York began their domination over Brooklyn back in 1941, cleanly fielded the ball and threw to Hodges at first. Howard was out, and Podres had thrown an improbable complete-game shutout. The Yankees were forced down to their knees, but they were not broken. Nevertheless, the Brooklyn Dodgers won, 2–0, and were World Series champions for the first time. It *was* Next Year.

8

1956: BACK TO NORMALITY

THE BROOKLYN DODGERS had finally done it. They were World Series champions at last, and in doing so they beat the New York Yankees, their tormenters for well over a decade. This made the victory extra special. The Brooklyn natives partied like those who win their first title do. People spilled out on the streets throughout the borough; it was finally next year. But one championship does not make a dynasty. Nor does losing a fiercely fought contest spell the end of the days for the vanquished. It was next year in 1955, but 1956 would restore the "natural" order of the baseball world. And while there were more than hints of it at the time, the people celebrating Brooklyn's championship would soon be condemning the Dodgers for the rest of their days. There was change coming, but not a change that Brooklyn fans would welcome.

THE YANKEES' 1956 SEASON

Rather than have a relaxing offseason at home, the Yankees went on a 25-game goodwill tour of Hawaii, Guam, Japan, and the Philippines. While three newlywed players used the trip as a honeymoon and Stengel and his wife celebrated their thirty-fifth wedding anniversary, the tour was mandatory for the majority of the players. It was a goodwill tour for the Yankee brand name, but playing in meaningless games around the world after a long season was not the best way for tired players to start their offseason. Nor were they in a position to refuse going on the tour. While one may look back to the 1950s and think players played baseball for the love of the game, the reality is the players had few rights and the vast majority did not earn a fair wage. Yet come the new season, the players were ready to give it their all.

One player looking forward to another season in pinstripes was Don Larsen. Larsen, nicknamed "Gooney Bird" early in his career, was a man of contradictions. As Charles F. Faber writes for the Society for American Baseball Research, Larsen "married out of a sense of duty; yet he refused to support his wife and baby daughter. He kept his marriage secret as long as he could, preferring to be viewed as a carefree bachelor. He loved the night life; yet he was living out his retirement years . . . in a quiet village in northern Idaho, far from the crowded bars of his youth. This man who turned down college scholarships because he didn't like to study, the same man who had to be compelled by a court order to support his family, auctioned off one of his most prized possessions to raise money to support his grandchildren's college education."

Larsen signed with the St. Louis Browns as a teenager and was slowly working his way toward his big-league debut when he was drafted into the military in 1951. He was discharged from the military early enough in 1953 that he was able to participate in spring training. Larsen made his debut in April and had a decent first season in the majors with a 7–12 record and an ERA of 4.16. The following year, the Browns moved to Baltimore and became the Orioles. Larsen's first, and only, year in Baltimore was one to forget. While his ERA increased slightly to 4.37, he only collected three wins, with 21 losses. However, two of the three wins were against the Yankees, and Larsen was part of the massive seventeen-player trade between New York and Baltimore after the season. In 1955, a sore shoulder in spring training saw him start the season in the minors before eventually joining the big-league club. He finished with a 9–2 record, and, more important, his ERA dropped down to 3.06.

Larsen's spring training for the new season did not get off to a promising start when he crashed his new car early one morning. Larsen had spent the night drinking and fell asleep at the wheel. He enjoyed the nightlife, and Mantle noted that Larsen was the biggest drinker he knew. As an unnamed teammate noted, Larsen "probably had a lot more ability than 95 percent of all the pitchers in baseball. He was a good hitter. He could run the bases. He could field the ball. But he was a lazy type." Or, as Larsen himself admitted, "Let the good times roll. You give the best you can on the field. Who cares what you do afterwards, as long as you show up and do well." On the field, while he only appeared in 19 games in 1955, Larsen doubled that amount in the '56 season (with 20 starts) and went 11–5 with a 3.26 ERA.

It was a decent enough season, but Larsen's crowning achievement in his baseball life was still to come.

Johnny Kucks was another second-year Yankee looking to improve on his first campaign. Kucks signed with the Yankees in 1952 and was presented with a check for $13,000 (there are some claims the amount was $18,000; by comparison, Larsen received $850 when he signed with the Browns). Kucks was an All-Star in his first professional season with Norfolk of the Class-B Piedmont League. He then spent the 1953 and 1954 seasons in the military. After being discharged in time for spring training in 1955 and impressing the front office enough, Kucks made his major-league debut in April. Stengel said, "This here Kucks, with a natural sinker, and the ability to field well and hold men on bases, is justifying my decision not to ship him to Denver. I have great faith and confidence in this Kucks kid, and Ol' Case ain't wrong all the time. I have been known to make the right decisions very often." Used mainly in a relief role, Kucks appeared in 29 games (13 starts) and had a record of 8–7 with an ERA of 3.41. In his second campaign in pinstripes, Kucks became a regular starter. His ERA increased slightly to 3.85, but he picked up 18 wins and had 12 complete games. Kucks was an All-Star (selected by AL manager Stengel), and, perhaps mesmerized by the win total, several writers gave him MVP votes. The reality was that Kucks was an average pitcher; indeed, his WAR for the year was 0.0. Kucks was replacement level and benefited because he pitched for a great team. As such, when he took the mound, he usually received a great deal of run support. In only six of his 31 starts did the Yankees score fewer than three runs. Kucks was an average pitcher and only played for six seasons in the majors. Yet, as we shall see, even an average player can have their moment of glory.

One decidedly non-average player was looking for one more moment in the sun. Phil Rizzuto was in his 13th major-league season. No longer a regular starter, his career was barely hanging by a thread. Truth be told, he should have retired after the 1954 season when he hit an anemic .195 with an OPS of .541. Yet it is hard for almost every athlete to say good-bye. Rizzuto did not want to hang up his pinstripes, but in the end it was not his decision. On Old-Timers' Day, August 25, 1956, Rizzuto was summoned to a meeting with Stengel and Weiss. They gently let Rizzuto know that the team needed an incoming bat for the remainder of the season, and who did he think should make way? Rizzuto listed a few players before coming to the conclusion that it was he who was being let go. Not helping matters was that the new player the Yankees brought up was older than Rizzuto—forty-year-old Enos Slaughter. Rizzuto eventually calmed down, did not bad-mouth the Yankees on his way out, became a beloved announcer, and was eventually elected to the Hall of Fame.

While Rizzuto's career was over, Mantle's was taking off. Coming off a season where he should have been the MVP, Mantle became even better. He led the AL in slugging (.705), OPS (1.169), total bases (376), and runs (132). Mantle also led the AL in three other categories: those that make up the Triple Crown. Mantle had 130 RBIs. There was also a chance he would break Ruth's home run record, but he had to "settle" for 52 after hitting just five long balls in September. As for the batting title, with eight games left in the season Ted Williams had a narrow lead over Mantle, .356 to .352. However, Williams went into a minislump. Mantle ended the season with a batting average of .353 compared to Williams at .345. The twenty-four-year-old emerging superstar won the Triple Crown and was later rightfully named MVP.

In addition to Mantle, both Berra and Skowron had great years with the bat. Berra had a slash line of .298/.378/.534 with 29 doubles, 30 home runs, and 105 RBIs. Skowron went .308/.382/.528 with 23 home runs and 90 RBIs. On the pitching side, the star of the staff was Ford. He led the majors with an ERA of 2.47 while winning 19 games. He was an All-Star and finished third in Cy Young voting (he arguably should have won).

As for the season itself, once again the Yankee offense led the AL in slugging and OPS while only being middle of the pack in OBP. At times, the team may have struggled to get on base, but they were always a power threat. Yankees pitchers had the second-best ERA amongst AL teams. On April 20, with a record of 3–1, New York was a half-game out of first. That was the last time the Yankees did not lead the pennant race for the entire season. Apart from a hiccup in late June where four straight losses cut their lead to one game, the Yankees, as they often did, cruised. They finished with a record of 97–57 and easily won the AL pennant by nine games over Cleveland.

THE DODGERS' 1956 SEASON

When he fielded Howard's grounder and threw to first ensuring the Dodgers its first World Series title, Harold Henry Reese, or as he was more commonly known, Pee Wee Reese, ended the years of suffering in Brooklyn as well as his own baseball heartache.

While not the largest player around, Pee Wee Reese got his nickname not because he was only 5-foot-9 and weighed a buck forty when he signed as a shortstop with the American Association's Louisville Colonels, but because he enjoyed playing marbles (a "peewee" is a type of marble). Reese quickly became a star. After signing with them, the Colonels were bought by the Red Sox. With Joe Cronin entrenched as Boston's shortstop and manager, Reese was sold to the Dodgers in 1939 for $35,000 and four players to be named later; each of the four players had to have a value of $10,000. To say Reese was not happy to be traded would be an understatement. When told of his sale to the Dodgers, Reese responded, "Oh, not Brooklyn!" Very few people wanted to play for Dem Bums in those days. However, being traded was the best thing to happen to him. Beginning in 1940, Reese became a regular and was a perennial All-Star. More than any other Dodger, Reese understood the pain of constantly losing the World Series to the boys from the Bronx. Reese was the only Dodgers player who appeared in all five World Series losses to New York. Thus, fielding that final groundout, Reese smiled. It was time to celebrate.

Reese was a Hall of Fame player, but more important, he was a great man. Reese was shocked when he heard that the Dodgers had signed a black player. Like many white players, it was drummed into Reese that black players were simply not good enough to play in the majors. However, rather than accept the prevailing "wisdom," Reese noted that "if he's man enough to take my job, I'm not gonna like it, but, dammit, black or white, he deserves it." When a number of Dodgers players were trying to get their teammates to sign a petition saying they did not want to play with Robinson, Reese refused to sign it. Reese often was seen chatting with Robinson on and off the field. One particular incident stands out. In May 1947, during infield practice before a game in Cincinnati, both fans and a number of Reds players were shouting insults at Robinson. Reese responded by walking over to Robinson and putting an arm around him. There is now a statue outside MCU Park in Coney Island commemorating this moment.

However, while it is undoubtedly true that such an action took place, when and where is open to debate. Rob Edelman, writing for the Society for American Baseball Research, states, "Duke Snider, for one, recalled that the incident took place in Boston. According to an account in *The Sporting News* published in 1956, it first occurred during a 1947 exhibition game in Fort Worth, when 'a foghorn-voiced Texas fan got on Jackie with the kind of comments that need not be described' and, later on in the season, in Boston, Reese 'made almost an identical gesture—the gesture that told the world that Robinson was his teammate.' Then in 1984 the very same paper reported that the incident took place in Cincinnati. In a 1952 magazine article and his book *Wait Till Next Year*, published in 1960, Robinson himself recalled that the incident took place in Boston—in 1948. Carl Erskine claimed to be present when it happened, and he did not become a Dodger until 1948. According to some recollections, Reese made his gesture during infield practice. Others recalled that it occurred during the game, prior to the home team's at-bat. The 1984 *Sporting News* account had it taking place in-game, when the Dodgers were in the field, after Jackie had committed an error."

No matter when or where it occurred, Reese's actions solidified his and Robinson's friendship. It also had the effect of resonating throughout baseball. Such a simple gesture of friendship and camaraderie went a long way. Reese had a wonderful career, and following his playing days he became a broadcaster before staying in baseball as an employee of the Hillerich & Bradsby Company, makers of the famed Louisville Slugger bat. Reese died in 1999 at the age of eighty-one. But his contribution to race relations was not forgotten. At Reese's funeral, Joe Black told the mourners that "Pee Wee helped make my boyhood dream come true to play in the majors, the World Series. When Pee Wee reached out to Jackie, all of us in the Negro League smiled and said it was the first time that a white guy had accepted us. When I finally got up to Brooklyn, I went to Pee Wee and said, 'Black people love you. When you touched Jackie, you touched all of us.' With Pee Wee, it was No.1 on his uniform and No. 1 in our hearts."

While Robinson and Reese were friends almost from the beginning, a new teammate had several prior run-ins with number 42 and other Dodgers. In May, Loes was sold to Baltimore. Needing another starter, the Dodgers turned to Sal Maglie. Salvatore Anthony Maglie was a fearsome intimidator for the New York Giants. He did not make his major-league debut until he was twenty-eight but only lasted one year in the bigs. It was his own choosing. He jumped to the Mexican League and played there for the 1946 and 1947 seasons. Baseball Commissioner Happy Chandler banned Maglie and other American players who participated in the Mexican League from the majors for five years. With the Mexican League on the verge of collapse, Maglie was part of a group of pros touring the US playing in exhibition games. Following the tour, and being unable to cover expenses, Maglie purchased a gas station before playing in the Provincial League in Quebec. The major league ban was eventually lifted, and Maglie returned to the Giants in time for the 1950 season. While initially pitching out of the bullpen, Maglie eventually became a starter and finished the year with an ERA of 2.71, the best in baseball.

Maglie was not just a good pitcher, he was a fierce competitor. Cincinnati's Danny Litwhiler claimed that Maglie "scares you to death. He's scowling and gnashing his teeth, and if you try to dig in on him, there goes your Adam's apple. He's gonna win if it kills you and him both." And as a Giant, there was arguably no team that Maglie hated more than the Dodgers. Maglie often threw hard, up, and tight to Campanella, Furillo, Hodges, and Robinson. There was a reason why Maglie had the nickname of "The Barber." There was no love lost between Maglie and the Dodgers.

Maglie had a great career with the Giants and was a key part of their 1954 world championship. The following year, Maglie was still pitching well, but as he was thirty-eight, Father Time was beginning to catch up with him. He was somewhat surprisingly traded to Cleveland midway through the season, and he began contemplating retirement. However, Maglie and his wife adopted a boy, and the prospect of his son seeing him play renewed the fire within. After only two appearances with Cleveland at the start of the 1956 season, he was sold to Brooklyn for the measly sum of $100. Brooklyn fans could not believe that the hated Maglie was now a Dodger and wondered how the players would respond. When Maglie walked into the Ebbets Field clubhouse, Furillo greeted his fellow Italian with "Hey, paisan." The two became friends. As for Robinson, he warmly welcomed him. Maglie may have played hard, but now he was a Dodger.

Maglie had an outstanding season for the boys in blue. He had a 13–5 record with an ERA of 2.87 and finished second in both Cy Young and MVP voting. His finest performance as a Dodger during the regular season came on the night of September 25 in a tight pennant race. In front of an anemic crowd of 15,204 at Ebbets Field, Maglie pitched a complete-game shutout against the Phillies. Maglie walked two, struck out three, while not allowing a hit. A no-hitter at such a crucial point of the season was truly superb.

Apart from the addition of Maglie, the Dodgers were virtually unchanged from the previous season. Once again, the front office was happy to rest on its laurels. While Brooklyn was world champions, age was catching up to a number of players. In addition, World Series hero Johnny Podres was drafted into the military, causing him to miss the entire 1956 campaign.

Offensively, the team was still led by Snider. He led the Dodgers and the entire NL in home runs (43), walks (99), OBP (.399), slugging (.598), and OPS (.997). Sandy Amoros had a career year with a slash line of .260/.385/.517 and 16 home runs. Hodges was as solid as ever, going 265/.354/.507. However, age and injury caught up with Campanella, who followed up his MVP season by hitting only .219 (101 points lower than 1955) and had an OPS of .727 (an astonishing 251 points lower).

On the pitching side, apart from Maglie, Newcombe was magnificent, finishing with an ERA of 3.06 on the way to winning both the MVP and the very first Cy Young Award. Newcombe was great, but what mesmerized voters is that he ended up winning 27 games. By contrast, no other Brooklyn pitcher won more than 13 games. Carl Erskine had a 13–11 record and an ERA of 4.25, a disappointing season all around.

But he did have a career highlight. On May 12 at Ebbets Field against the Giants, Erskine threw a no-hitter. Coincidentally, in the two no-hitters thrown by Dodgers pitchers in the 1956, both Erskine and Maglie only struck out three batters while allowing two walks.

Individually, some Dodgers players had career highlights, but overall the team struggled over the first half of the season. The Dodgers went 42–32, but most of the NL was so mediocre that Brooklyn was only two games out of first. They then proceeded to lose four straight, and as late as July 26 Brooklyn was six games out. With no team dominating the league, the Dodgers still found themselves, somewhat miraculously, in a pennant race. A great run where they won eight of nine saw Dem Bums sitting atop the NL, but the team was once again inconsistent, and they were one game out of first with three games left. The Milwaukee Braves lost two out of their final three, while Brooklyn was perfect, winning their final three games. As such, Brooklyn had won another NL pennant, with the Braves one game behind and the Reds two games back.

THE 1956 WORLD SERIES

It was time for another Dodgers-Yankees World Series, but this time Brooklyn was the defending champions. Another Dodgers triumph could have finally broken the Yankees' domination over baseball. New York had not won the World Series since 1953, and as Brooklyn knew all too well, back-to-back fall classic losses are difficult to recover from. Unlike the previous World Series, Mantle was fit and looking to avenge the heartbreak of 1955, while the Dodgers were beat up and tired coming off a tight pennant race. In 1955, Dem Bums cruised to the pennant and were well rested heading into the World Series, while the Yankees were fighting until almost the end of the season in the AL. The roles were reversed this time around.

One advantage for Brooklyn was that they had home field advantage. In Game One at Ebbets Field, Alston decided to go with Maglie. In somewhat of a surprise because the Dodgers feasted on left-handed pitching, Stengel went with Ford. Ford was the undoubted Yankees ace, but the one thing Brooklyn did better than any team in the majors was eat up left-handed pitching at Ebbets Field. It was, however, New York that opened the scoring. Wasting little time, Enos Slaughter singled with one out in the top of the first. This brought up Mantle, and looking to atone for his injury-plagued fall classic from the previous year, he launched a ball completely out of Ebbets Field and into a parking lot across the street. The Yankees were up by two. The lead did not last long. After a perfect first inning, Ford had to be feeling confident. However, Robinson opened the bottom of the second with a solo shot to left. Hodges then singled before Furillo hit a gapper to left-center, scoring Hodges to tie the game. But once again the Dodgers struggled with runners in scoring position, and Ford got out of the inning without further damage. Nevertheless, the game was effectively over the next inning. With one out, Reese and Snider singled, but Robinson lined out to center and the runners had to hold. This brought up Hodges, and he homered to deep left. The Dodgers led by three. While Martin cut the deficit next inning with a solo shot of his own, Amoros doubled home Campanella in the bottom of the inning. That was all the scoring for the game, as the Dodgers won, 6–3. While Ford only lasted three innings, Maglie pitched a complete game while striking out 10. The $100 it cost to pry Maglie from Cleveland looked like the bargain of the century. New York had chances throughout the game but could not get even one hit with runners in scoring position, going 0-for-6. Just like last year, the well-rested team coming into the World Series lost Game One. And history was to repeat itself in Game Two.

Starting for the Yankees was Larsen, looking for his first World Series win after taking the loss in Game Four in 1955. Likewise, Dodgers starter Newcombe, who failed to record a victory in his three previous World Series games. Although, to be fair, one of his losses was when he went eight innings and only gave up one run. As fate would have it, neither Larsen nor Newcome would be credited with the win. Once again, New York scored in the top of the first. With a runner on first and two out, Berra walked before Collins singled the runner home. Newcombe then imploded in the second. Martin singled to open the inning before being moved to second on a Coleman bunt. This brought up Larsen, and he was a decent hitter, at least for a pitcher. He singled to left, scoring Martin. McDougald followed with a single of his own. With two out, Mantle walked to load the bases. Showing faith in his starter, Alston left Newcombe in to face Berra. It was a mistake. Berra hit a grand slam, Newcombe was out, New York led by six, and the game was effectively over. Or was it?

In the bottom of the inning, the first three Dodgers reached to load the bases. Hodges then scored on a Campanella sacrifice fly. Pinch-hitter Dale Mitchell popped up, and with two out Larsen was looking to get out of the inning without further damage. But he walked Gilliam, and Stengel had seen enough. He pulled

Larsen and inserted Johnny Kucks. However, Reese singled, scoring Amoros and Furillo. With Snider due to bat, Stengel pulled Kucks and put in lefty Tommy Byrne. While Snider hit righties better than left-handed pitching, he still had prodigious power. And it showed as he homered to right-center and somewhat miraculously the game was tied. Brooklyn had all the momentum, and it continued for the rest of the game. Reliever Don Bessent held New York to two runs across seven innings. Meanwhile, the Yankees relievers were a dumpster fire. Every New York pitcher inserted into the game gave up at least one run, apart from Turley, who faced just one batter. The Dodgers ended up destroying the Yankees, 13–8. Despite all their power, Brooklyn only recorded three extra-base hits: Hodges doubled twice and Snider homered. It was through singles (nine) and walks (eleven) that Dem Bums put the sword to their crosstown rivals. The Dodgers won the first two games, and back-to-back World Series triumphs could have spelled the end of Yankees domination. Only one team had lost the first two games of a World Series and ended up winning it all: the 1955 Dodgers. Would history repeat itself, but this time in New York's favor?

One sour note for Brooklyn was that Newcombe looked horrible. And making things worse, he got into an altercation with a parking attendant while the game was still underway. The attendant, Michael Brown, told reporters, "Newcombe and his brother were coming out of the ballpark and going toward their station wagon. I hollered to him: 'What's the matter, Newk? A little competition too much for you? Do you fold up?' He called me a couple of foul names and with that he punched me. Then somebody stopped him. He accused me of razzing him all season and I said I only did it twice before." Both Newcombe and Brown were hauled to a police station, where they eventually apologized to each other. The incident and his Game Two performance affected Newcombe, and Alston was loath to use him for the rest of the World Series.

Another pitcher looking to atone for a less-than-stellar World Series outing was Ford. Due to his abbreviated start in Game One, Stengel gave Ford the ball in Game Three. In Game One, Ford was reluctant to go to his off-speed stuff due to the power of the Dodgers' right-handed hitters and the short left-field fence at Ebbets Field. Home runs to left at Ebbets Field were only routine fly balls at Yankee Stadium. As such, Stengel had faith that Ford would rebound. As for Brooklyn, second-year righty Roger Craig got the ball. Craig had an average season with a 12–11 record and an ERA of 3.71. In contrast to the Game Two slugfest, Game Three was more of a pitchers' duel, at least for the majority of the game. Brooklyn opened the scoring in the top of the second on Campanella's sacrifice fly, but New York came right back in the bottom of the inning as Martin's home run tied the game. Both pitchers then cruised until an eventful sixth inning. In the top of the inning, Reese tripled with one out and was brought home thanks to Snider's sacrifice fly. The Dodgers had a lead relatively late in the game. If they could hold on, they would have taken an almost unassailable lead in the World Series. But it was not to be. Bauer led off the bottom of the inning with a single before Craig got the next two outs. Berra kept the inning alive with a single of his own. And up to the plate came forty-year-old, 10-time All-Star and future Hall of Famer Enos Slaughter, who was acquired when New York released Rizzuto. Slaughter had a slash line of .281/.354/.392 in 24 games for the Bronx Bombers. He was not exactly a power threat, as he had not hit more than two home runs in a season since 1952. In 115 total games in 1956 Slaughter hit all of two homers, none for New York. Of all the things going through Craig's mind as he waited on the mound, giving up a homer to Slaughter was not one of them. But that is exactly what he did. On a 3-1 count, Slaughter hit a bomb to right for a three-run jack. New York had a 4–2 lead. Slaughter's homer was the only Yankees hit with runners in scoring position for the game; to be fair, they only had two opportunities. In contrast, Brooklyn was woeful, going 0-for-5. The Dodgers' performance can be summed up by the baserunning gaffe by Furillo in the top of the ninth. With Ford on the mound, New York led, 5–3. Furillo led off the inning with a hit to the gap in right. Rather than settle for a double, he tried to stretch it into to a triple. Big mistake. Bauer gathered the ball and threw to Martin, who fired a bullet to third baseman Andy Carey, who applied the tag. Furillo was out and with it the Dodgers' chances. Never make the first or last out at third. Campanella struck out, and Charlie Neal grounded out. Ford atoned for his Game One loss, striking out seven on the way to a complete game. New York was back in the Series.

Following his short start in Game Two, Newcombe could have gotten the ball for Game Four, but Alston decided to stick with the original game plan. Game Four was coincidently enough a battle of fourth starters as Carl Erskine was matched up against Tom Sturdivant. Erskine had a disappointing year as his ERA ballooned to 4.25. Sturdivant was in his second year in the majors and first as a semi-regular starter. In 1955, he was a reliever and only made one start. In the 1956 campaign, Sturdivant appeared in 32 games with 17 starts and had a 16–8 record and a 3.30 ERA. Stengel got Sturdivant ready for the World

Series by starting him in his final eight appearances of the regular season. Sturdivant pitched in the Game Two slugfest, allowing a run on two hits and a walk in two-thirds of an inning. Thus, Brooklyn must have felt confident in their chances, but likewise, Erskine did not put any great fear into the Bronx Bombers.

New York took the lead in the first, as Berra hit a two-out RBI single to drive home Joe Collins, who had doubled earlier in the inning. Brooklyn came back and tied the game in the fourth; Snider doubled to open the frame, and a Hodges single brought Brooklyn back in the game. Once again, it did not last. Mantle led off the bottom of the inning with a walk and stole second. Slaughter was intentionally walked to bring up Martin and the chance of a double play. It did not work out that way. Martin singled home Mantle, and Slaughter moved to third. Slaughter then scored on a McDougald sacrifice fly. New York added to their lead in the sixth when Mantle homered to start the inning. In the seventh, Bauer homered to left with a runner on first. The Dodgers threatened in the top of the ninth, but it was too little too late. New York won, 6–2, and the Series was tied. Erskine lasted only four innings, giving up three runs. By contrast, Sturdivant was magnificent, pitching a complete game while striking out seven. Brooklyn, though, had their chances. They were 2-for-9 with runners in scoring position and stranded eight. Once again, Brooklyn's inability to get the big hit cost them in the World Series. Of course, in Game Five, the Dodgers did not get the big hit, or a hit at all.

Maglie was great for Brooklyn on October 8 at Yankee Stadium. He was cruising through 3 2/3 innings before Mantle hit a ball that somewhat improbably stayed fair and landed in the stands just inside the right-field foul pole. The Yankees were up by one. They doubled the lead in the sixth when Carey led off with a single, was bunted over, and Bauer singled to left, driving in Carey. Across eight innings, Maglie gave up just those two runs on five hits, while striking out five. For him and the Dodgers, there was just one problem; Don Larsen was *perfect*.

Following Game Four, Larsen, relaxed as always, went out for a few drinks with the *New York Mirror's* Arthur Richman. He did not know whether he would be pitching the following day. Larsen first learned that he would be taking the mound when he arrived at the stadium and found a baseball in his pitching shoe put there by pitching coach Jim Turner. Larsen pitched well, but, as he admitted, if the game were at Ebbets Field, no one would have been talking about his performance. Larsen was being modest. His stuff that day was outstanding, and it was more than good enough on that historic day. Just like Maglie, Larsen cruised early. But unlike his Dodgers counterpart, Larsen kept cruising. In the fifth, Hodges drove a ball to left-center, where Mantle, bad legs and all, got a good jump and made a fine running catch. While time has led to the myth that Mantle's catch was out of this world, the reality is it was a good catch, certainly not special. But Larsen was special. Heading into the ninth inning, no Dodger had reached base. On a 1-2 pitch, Furillo hit a lazy fly ball to right. One out. On an 0-1 pitch, Campanella grounded out to second. Two out. This brought up the pitcher's spot. Alston called upon pinch-hitter Dale Mitchell, a two-time All-Star with Cleveland. Now in his 11th year in the bigs, Mitchell was traded to Brooklyn during the season. He had 24 plate appearances for the Dodgers and would be out of the majors at the end of the season. Mitchell stood between Larsen and baseball immortality. The first pitch was a ball. The second was a called strike. Then a swinging strike followed by a foul ball. The next pitch would be Larsen's 97th. Larsen delivered, and Mitchell checked his swing. Home-plate umpire Babe Pinelli rung Mitchell up for strike three! A number of fans ran out onto the field. On October 8, 1956, in the Bronx, Larsen was sublime. He pitched a perfect game. Nobody could quite believe it. Yankees public address announcer Bob Sheppard later noted that "if Nolan Ryan had done it, if Sandy Koufax had done it, if Don Drysdale had done it, I would have nodded and said, 'Well, it could happen.' But Don Larsen?" Was the called strike three really a strike? Not that it matters, but Berra was adamant that the pitch was indeed a strike. He said, "No question about it. People say it was a ball and that I rushed the mound to hug Larsen to make the umpire think it was a strike. Nonsense. It was a perfect strike." As for Larsen himself, he was somewhat in shock. He was overheard hours after the game saying, "Last night I was a bum and tonight everybody wants to meet me." This included Dodgers owner Walter O'Malley, who came into the Yankees clubhouse to congratulate Larsen and get a baseball signed. There has not been another no-hitter in World Series history, let alone a perfect game since. Larsen did the seemingly impossible, and his heroics pushed New York to the verge of once again riding roughshod over Dem Bums. Larsen passed away on January 1, 2020. He was ninety years old.

While New York needed only one more win to reclaim their throne, Game Six and, if necessary, Game Seven would be at Ebbets Field. And considering Brooklyn's dominance at their home ground, they had to like their chances to go back-to-back. Stengel gave the ball to Turley, who had appeared in the opening two games in relief. Considering Game Six was a must win, one would assume that even with his struggles, Newcombe would take the mound for the Dodgers. Instead, Alston decided on Clem Labine. Labine, who began his career with Brooklyn back in 1950, was predominantly a reliever, never making more than nine starts in a single season. In 1956, he made three starts. Even though he had a good year in relief and was an All-Star, the fact that he started for Brooklyn was somewhat of a shock. More of a shock was to follow. Game Six, just like the previous game, was a pitchers' duel. While both teams had chances to score after nine innings, neither team had put a run on the board. The Yankees went down in order in the 10th. In the bottom of the inning, Gilliam walked and was bunted over by Reese. New York elected to intentionally walk Snider to bring up Robinson. On a 0-1 count, number 42 lined a ball to left, his last hit in the majors. Slaughter got a bad read on the ball, and as a result Gilliam scored easily. A walk-off victory provided by legend Jackie Robinson must have had Dem Bums primed for Game Seven. However, momentum just like happiness can be fleeting. And so it proved to be.

Both managers had pitching conundrums. Stengel could have gone with Ford, but considering the shellacking Ford took in Game One at Ebbets Field, he decided to turn to Kucks. Kucks had appeared in relief in Games Three (two innings of work) and Five (faced one batter) and was well rested heading into the decider. Alston had a choice between Craig, Erskine (on short rest), or Newcombe. Three pitchers who were unimpressive in the Series so far. Alston very reluctantly went with Newcombe. And the rest was history. Bauer singled to open the game before stealing second. Newcombe came back to strike out Martin and Mantle. All Newcombe had to do was get past

Berra. Unfortunately—or fortunately—due to one's perspective, Berra had a history of feasting on Newcome. And history repeated itself. Berra homered to right, the Yankees led, 2–0, and the Dodgers imploded. Indeed, history repeated itself in the top of the third. With a runner on and two out, Berra stepped to the plate. There is no earthly reason why Alston should have let Newcombe pitch to Berra, but he did. You can guess the result. Berra hit the ball out of the ballpark; New York now led, 4–0. Alston allowed Newcombe to start the fourth. Brooklyn was down by four, but with their power and playing at Ebbets Field, the game was not over. Nevertheless, once again a Dodgers manager was slow to pull his starting pitcher and paid the price. Howard homered to open the inning, and the Dodgers players and fans were demoralized. Only then did Alston come out and get Newcombe. While Newcombe struggled, Kucks was having no problems with the Brooklyn hitters. The Yankees broke the game wide open in the seventh. Craig came on to pitch and loaded the bases with nobody out. Skowron then proceeded to hit a grand slam, and the men in pinstripes pounded Dem Bums into the ground.

In the bottom of the ninth with two outs and the Yankees ahead, 9–0, up to the plate stepped the tired warrior number 42, Jackie Robinson. Kucks was still on the mound. And on the final pitch ever between New York and Brooklyn, he struck out Robinson. Berra dropped the pitch, and, rather than meekly accept Brooklyn's fate, Robinson raced to first. But this time Robinson was not fast enough, and Berra threw to first for the final out. Kucks was superb. He threw a three-hit shutout. People look back at the 1956 World Series and remember Larsen's perfect game, while Kucks's performance is somewhat an afterthought. But in some ways, what Kucks did was more spectacular: holding the Dodgers scoreless at Ebbets Field in the biggest game of the season was no small feat. Kucks later noted that "I didn't know I was going to start that game until about an hour before, when I found the ball in my glove in my locker. . . . It was going to be either me, Whitey Ford, or Tom Sturdivant, and I think the reason Casey [Stengel] picked me was because Ebbets Field was such a small ballpark and I had that good sinkerball." On October 10, 1956, it was not just a good sinkerball, but a virtually unhittable pitch.

It is easy to say that the difference between 1955 and 1956 was a fit Mantle, and he did have a great Series this time around with an OPS of 1.067 and three home runs. But the reality is once again when there was everything to play for, New York outmanaged, outhit, and outpitched the Dodgers. New York dominated Brooklyn in the crosstown World Series not because they were lucky, had devil magic, or the baseball gods favored them, but because they were simply a much better team.

New York was once again world champions. The greatest baseball franchise in the history of the game was sitting on top of the mountain. As for the Dodgers, they were beaten, heartbroken, and soon to say good-bye to Brooklyn.

9

1963: LOS ANGELES DOMINATION

THE YANKEES AND the Dodgers would not meet up again until 1963. In the years since their last Series meeting, New York was still at the top (or very close) of the mountain. In 1957, the Bronx Bombers cruised to the AL pennant by eight games. They met the Milwaukee Braves, who won the NL pennant by the same margin, in the World Series. In somewhat of a shock when all was said and done, Milwaukee defeated New York four games to three and were crowned world champions. The two teams met again in the World Series the following year. A Milwaukee victory could have altered the balance of power. However, while it was rare for New York to lose in the World Series, it was exceeding rare for them to lose back-to-back World Series. Like 1957, it came down to Game Seven. The game was tied, 2–2, in the eighth. This time, the men in pinstripes asserted their power. A Howard RBI single and a three-run blast off the bat of Skowron settled matters as New York regained their crown.

DODGERS VS. YANKEES

The 1959 Yankees were a shell of their former selves, finishing with a dismal 79–75 record, "good" enough for third place in the AL, 25 games off the pace. Other teams would have taken years to recover from such a horrid season, but other teams are not the New York Yankees. In 1960, New York recaptured the AL pennant by eight games. This time they would face the Pittsburgh Pirates in the fall classic. As was becoming the norm, a seventh game was needed. Heading into the bottom of the eighth, the Yankees had a comfortable 7–4 lead. This time, however, shockingly, New York imploded, conceding five runs. The Yankees came back in the ninth to tie it. However, with Ralph Terry on the mound, Bill Mazeroski homered to deep left in the bottom of the inning, and the Pirates walked it off and were on top of the world. The heartbreaking loss spelled the end of Stengel's time in New York, as he was replaced as manager by Ralph Houk.

The 1961 Yankees won 109 games and the AL by, you guessed, eight games. The season was highlighted by the home run race between teammates Mickey Mantle and Roger Maris, whom New York acquired from the Kansas City Athletics after the 1959 season. Mantle had 54 home runs before being hampered by a late-season hip injury, while Maris broke Babe Ruth's 1927 record of 60 homers in a season when he slammed his 61st on the final day of the season. This time they faced the Cincinnati Reds, in the World Series. It was not total annihilation, but close to it. New York was once again back on top after thumping the Reds four games to one. The 1962 Yankees "only" managed to win 96 games and the AL pennant by a "paltry" five games. Awaiting them in the World Series was their old New York nemesis, the Giants. In 1958, the Giants followed the Dodgers to California, relocating to San Francisco. Game Seven was needed to separate the two teams. On the mound for New York was 1960 "villain" Ralph Terry. Terry was charged with two losses in the 1960 World Series, one in 1961, and he lost again in Game Two of the 1962 World Series. However, the world does love a good redemption story. In Game Five, Terry pitched a complete game as New York won, 5–3. And here he was again on the mound in Game Seven, his third start of the Series. Terry was able to take the ball because rainouts meant there were six days between Game Five and Seven. Terry was superb, only giving up four hits, while striking out four on the way to a complete-game shutout. The Yankees won, 1–0, with the only run coming courtesy of a groundball double play with the bases loaded in the fifth, scoring Skowron from third. Nevertheless, New York won back-to-back World Series. Heading into the 1963 season, New York's authority over the baseball world, while at times threatened, remained intact.

While the Yankees were riding roughshod over baseball, it was a different story for the Dodgers. Following their 1956 World Series loss, the majority of the team went on a goodwill tour of Japan. It was fine PR for the Dodgers, but most players would have rather stayed home and recovered from another grueling season. One player who did not go was Jackie Robinson. Injuries and age had finally caught up to the Brooklyn legend, who was contemplating retirement. Rather than celebrate all his accomplishments and praise him to the moon, before Robinson officially announced his decision, he was traded to the Giants for $30,000 and Dick Littlefield. Let that sink in. The Dodgers traded Jackie Robinson to the Giants. Considering that the Giants were offering Robinson substantial money to play for one year, number 42 was tempted. However, he decided to officially announce his retirement, and the trade was off. While the Yankees were celebrating their history with Old-Timers' Day, Brooklyn was disloyal to a legend.

The 1957 Dodgers was a decent team and was still in contention at the start of August. But it soon fell by the wayside and ended up 11 games out of first with an 84–70 record. What was happening on the field, though, was a just a backstory to the real story with the team. Since 1953, Dodgers owner Walter O'Malley was looking to build a new stadium in Brooklyn. Ebbets Field was crumbling, and even if it could be renovated, there was only room for 700 parking spaces. Something unsaid, though, was the changing demographics of Brooklyn. There was an influx of African Americans moving into the borough, and at the same time whites were leaving. The media also portrayed the borough as a crime-ridden hotspot. In August 1955, O'Malley issued the city with an ultimatum: beginning in 1958, the Dodgers will be playing in a new stadium in the borough or the team will relocate. O'Malley was proposing that the Dodgers pay for the new stadium themselves. In a letter to the vice chairman of the Triborough Bridge and Tunnel Authority, O'Malley wrote, "It is my belief that a new ball park should be built, financed and owned by the ball club. It should occupy land on the tax roll. The only assistance I am looking for is in the assembling of a suitable plot and I hope that the mechanics of Title I (of the Housing Act of 1949) could be used if the ball park were also to be used as a parking garage." However, New York City officials were seemingly not interested in keeping the Dodgers. Faced with the indifference and with dollar signs in his eyes, O'Malley began looking west. To Los Angeles. In

May 1957, the National League owners gave formal approval to the Dodgers if O'Malley decided on that course of action. And he did. On September 24, 1957, a paltry crowd of 6,702 at Ebbets Field saw the Dodgers' last game in Brooklyn. On September 29, the Dodgers lost to the Phillies in Philadelphia, thus spelling the end of the Brooklyn Dodgers. It was made official on October 8. Dodgers official Arthur Patterson told the assembled media, "In view of the action of the Los Angeles City Council yesterday, and in accordance with the resolution of the National League made October 1, the stockholders and directors of the Brooklyn Baseball Club have today met and unanimously agreed that the necessary steps be taken to draft the Los Angeles territory." Good-bye Brooklyn, hello Los Angeles.

The Dodgers' first order of business was finding a home stadium. The team considered the Rose Bowl and the minor-league Wrigley Field, not the infinitely more famous one in Chicago, but a stadium with the same name that the Dodgers bought in February 1957. O'Malley finally settled on the Los Angeles Coliseum. The LA Coliseum as a baseball stadium left a lot to be desired. Home plate was only 250 feet from the left-field fence, while 440 feet from right-center. In 1958, only seven home runs were hit to right. The Coliseum's dimensions destroyed Snider as a power threat. In 1958, while hampered with a knee injury, Snider hit only 15 home runs. Money-wise the move to LA was great. In 1957, the Dodgers drew 1,028,258 paying fans to Ebbets Field. In 1958 at the Coliseum, the team drew 1,845,556 fans. And this was to see a team that was a horrid 71–83. Yet somehow a miracle occurred the following year. The 1959 team was much improved, winning eighty-eight games. A good turnaround made even better because the NL was pretty weak that year. So much so that the 88 victories were good enough for the Dodgers to win the pennant following a playoff with the Braves. In the World Series, Los Angeles defeated Chicago, four games to two. They were World Series champions. The Dodgers were clutch: they scored twenty-one runs in the Series; nineteen came with two outs.

Lighting very rarely strikes twice, and the 1960 Dodgers came back to Earth. They won 82 games, finishing in fourth place, 13 games off the pace. The team improved to 89–65 in 1961, but the Reds were better, winning the pennant by four games.

Nineteen sixty-two was a good year off the field for Los Angeles as they moved to their new home, Dodger Stadium. All players, with the possible exception of Wally Moon, who perfected hitting home runs to left field, were happy to be leaving the LA Coliseum. The team responded by playing magnificent baseball, finishing the regular season at 101–61. There was just one slight problem. With seven games remaining in the season, the Dodgers led the NL by three games. LA then proceeded to go 1–6, including four straight losses to end the season, and finished tied with the Giants. Like in 1951, a three-game playoff would decide the pennant. The Giants thumped the Dodgers, 8–0, in Game One. Game Two saw the Dodgers walk it off in the bottom of the ninth, winning, 8–7. And in Game Three, the Dodgers collapsed again. At Dodger Stadium, the home team led, 4–2, after eight. Dodgers ace Don Drysdale told Alston that he wanted to pitch the ninth. Alston told Drysdale that he would be on the mound to start Game One of the World Series against the Yankees. Instead, Alston turned to three different relievers during the inning. All of them were ineffective as the Giants piled on four runs and eventually ran out winners, 6–4, and headed to the World Series. To say there was heat on Alston was an understatement; many players were furious he did not pitch Drysdale. Tommy Davis continually screamed, "You stole my money!" (you, of course, being Alston and the money the players' World Series share). Wally Moon asked reporters, "How the hell would you feel if you all just lost $12,000?" Grumbling within the ranks would continue the following season.

THE DODGERS' 1963 SEASON

Baseball players are meant to be loyal to their team. If they leave for a better opportunity, they are called "sellouts" and other less flattering names. Yet teams are usually never loyal to their players, even stars. On April 1, Dodgers legend and future Hall of Famer Duke Snider was sold to the New York Mets, who joined the league in 1962 to fill the void left after the Dodgers and Giants fled to the West Coast. While Snider was not the same player in his prime as near the end of his career, he deserved a lot better than being sold to a team that had no chance to contend. At least the Dodgers promised Snider a job with the team once his playing days were over. Nevertheless, Snider should have played his entire career with the Dodgers. That he did not was a disgrace.

Back in Los Angeles, adding fuel to the pressure on Alston was third-base coach Leo Durocher. There was a belief that the reason why Drysdale never got the ball in the infamous ninth inning was that Durocher was an advocate for it. After the game, Durocher allegedly told journalists that the Dodgers would have been going to the World Series if he were their manager. Before the 1963 season got underway, *Sport* magazine splashed on its cover "Will Dissension Destroy the Dodgers?" Inside the magazine, Drysdale was quoted as saying, "You're damn right I would have liked to pitch. Only they [Alston] didn't ask me."

That the Dodgers were mediocre in April and early May led to the knives once again being out for Alston. Following a series loss to the Pirates in Pittsburgh, a number of players were not impressed by the old bus they had to take to the airport, especially as it did not have air conditioning. And as fate would have it, they saw their Pirate counterparts being transported in a luxurious bus. That led to more grumbling. Alston snapped. First baseman Ron Fairly retold the story in *True Blue*. He wrote that Alston said, "Anybody who doesn't like this bus? Get off it and come outside. We'll settle it right there." Alston got off the bus walking back and forth staring at the players through the windows. The players remained in their seats. Alston went back inside and stared down the players, telling them, "Anybody got anything to say?" Nobody said a word. The team then proceeded to go on a 13–2 run, and all was right with the world. Except a five-game losing streak in late May and early June led to more calls for a managerial change. And they were still being discussed by the media as the Dodgers went 16–12 for the month of June. Luckily for Alston, he had two superstar pitchers on the roster; Drysdale and Sandy Koufax.

Donald Scott Drysdale's father was a baseball coach. But rather than push Don into the game, he did not allow his son to pitch until he was sixteen. The thought being that it was better to save the arm for hopefully the pros rather than meaningless games. It was a good strategy that paid off rather quickly. Drysdale signed with the Dodgers when he was seventeen. In 1954, he was sent to Bakersfield in the California League. The following year, he went to Montreal. He impressed the Dodgers' hierarchy enough that on April 17, 1956, at the ripe old age of nineteen, Drysdale became one of Dem Bums. Pitching in relief, he went one inning and only gave up a walk. On April 23, he made his first start. Drysdale pitched a complete game, giving up one run while striking out nine as the Dodgers beat the Phillies, 1–0. While there were some teething pains along the way, Drysdale had *ace* written all over him. In 1962, Drysdale had a magnificent season, going 25–9 with an ERA of 2.83. He was an All-Star, finished fifth in MVP voting, and won the Cy Young Award. Yet for him the 1962 season was always one of missed opportunities, and that he did not get to pitch the fateful ninth inning against the Giants gnawed away at him. It is fair to say that Drysdale was ruthless on the mound. As he said, "My own little rule was two for one—if one of my teammates got knocked down, then I knocked down two on the other team." Drysdale hit 154 batters during his career, an NL record. Or, as journalist Dave Anderson noted, "Home plate is 17 inches wide. But to Don Drysdale it is divided into three parts—the inside four inches, the middle nine inches and the outside four inches. To him only the middle part belongs to the hitter; the inside and the outside part belong to the pitcher." Looking at won-lost record alone, in 1963 Drysdale had a "bad" year, going 19–17. Yet his ERA declined to 2.63. Drysdale received two or less runs of support in 15 of his 42 starts. Nevertheless, that the Dodgers could count on Drysdale to give them a lot more than a fighting chance every time he took the mound went a long way to ensuring that the 1963 season would not end up as disastrous as the previous year. This was especially true, as alongside Drysdale in the pitching rotation was Sandy Koufax.

When one thinks of Koufax, or as he is still known "The Left Arm of God," a person remembers one of the greatest pitchers of all time. Hall of Famer Ernie Banks of the Chicago Cubs claimed that facing Koufax "was frightening. He had that tremendous fastball that would rise, and a great curveball that started at the eyes and broke to the ankles. In the end you knew you were going to be embarrassed. You were either going to strike out or foul out." However, for a number of years Koufax struggled to put it all together. Between 1955 and 1960, he had a record of 36–40 and a decidedly average ERA of 4.10. Indeed, at the end of the 1960 season, so despondent with how things were going and that Alston seemingly did not have faith in him, Koufax threw his glove, among other things, in the bin and left the clubhouse.

One of the issues with Koufax is that he did not spend any time in the minors honing his craft. After a good first year playing college ball, he was scouted by a number of teams. Koufax had a tryout with the Giants but did not perform well. The Yankees offered a signing bonus of only $4,000 and said Koufax would start out in Class-D ball. If the Yankees had not been so frugal, Koufax may well have ended up in pinstripes. But the low signing bonus and playing in Class D did not appeal to Koufax and his family. Koufax also had a tryout with the Dodgers. Brooklyn officials, including Alston, were impressed. The Dodgers offered Koufax a $6,000 annual salary and a $14,000 signing bonus. Koufax accepted the offer. After he verbally agreed to join the Dodgers, the Pirates offered an extra $5,000, and the Milwaukee Braves offered Koufax $30,000, but as he had already accepted terms with Brooklyn, Koufax signed with the Dodgers. Under major-league rules at the time, any player who signed for more than $4,000 had to be on the big-league team's roster. As such, even though Koufax should have played minor-league ball because he was still effectively wild, he joined the Dodgers beginning with the 1955 season. Koufax was injured at the start of the season. When he returned, he replaced future Dodgers manager Tommy Lasorda on the roster. Lasorda liked to joke that "it took the greatest left-handed pitcher in baseball history to get me off that Brooklyn club—and I still think they made a mistake."

Koufax was so disillusioned with the Dodgers that at times he hoped to be traded to another team. Luckily, that never happened. During spring training in 1961, backup catcher Norm Sherry told Koufax to relax and maybe not to try to blow every pitch past the batter. Koufax was scheduled to start and maybe pitch five innings, but another Dodgers pitcher missed the flight, so Koufax was now required to pitch as long as possible. After a less than promising start, Sherry visited Koufax on the mound. In the book *True Blue*, Sherry recounted what he told Koufax: "Sandy, we only got one other pitcher here. And at this rate, you're gonna be out here all day. Why don't you take something off the ball? Don't even try and strike these next guys out. Just throw it over the plate and let them hit it." And the rest is history. Koufax had a vastly improved season, going 18–13 with an ERA of 3.52, making his first All-Star team.

Koufax was even better in 1962. He went 14–7 with a league-leading ERA of 2.54. Unfortunately, Koufax had a hand injury that he first sustained batting the previous year. In a 1963 *Sports Illustrated* article by Robert Creamer, Koufax noted that "the trouble was down here in the palm, here where the fleshy part of the thumb joins the palm. There was a blood clot right there, and that cut off the circulation to the index finger and partly to the next finger and thumb." It got worse, and in July Koufax had to go on the disabled list. Koufax said that "the doctors told me later that at the time they weren't worried so much about when I was going to pitch again as they were that they might have to amputate the finger." While Koufax returned in September, he was not the same pitcher he was earlier in the season. If Koufax had been fit, it is beyond a shadow of a doubt that the Dodgers, and not the Giants, would have faced the Yankees in the World Series.

Koufax was sufficiently healed heading into the 1963 season, and he truly was The Left Arm of God. Koufax had a record of 25–5 with an ERA of 1.88, with 11 shutouts and 306 strikeouts. He was an All-Star, was the unanimous pick for the Cy Young Award, and was also named the NL MVP. And Koufax also pitched his second no-hitter (his first was in 1962). On May 11 against the Giants at Chavez Ravine, Koufax walked two, struck out four, while not allowing a hit as the Dodgers beat the Giants, 8–0. It truly was a stellar season.

Indeed, the Dodgers' entire pitching staff was great. They led the NL in wins, ERA, shutouts, and strikeouts. In addition to Koufax and Drysdale, special mention should go to reliever Ron Perranoski. In his third season with the Dodgers, Perranoski went 16–3 with a career-best ERA of 1.67 while appearing in an NL-leading 69 games. He finished fourth in MVP voting.

While Los Angeles's pitching was outstanding, their offense was woeful. The Dodgers were fourth in batting average (.251), fifth in OBP (.309), eighth in slugging (.357), and sixth in runs scored. The two things they did well were stealing bases and not striking out; they led the NL in both categories.

Their wonderful pitching was able to overcome their mediocre hitting. Despite all the noise about Alston being in trouble and a managerial change being imminent, the Dodgers were never more than five games off the pace in the early going, and entering July they were only 1 1/2 games out of first. And despite a run of only three wins out of ten games as the month drew to a close, the Dodgers finished July leading the NL by 4 1/2 games. While there was some hiccups along the way (after a bad run, their lead were cut to one game on September 15, and there was fear another collapse was on the horizon), the Dodgers steadied and ended up winning the NL by six games.

THE YANKEES' 1963 SEASON

New York's 1963 season began with Ralph Houk at the helm looking for a three-peat of World Series victories. Houk was a fringe player with the Yankees between 1947 and 1954. Being a catcher, his opportunities were limited. In his rookie year, he played in 41 games, the following year 14. He never again played more than 10 games. In his final season, he only made a single appearance. Nevertheless, Houk said, "I liked catching. I had the whole game in front of me. I was in on every pitch. At fifteen I was solid as a rock, 170 pounds of hard-muscled flesh. I could block onrushing base runners at home plate. In fact blocking was easy for me."

In his two final seasons for New York, Houk did some coaching for the team. In 1955, the Yankees appointed him as manager for their Triple-A affiliate in Denver. He stayed there until 1957 and impressed the Yankees' hierarchy with his performance. Houk joined New York's coaching staff in 1958. In 1960, he got his first taste of managing in the majors as he filled in for Stengel for 12 games. At the end of the season, following

New York's loss to the Pirates in the World Series, Stengel was fired, and Houk became the manager. While he inherited a great ballclub, he made them better. He told Ford that he would no longer be protected and only pitch in favorable stadiums. Ford was expected to be the true Yankees ace. The lefty responded by having a magnificent season and winning the Cy Young Award. While the Yankees did not have an official captain since Lou Gehrig's death, Houk told Mantle the he was the unofficial captain of the team. Another major move was installing Johnny Sain as the pitching coach and Wally Moses as hitting coach. The players loved Houk, responded accordingly, and two World Series titles followed with Houk also winning the 1961 *Sporting News* Manager of the Year award.

In March 1961, the NL expansion team New York Metropolitans hired Weiss to become their new GM. And in October of that year, Weiss announced that Stengel would be the Mets' first manager. The Mets finished dead last every year Stengel was in charge. He was replaced by Wes Westrum during the 1965 season. Stengel never managed in the majors again.

With two World Series titles already, Houk's place in Yankees history was even now set. One second-year player, though, was trying to carve his own slice of New York folklore. Jim Bouton, also known as Bulldog (a more famous pitcher with that nickname, Orel Hershiser, would come along in the 1980s), had a decent rookie season in New York. He appeared in 36 games, making 16 starts. Bouton went 7–7 with an ERA of 3.99. However, he did not make an appearance in the 1962 World Series. Nevertheless, Bouton overachieved, as he was not expected to make the Opening Day roster; indeed, he was assigned number 56. Rather than view such a high number as a negative and change it to a lower number at the first opportunity, Bouton kept number 56 for the rest of his career. As his nickname indicates, Bouton was extra competitive. He said, "I would smash into a second baseman to break up a double play, or do anything I possibly could to win."

Bouton had a career year in 1963. He won 21 games, and his ERA was a minuscule 2.53. He finished 16th in MVP voting and was an All-Star. Yet no matter how good Bouton was on the field, he will always be remembered for lifting the lid on the baseball world through his book *Ball Four*. I remember reading it and being blown away. When it was released in 1970, there were few books like it, let alone from ex-players. Bouton was shunned by most of the baseball world, and especially by the Yankees. He was not invited back to participate in Old-Timers' Day for a number of years. New York is big on tradition, but through their own rose-colored glasses. In this, they are no different from any other major-league team. Bouton was not exactly a popular player because he spoke his mind (always a bad thing in baseball, where conformity is sacred). Also, management was not happy that during contract negotiations Bouton went to the media to alert them how much (or, more to the point, how little) he was making. Moreover, because he did not sugarcoat things, he did not bow down to the cult of personality. In his follow-up book, *I'm Glad You Didn't Take It Personally*, Bouton wrote that "After two or three years of playing with guys like Mantle and [Roger] Maris . . . I was no longer awed. I started to look at those guys as people and I didn't like what I saw. They were fine as baseball heroes. As men they were not quite so successful. At the same time I guess I started to rub a lot of people the wrong way. Instead of being a funny rookie, I was a veteran wise guy.

I reached the point where I would argue to support my opinion and that didn't go down too well either."

Bouton was eventually invited to Old-Timers' Day in 1998 following a piece in the *New York Times* from his son asking for the Yankees' forgiveness, not that Bouton had anything to forgive. In addition to being a trailblazer with his writing, Bouton also is the cocreator of the popular bubble gum Big League Chew. As I was writing this book, Bouton passed away. He was eighty. It was a sad day for baseball. There have been very few players like Jim Bouton, and the baseball world is a worse place because of it.

In addition to Bouton, there was another second-year Yankee looking to build on his rookie year. Brooklyn-born first baseman Joe Pepitone was a high school baseball star, but he did not have an easy life growing up. He was constantly verbally and physically abused by his father. In his autobiography, *Joe, You Coulda Made Us Proud*, Pepitone wrote that his father "had a furious temper and, when he wasn't spoiling the shit out of me, he was beating the shit out of me." The beatings stopped after an incident with a heavy glass ashtray. Pepitone recounted that his father threw the ashtray, it hit a door, and "smashed into a hundred pieces, and a dozen shards richocheted [*sic*] into my eyes and face. I had searing pains in my eyes and I couldn't open them. I thought I was blind, and I could feel the blood running down my face and dripping off my clothes." His father was so scared about what happened that he stopped beating his son. But the verbal abuse continued. Bruises heal, but emotional pain can last a lifetime. Pepitone noted his father "couldn't stop yelling at me any more than he could stop beating me all those years. I knew he didn't mean it, that all he wanted was for me to do well. But the yelling really got to me because it stuck with me longer than a punch, the words crouching in my head and repeating themselves, the things he called me." Pepitone's father died of a heart attack while Pepitone was still in high school. Not long after his father died, Pepitone was shot in a prank that went horribly wrong. In a 1962 Associated Press article, Pepitone explained what happened: a classmate found a gun, took it to school, and "stuck the gun in my stomach and barked, 'Hands up.' I was so frightened, I backed right into the clothes closet. The next thing I knew he had pulled the trigger. I didn't feel a thing. I looked at my stomach and saw a hole. There was no blood. That's all I remembered until after the operation." Not an easy life growing up at all.

Pepitone signed with New York in 1958 for a bonus of $25,000 and was assigned to the Auburn Yankees of the Class-D New York–Pennsylvania League. Moving up the minor ranks, Pepitone continued to excel and after a good showing in spring training made the big league team in 1962. Pepitone appeared in 63 games, hitting .239 with an OPS of .697. He became a regular starting with the 1963 season, when he led the team in games played (157) and hit .271 with 27 home runs (second best on the team).

Yet Pepitone was arguably known for his exploits off the field. Such exploits were not in his or his family's best interests. In his 1975 autobiography, Pepitone wrote he gave his family "ample reason to be concerned about me, about my self-destructiveness, and I'm sorry about that. Truly sorry that I brought them down so many times. I know now that you can't fuck over yourself without messing up the people you care about most, and with that knowledge comes the greatest pain of all. You do what you have to do, and you pay the price—but you pay it doubly when you see how it has hurt others you love." Unfortunately, Pepitone caused more anguish for his loved ones as he struggled with his demons throughout the decades. However, in 2018, Pepitone told writer David Krell that he "began seeing a psychiatrist and I learned that I'm bipolar." Pepitone further noted that he then "rebuilt my relationships with my family."

While Bouton and Pepitone were looking to make their mark, two thirty-four-year-olds had stellar seasons. Ford, now ensconced as the Yankees ace, went 24–7 with an ERA of 2.74 and finished third in MVP voting. In other years, he would have been a worthy recipient of the Cy Young award. But as noted earlier, 1963 was the Year of Koufax. Ford benefited from having Howard behind the plate. In addition to being a good defensive catcher, Howard had a great offensive year. He had a slash line of .287/.342/.528 and led the team with 28 home runs (one more than Pepitone). Howard was an All-Star, a Gold Glove winner, and the first black player to win the AL MVP award. By that time, black players had already won eleven NL MVP honors.

The great seasons by Ford and Howard were offset by the injury-riddled years of Maris and Mantle. Maris was restricted to 90 games, while Mantle only appeared in 65. Considering that these two star offensive threats were often injured, one would have expected New York to have had a mediocre year. The reality was vastly different. After a slow start in April, the Yankees turned it on from then on. It was close for a while; New York did not take the outright lead in the AL until June 18. After that it was very much smooth sailing. The Yankees finished with a record of 104–57 and won the pennant by 10 games. The men in pinstripes would have been favored to add another World Series crown against any NL team, let alone Dem Bums. The Dodgers were the Yankees' whipping boys; it would have been foolish to bet against New York. Except the Dodgers in Los Angeles were Dem Bums no more.

THE 1963 WORLD SERIES

Sixty-nine thousand fans packed into Yankee Stadium for Game One hoping and expecting to see the Yankees continue their domination over the Dodgers. The New York players were exceedingly confident before the start of the Series, but so was their opposition. But nerves were only natural before such a big game. To calm their nerves, catcher John Roseboro and short-stop Maury Wills had a few shots of brandy. Alston caught the players indulging, but rather than go ballistic, he simply smiled and walked away.

It was a marquee matchup pitting Ford against Koufax. Ace versus Ace. Both pitchers breezed through the first, with Koufax striking out the side. In the second, Ford got the first batter and then ran into serious problems. Frank Howard doubled, bringing up Skowron. Skowron had been traded to the Dodgers from the Yankees following the 1962 season. He was heart-broken at being traded, and now was his moment to make New York pay. Skowron singled, bringing home Howard. That was followed by a single from Dick Tracewski, moving Skowron to second. Up to the plate stepped Roseboro. He may well have had a bit of a buzz still going after his pregame drink. Rose-boro was definitely feeling something after launching a pitch into deep right field for a three-run homer, and the game was as good as over. Skowron added another run with an RBI single in the third. A five-run lead could have been overcome if there were a lesser pitcher on the mound for the Dodgers, but Koufax struck out 15 (a new World Series record), and his only blemish was allowing a two-run shot to Tom Tresh in the eighth. The Dodgers won, 5–2, with Koufax pitching a complete game.

Yankees second baseman Bobby Richardson had struck out only 22 times in 668 plate appearances in the regular season; Koufax fanned him three times. Koufax struck out Mantle twice. Koufax was told not to throw curveballs to Mantle. The first time, Koufax threw nothing but heat. The second time, with two strikes, Koufax wanted to see how good Mantle really was. He threw him a curveball. Strike three. Mantle turned to Roseboro and said, "How the fuck is anybody supposed to hit that shit?" Reflecting on the game in 2013, Bouton told Rob Neyer in a *SBNation* article that "I was looking forward to watching Sandy Koufax pitch. It was unbelievable. He had such a graceful pitching motion, almost a lazy motion. It was like one of those jumbo jets. You see them taking off, they're so huge and they look so slow, and then *whoom*. Mickey just couldn't catch up to Koufax's high fastball." Yet Koufax was not that impressed with his game. He said, "I just felt a little tired in general early in the game. Then I felt a little weak in the middle of the game. Then I got some of my strength back, but I was a little weak again at the end." The last word about Game One goes to Berra. Supposedly after the game he said about Koufax, "I can understand how he won twenty-five games. What I don't understand is how he lost five." Koufax has put the fear into the Yankees.

New York players were still confident bordering on arrogant, though. Tresh said about Koufax, "now that we've had a chance to look at him, we'll get to him easier next time." Easier said than done. Before the Yankees had a chance at redemption against Koufax, they could get revenge on the 1955 nemesis, Johnny Podres, who was scheduled to start Game Two. Alston preferred using Drysdale at home. Podres, who starred in Brooklyn's only World Series title, exclaimed back then that "I can beat New York any day of the week." On the mound for New York was neither Ralph Terry nor Bouton, but lefty Al Downing. Downing made his debut in 1961, appearing in five games, while only making a single appearance in 1962. In 1963, he did not pull on the pinstripes until June 7. From then on, he was a regular, appearing in 24 games, with 22 of them being starts including 10 complete games. He went 13–5 with an ERA of 2.56. Houk's mind-set in starting Downing was the belief that the Dodgers did not hit left-handed pitching that well. The manager's gamble did not pay off.

In the top of the first, Wills singled and stole second. Gilliam followed with a single of his own, moving Wills to third, and with smart baserunning, Gilliam went to second on the throw. Dodgers center fielder Willie Davis played great defense, but he did not have a good season at the plate; his OPS was an anemic .646. Yet here he was, a left-handed hitter batting third in the lineup against a lefty. It was not a good matchup for Los Angeles, but it worked out for them. Such is baseball. Davis doubled home Wills and Gilliam, and the Dodgers had an early 2–0 lead. And that was enough for Podres. He was magnificent, going 8 1/3 strong innings, allowing just six hits and a walk. Downing only lasted five innings, giving up three runs. Following his two RBIs in Game One, Skowron made the Yankees further pay for trading him by hitting a solo shot in the fourth. Yet New York had their chances: as good as Podres was, the Yankees were a hopeless 1-for-7 with runners in scoring position. By contrast, the Dodgers were a solid 3-for- 8. Unlike past World Series, the Dodgers were the team whose starters went deep into games, who got the clutch hits, and who made the correct managerial decisions. Los Angeles won Game Two, 4–1. The Dodgers came back to New York and put a hurting on their former crosstown rivals. Nevertheless, in the 1955 and 1956 World Series between the two teams, the club that won the first two games when all was said and done were on the losing end come Game Seven. Would history repeat itself?

Some Yankees players were very sure, or at least pretending, that they had the Series in the bag. On the day of his start in Game Three, Bouton and infielder Phil Linz printed a fake newspaper with the headline "BOUTON SHUTS OUT THE DODGERS . . . LINZ WINS GAME WITH HOMER." The players showed their teammates the fake newspaper on the way to Chavez Ravine, and much laughter followed. There was just one problem for New York: for as good as Bouton was, he was not as good as the Dodgers' Game Three starter, Don Drysdale.

Bouton was superb, only allowing four hits and five walks in seven innings of work. Los Angeles only managed to score one run against him. In the bottom of the first, Gilliam walked, took second on a wild pitch, and Tommy Davis singled him home. However, while Davis is credited with the hit and an RBI, second baseman Richardson should have made the play; the ball caromed off him into center field. That would be the only run the Dodgers scored for the entire game. Once again, Drysdale got very little run support. This time, though, it did not matter. The Yankees could only manage three hits and a walk, while striking out nine times. As in Game Two, they had their chances but were a woeful 0-for-5 with runners in scoring position. Drysdale was absolutely magnificent in pitching a complete-game shutout as Los Angeles defeated New York and took a very commanding 3–0 lead in the Series. Bouton was pragmatic about the loss, telling Neyer, "I'm just happy to be in the big leagues, happy to win 20 games. It was just a thrill. Sure, it was too bad that we lost the game, but damn, what a thrill."

Considering that Koufax was geared up to start Game Four, the Yankees knew the writing was on the wall and had their bags packed prior to the game ready to leave Los Angeles and this nightmare of a World Series. Yet New York still had some hope, because as good as Koufax was, they had their own ace, Ford, looking to avenge his Game One loss.

And just like Game Three, Game Four was a great pitching duel. Both teams had very few opportunities to score. It would take one moment of brilliance and one error to decide the game. Both Koufax and Ford had little trouble in the first four innings. Koufax easily navigated around a leadoff single in the fifth, retiring the next three batters in order. Ford began the bottom of the inning by getting Tommy Davis to ground out. Up to the plate stepped man mountain Frank Howard. Despite being 6-foot-8 and at his peak weighing 275 pounds, Howard had an issue dealing with people. In a 1964 *Sports Illustrated* article, he said, "Five years ago I couldn't sit down and talk to anyone I didn't know well. I would run and hide to avoid publicity. I still don't get on easily with people that I don't know. I'm a moody guy, and I've done some stupid things." Even with the Dodgers on their way to winning the NL pennant, Howard wanted to quit baseball during the 1963 season and again before the start of the following season. Luckily for the Dodgers, he was convinced to stay on. He was traded to the Washington Senators at the end of 1964, was a four-time All-Star, and had a great career before retiring after the 1973 season. He also became a major-league manager. Despite all his accolades, Dodgers fans will always remember his at-bat against Ford on October 6. Ford left a curveball hanging, and Howard blasted a mammoth 450-foot home run to left field, giving Los Angeles a 1–0 lead. The lead lasted to the top of the seventh. With one out and the bases empty, Mantle temporarily worked out the riddle of Koufax and blasted an opposite-field homer to tie the game. Even "The Left Arm of God" is not perfect. Somewhat shockingly, it was the first time in the Series the Yankees managed to tie the game after the Dodgers scored. However, they would never take the lead.

In the bottom of the seventh, Gilliam hit a grounder to third baseman Clete Boyer. Boyer promptly threw to first, but Pepitone lost the ball against the backdrop of white shirts in the crowd, and smart baserunning saw Gilliam hustle to third. Willie Davis then followed with a nice lazy fly ball to center, and Gilliam easily beat the throw to score. The Dodgers regained the lead, and this time they held it for good. Of course, the Dodgers do like to make their fans sweat. Richardson led off the ninth with a single. Koufax then struck out both Tresh and Mantle looking. Howard grounded to short, but second baseman Dick Tracewski dropped the throw, and the runners were safe. Luckily for the Dodgers, Koufax was on the mound. He did not panic and was helped when Hector Lopez went after the first pitch and grounded weakly to short. There were no mistakes this time. Maury Wills threw to first, where, perhaps fittingly, Skowron held onto the ball for the final out. Koufax pitched another complete game, giving up one run on six hits, no walks, while striking out eight. The Dodgers swept the Yankees. Los Angeles was World Series champions. In the history of Dodgers-Yankees baseball, it was the only time that a team swept their rival. Los Angeles was just that great in 1963, and they were special because of their pitching, Koufax and Drysdale in particular. In the World Series, it was the Dodgers who got the crucial hits from their mediocre offense, and Koufax, Drysdale, and Podres dominated the Yankees from the mound. Three complete games, another of 8 1/3 innings, and they allowed just five runs in four games. The 1963 Los Angeles Dodgers were just that damn good. Yet unlike the Yankees' domination of the previous decades, the Dodgers' stay at the top of the baseball world was fleeting.

10

1977: FIRST OF BACK-TO-BACK MEETINGS AND THE CROWNING OF MR. OCTOBER

WITH THE ANNIHILATION of the Yankees in the World Series, many Dodgers fans were thinking that it was Los Angeles's time to sit alone atop the baseball world. That dream turned into a nightmare. Their 1964 season was marred by injuries, and many of the players seemed to have a World Series hangover. The Dodgers ended up in sixth place with a record of 80–82, 13 games out of first. Yet a ballclub with Koufax and Drysdale on it would not be average for any length of time. The 1965 season saw the Dodgers reclaim their place atop the NL standings, winning the pennant by two games over the Giants. That Los Angeles was headed to another World Series was remarkable considering that their offense was not just mediocre, it was bad. The Dodgers were seventh out of the ten NL teams in batting average, eighth in OPS, and ninth in slugging. The Dodgers hit neither for average nor for power. Nevertheless, with Koufax and Drysdale once again leading the way, Los Angeles was good enough to win. And the season was capped off by beating the Minnesota Twins in seven games to win the World Series. Koufax pitched a complete game shutout, while striking out ten, in the decider.

Nineteen sixty-six saw the Dodgers heading back to the World Series. The offense was even worse, but Koufax was arguably even better, finishing with a record of 27–9 with a 1.73 ERA. But he was hurting; numerous injuries and being treated like a pack mule by the Dodgers had taken a heavy toll. Baltimore swept the Dodgers in the fall classic, Koufax retired, and the Dodgers went back to being Dem Bums, afterthoughts in the baseball world. Los Angeles was horrid in 1967, finishing eighth in the NL, 28 1/2 games out of first. While they moved up to seventh the next year, they won three fewer games than the year before. Even when divisional play was introduced in 1969, it took until 1974 for Los Angeles to once again reach the postseason. The Dodgers beat the Pirates in the NL Championship Series and faced the Oakland Athletics in the World Series. While Los Angeles had their chances, the Athletics outclassed the Dodgers, defeating them, four games to one. Another World Series loss for the Dodgers. The 1975 and 1976 Dodgers were not bad teams, but they had the misfortune of being in the same division as the Big Red Machine. The Cincinnati Reds won the NL West by 20 games over the Dodgers in 1975 and 10 games the following season. Very few people expected the Dodgers to challenge the Reds in 1977, but the Dodgers often had a habit of overachieving when it was least expected.

As for New York, as the cliché goes, all good things must come to an end. Houk retired after the 1963 season to become GM and was replaced by Berra. New York struggled, but still had enough talent to win the pennant by one game. However, they lost in the World Series to the Cardinals in seven. And even though he had a very good first year as manager, Berra was fired the day after Game Seven. Houk told reporters, "Losing the World Series had nothing to do with [this]. The decision was made before the World Series." Treating a Yankees legend so shabbily was not a good look for the team, and fans were irate.

Moreover, back-to-back World Series losses are tough to deal with. And it took a long time for New York to recover. If the team had a lot of good young prospects in the farm system, the inevitable rebuild as their starters got older would have been accelerated. Instead, the farm system was barren, the introduction of the amateur draft meant a slightly more level playing field, and the Yankees being very slow in signing black players (as were many AL teams) put them in a distinct disadvantage to NL teams. As Appel notes, "National League teams had been signing African-American players the caliber of Mays, Aaron, Banks, McCovey, Gibson, Frank Robinson, Billy Williams, Lou Brock, Ferguson Jenkins, and Willie Stargell and dark-skinned Latino stars like Clemente, Orlando Cepeda, Juan Marichal, Tony Perez, and more. . . . The Yankees had let all those players get away." The Yankees were no longer atop the pantheon; they were just another baseball team. Their ruling-class days were gone.

In 1965, New York plummeted to 77 wins, only good enough for sixth place, 25 games out of first. Yet that was a "good" season" compared to 1966, when the team won 70 games and finished dead last. The lowlight occurred on September 22. A makeup day game against the White Sox attracted only 413 fans to Yankee Stadium. The Yankees no longer ruled baseball; they were merely afterthoughts in the AL and then the AL East. In 1974, New York finished second in the AL East; it was their closest brush with the postseason in a decade. Postseason play was once again realized in 1976. The Yankees defeated the Royals, 3–2, in the AL Championship Series but were swept by the rampaging Reds in the World Series. New York was outclassed in every aspect. Yet the Collective Bargaining Agreement between MLB and the MLB Players Association that was signed on July 12, 1976, brought a form of free agency to the game. And New York was ready to spend.

THE YANKEES' 1977 SEASON

The onset of free agency led to a dramatic increase in player salaries. As Robert F. Burk notes in *Much More Than A Game,* "In 1977, the first year of widespread free agency, the average big league salary jumped nearly 50 percent to $76,066. Even when adjusted for inflation, real wages registered a 39 percent rise and went up another 31 percent the next season. By 1979 the mean major league salary stood at $113,558, more than double the pay since the inauguration of free agency." Moreover, players received enhanced job security as teams began offering multiyear contracts. Prior to 1975, all players received contracts for a single year. In 1980, approximately 40 percent of players had multiyear contracts. Free agency was good for players, good for baseball, and it was *good* for the Yankees.

While some teams were wary of spending big money on free agents, the Yankees were not. Say what you will about George Steinbrenner, who became principal owner of the Yankees in 1973, but he was ahead of the game when it came to realizing how free agency would change baseball.

The biggest free agent hitting the market was Reggie Jackson. Jackson was a multisport star in high school and went to Arizona State University on a football scholarship. However, he also asked to play baseball. After a summer playing with an amateur team in Baltimore, Jackson became the starting center fielder on his college team when he was a sophomore. He had a great season, and the Kansas City Athletics picked him second overall in the 1966 amateur draft. Jackson breezed through the minors and made his major-league debut the following year. Yet he struggled in Kansas City, hitting only .178 with one home run in 35 games. Kansas City was not for him, but Oakland was. The Athletics relocated to Oakland following the 1967 season, and Jackson found a home there. Jackson wrote in *Reggie: the Autobiography* that "the eight years I spent in Oakland were the best baseball years of my life." Following the 1975 season, Jackson was traded to Baltimore. Jackson missed the first few weeks of the season, as he could not agree to contract terms with the Orioles, and when he did sign, he was not in his best shape. Even then, he still led the AL in slugging, and coming into the 1977 season, Jackson was a six-time All-Star and former AL MVP.

Steinbrenner personally led New York's efforts to get Jackson. Steinbrenner took Jackson to lunch, and then the two of them took a walk around Manhattan. Jackson signed a five-year deal worth $2.96 million and also received a Rolls-Royce. It is important to note that Jackson was not looking for the biggest payday; other teams offered more. Jackson wanted the money, but he also wanted to win it all. Nevertheless, that Jackson was the highest-paid player on the team rubbed a lot of Yankees players the wrong way.

Also, not helping matters was the fact that Jackson spoke his mind. Catcher Thurman Munson was the star and captain of the team and coming off being named the AL MVP. Munson wanted Steinbrenner to sign Jackson. He thought Jackson would help the team, and Munson also believed he and Steinbrenner had an agreement that with the exception of Catfish Hunter, Munson would be the highest-paid Yankee. But Steinbrenner did not adjust Munson's contract, and in *Sport* magazine, Jackson told reporter Robert Ward, "Munson thinks he can be the straw that stirs the drink, but he can only stir it bad." Jackson denied ever saying that. In his autobiography, *Reggie Jackson: Becoming Mr. October*, Jackson claimed, "It never happened. At least not like he said it did. . . . The whole time he [Ward] was trying to feed me that quote, but I know I never said it. . . . There's no way I'd be that dumb to knock the captain of the team—and, by the way, the guy who told George Steinbrenner to go get me on the free agent-market." However, Ward disputes this. He told the *New York Post*, "He's been lying about it since it happened. . . . He's just lied and lied. And now I think probably he's gotten to the age where he actually believes the stuff he says here. . . . I made nothing up. Not one thing." Regardless of who is telling the truth, the publication of the article led to resentment and anger within the Yankees clubhouse. The players were understandably aghast at Jackson's alleged comments, while Jackson was upset that very few players asked him whether the quote was true. There was also infighting between Jackson and Yankees manager Billy Martin.

After his playing career was over, Martin became a special scout for the Minnesota Twins, eventually becoming their manager for the 1969 season. The Twins made the playoffs but were swept by the Orioles. Martin copped some heat for some of his moves during the series, and especially his decision to start pitcher Bob Miller in Game Three. The Twins owner asked Martin why he started Miller, and Martin replied, "Because I'm the manager, that's why." Martin did not manage the Twins the next season. Martin was hired by the Tigers in 1971 and duly fired a couple of years later. The same was true with his tenure as the Texas Rangers manager. Martin became the Yankees manager midway through the 1975 season.

Age did not mellow the fiery Martin; far from it. And he had a particular issue with Jackson. Martin was not pleased that Steinbrenner did not get his input on whether the team should sign Jackson. Not to mention that Martin and Jackson did not like each other. In *Reggie Jackson: Becoming Mr. October,* Reggie wrote that Martin "lied to people. . . . That was his history. He lied to the general manager; he lied to the owner. He lied to players all the time, which was a big reason why he wore out his welcome." He also alleged that Martin made anti-Semitic comments to pitcher Ken Holtzman.

The Jackson-Martin feud was so bad that they also almost got into a fight on national television. On June 18 against the Red Sox in Boston, Jackson seemed not to run hard to field a base hit by Jim Rice that the Red Sox slugger stretched into a double. He was immediately benched by Martin, with the manager letting fly with a number of choice words. Jackson responded by yelling, "You never wanted me on this team," and calling Martin an "old man." The two were close to coming to blows, so Berra, who had been brought back as a coach the year before, intervened by placing Martin in a bear hug while fellow coaches Elston Howard and Dick Howser tried to placate Jackson. Jackson eventually left the dugout, then the clubhouse, and then the stadium. Martin told reporters, "If you don't hustle, I don't accept it. If a player shows up the club, I show up the player." Jackson made his own comment to a few trusted reporters in his hotel room later that day: "I'm a good ball-player and a good Christian and I've got an IQ of 160, but I'm a n———and I won't be subservient. The Yankee pinstripes are Ruth and Gehrig and DiMaggio and Mantle. They've never had a n———like me before." Following the confrontation there was continued rampant speculation that Martin would be fired. Yet the manager kept his job, and somehow, he and Jackson managed to coexist for the rest of the season. Despite, or maybe because of, all the infighting, the Yankees thrived.

Helping the Yankees capture the AL East title was another free-agent signing: starting pitcher Don Gullett. The lefty had spent his entire career with the Reds, winning two world championships with the team. While he was injury-prone, when he did pitch, he was pretty good. For the Yankees, he went 14–4 with an ERA of 3.58. By signing Gullett, New York not only strengthened its rotation, it weakened the Reds (which of course ended up benefiting the Dodgers).

Despite all the turmoil, on August 10, New York was only five games out of first; by the end of the month, they had a 4 1/2-game lead. Unlike in the 1950s and early 1960s, when New York mostly had an easy time winning the AL pennant, the 1977 AL East ended up being a dogfight between New York, Baltimore, and Boston. On September 11, the Yankees' lead was down to 1 1/2 games, and it increased to two games by September 21. New York then got hot, winning six in a row, and led by four with four games left. Of course, the Yankees then lost three straight, but neither the Red Sox nor Orioles could take advantage. The Yankees had a 100-win season and won the AL East by 2 1/2 games. The offense was led by Jackson. He may have been disliked in the clubhouse, but he still had a slash line of .286/.375/.550 with 39 doubles, 32 home runs, and 110 RBIs. Third baseman Graig Nettles only hit .255, but with 37 long balls (to lead the team) in 107 RBIs. In addition, Munson had another fine season both at and behind the plate. He had a slash line of .308/.351/.462 with 100 RBIs. Apart from Gullett, Ed Figueroa had a record of 16–11 and an ERA of 3.57. Mike Torrez, acquired during the season from Oakland, went 14–12 with an ERA of 3.82.

The standout starter, however, was Ron Guidry. Guidry made his major-league debut with New York in 1975, appearing in 10 games. In 1976, he only saw action in seven games. His breakout year was 1977. Guidry made the rotation and ended up going 16–7 and led all Yankees starters in ERA (2.82), strikeouts (176), and shutouts (five). Guidry finished seventh in Cy Young voting. The award was won by another Yankee, Sparky Lyle. New York's closer saved 26 games with an ERA of 2.17 and led the AL in games finished (60) and appearances (72). Lyle was a very good closer, but there is no way he should have won the Cy Young Award or finish sixth in MVP voting. There were many pitchers who would have been a more deserving Cy Young recipient. While WAR is not the be-all and end-all,

Lyle's WAR was 3.7, by far the lowest total of any of the nine pitchers who received Cy Young votes. Guidry's WAR was 4.8, runner-up Jim Palmer's was 7.4, while third-place finisher Nolan Ryan's WAR was 7.9. The pitcher with the highest WAR was California Angels starter Frank Tanana. He had a record of 15–9, with an ERA of 2.54, 20 complete games, and seven shutouts. His WAR was 8.3. Tanana finished ninth. Nevertheless, the record books will forever show that Lyle was the 1977 Cy Young Award winner.

Awaiting New York in the AL Championship Series was again the Kansas City Royals. The Royals had a much easier time in the AL West, winning the division by eight games, and had home-field advantage for the championship series. The first three games of the series were not close. In Game One, the Royals scored six times in the first three innings, running out winners, 7–2. In Game Two, Kansas held a 1–0 lead until the bottom of the fifth. New York scored two in the inning and another three runs in the sixth and eventually won, 6–2, with Guidry pitching a complete-game three-hitter. The series then moved to Kansas City. The Royals were never challenged, winning Game Three, 6–2. Game Four was reasonably close. The Yankees scored four times in the first three innings, but the Royals scored twice in the bottom of the third. New York added an insurance run in the top of fourth. This was to prove decisive as Kansas came back with two in the bottom of the inning. The Yankees eventually added another run in the ninth to win, 6–4, and force a deciding Game Five. Guidry started for New York and was decidedly subpar, giving up three runs in 2 1/3 innings. The score was 3–1 heading into the top of the eighth. Jackson, who was having a horrid series, so much so that Martin benched him for Game Five, came on as a pinch-hitter with one out and singled, bringing home a run. The Royals got out of the inning without further damage, but they were about to implode. In the top of the ninth, three outs away from a World Series berth and leading by a run, Royals manager Whitey Herzog brought in Game Three winner Dennis Leonard. Leonard led all AL starters in wins (20) and finished fourth in Cy Young voting. Leonard did not record an out, allowing the first two Yankees to reach. Herzog replaced him with lefty Larry Gura, the losing pitcher in Game Four. Gura was brought in to face left-handed hitter Mickey Rivers. The lefty-on-lefty matchup went to Rivers, as he singled, bringing home a run and tying the game. And with some good baserunning, Roy White went from first to third. Herzog then pulled Gura and replaced him with Mark Littell. Willie Randolph lined a ball to the outfield for a sacrifice fly, scoring White and giving New York the lead. Littell got the next Yankee. But with two outs, Lou Piniella reached on an error, and Rivers scored from second. Jackson grounded out to end the inning. Shell-shocked, the Royals put up no fight in the bottom of the inning. Lyle picked up the save as New York won, 5–3, and were headed to the World Series after one of the great ninth-inning comebacks in their history.

THE DODGERS' 1977 SEASON

On September 27, 1976, Walter Alston decided to retire even though there were still four games left in the season. There is still a debate on whether Alston retired on his own volition or he was pushed. Irrespective of whose choice it was, it was a good thing that Alston was no longer managing Los Angeles. This was perfectly illustrated by Alston's press conference announcing his retirement. Alston said, "We used to have 24 or 25 farm clubs. It would take six or seven years to reach the majors. A player had to beat out a dozen guys to do it. He was appreciative of what he had. Now they get a free ride through college and a bonus even before they've swung at a major league curve. They expect it to be that easy for them all the way." It was time for a change at top and to install a manger that actually liked the current generation of players. The Dodgers waited one entire day before announcing their new manager, Tommy Lasorda.

Thomas Charles Lasorda was a decent pitching prospect. However, while he made the majors, his time in the big leagues was fleeting. Lasorda debuted with Brooklyn in 1954 but only appeared in four games, all in relief. The following year, he also appeared in four games and made one start; he lasted one inning. His final season in the bigs was in 1956, when he appeared in 18 games for the Kansas City Athletics. Lasorda made five starts and had a record of 0–4 with an ERA of 6.15. Yet he loved baseball (and still does). He pitched in the minors for a total of 14 seasons and then remained in the game in a variety of roles. The Dodgers front office saw promise in Lasorda and installed him as a minor-league manager. At the start of the 1973 season, he became Los Angeles's third-base coach. Once Alston vacated his position, the Dodgers immediately turned to the man who bleeds Dodger blue. At the press conference heralding his appointment, Lasorda stated, "I think that when someone wakes up and finds that when he has inherited a position vacated by the greatest manager in baseball history, it's like waking up to find you have inherited the Hope Diamond." Despite the nice words Lasorda said about Alston, he always felt that Alston did not give him the opportunity to succeed as a player.

Lasorda wanted to put his stamp on the team early. Thus, before the commencement of spring training, Lasorda announced who his starting lineup would be for the regular season and that they would play together for the majority of the preseason. The players liked Lasorda's enthusiasm and that he was a fan of the game. But, of course, not every player likes change. There was one Dodger in particular who was not a fan of Lasorda.

Pitcher Don Sutton, who began his major-league career with the Dodgers in 1966, greatly preferred the managerial style of Alston. Sutton was not a fan of the over-the-top bombastic flair of Lasorda. Following Alston's retirement and before Lasorda was officially hired, Sutton was asked who he would like to be the new Dodgers manager. Sutton, despite knowing that Lasorda would be hired, endorsed Jeff Torborg. This did not particularly please Lasorda. Nor was Lasorda pleased when during spring training, rather than go out and catch fly balls during batting practice, Sutton did his customary laps. One day fellow starter Doug Rau joined Sutton in San Francisco. As retold by Lasorda in *I Live for This!: Baseball's Last True Believer*, he confronted Rau, who responded that "Sutton made me do it." Not exactly in the best mood, Lasorda ordered Sutton to his office and told him to knock it off. Defiantly, Sutton told his manager that he would continue to run laps during batting practice. Lasorda then locked the office door and told Sutton, "Fine, you want to change the rule, we'll change it right here. . . . Let's fight right here, you and me. If I beat you, the rule stays. If you beat me, I'll change it." Sutton changed his tune and told Lasorda he would follow the rules.

Sutton also had a problem with Lasorda continually using the phrase "Big Dodger in the Sky." In a 1982 *Sports Illustrated* profile, Sutton mused, "God may not even like baseball. He may be a football fan. Under any circumstances, I don't think He should be considered a pocket good-luck charm that you can pull out when you need it. I know Tommy didn't mean it disrespectfully. He's just a gung-ho, emotional man. He goes sky-high over a win and hits a deep depression over a loss. Walter always said you should never gloat on the peaks and never stay in the valleys. I spent so many of my years with Walter, the transition was very difficult for me. It took me years to understand Tommy. I still don't necessarily agree with him, but at least I think I understand him."

The two managed to coexist throughout the season, and Sutton had an All-Star campaign, going 14–8 with an ERA of 3.18. As good as Sutton was, he was not the best on the NL-leading pitching staff. Burt Hooton was superb, finishing with a 12–7 record. He was hurt by a lack of run support as he led all Dodgers starters with an ERA of 2.62. The Dodger with the most wins was Tommy John. He won 20 games with a 2.78 ERA. Thus, even though Hooton had a lower ERA, pitched more innings, and gave up fewer hits than John, he did not make the All-Star team, while John was an All-Star and finished second in Cy Young voting. In 1977 (and still in some circles today), wins were considered the defining factor in how good a pitcher was.

While the Dodgers had the best pitching in the NL, their hitting, while very good, relied on a few players. Steve Garvey hit .297/.335/.498 with 33 home runs and 115 RBIs; Dusty Baker had a slash line of .291/.364/.512 with 30 home runs, while Ron Cey went .241/.347/.450 with 30 home runs and 110 RBIs. And then there was Reggie Smith.

Smith was one of those players who, no matter how well he performed on the field, people expected him to do better. In a Society for American Baseball Research profile of Smith by Jeff Angus, former teammate John Curtis notes that "I will always remember Reg as one of the most complete players I ever saw. . . . I know he labored under the weight of everyone's expectations. In Boston, the sportswriters would wonder aloud why Reg wasn't playing up to his demonstrated abilities. . . . He once told me that the worst word in the English language was 'potential.'" Smith made his major-league debut with the Red Sox at the end of the 1966 season before becoming a regular the following season. Smith was a fixture for the Red Sox before being traded to the Cardinals in October 1973. Curtis states that Smith, as an African American, had it tough in Boston: "He said some people in the bleachers would throw batteries, heated coins, and other projectiles at him. He also told me about a night when some hooligans drove up to his house and emptied the garbage cans he'd placed by the driveway all over his front lawn. That's when I began to understand that Boston was a different town for him than it was for me." As a Cardinal, Smith had two good seasons before a down year in 1976 saw him traded to the Dodgers during the season. While he was born in Louisiana, Smith moved to Los Angeles at a young age and as such was happy to be a Dodger. Nineteen seventy-seven was his first full year on the team, and he was outstanding. Smith led the Dodgers in batting average (.307), OBP (.427: a NL-best), slugging (.576), and walks (104), while also hitting 32 home runs as Los Angeles became the first major-league team to have four players with 30 home runs.

The addition of Smith was too late for the Dodgers to win the NL West in 1976 but was one of the major reasons why Los Angeles ran away with the division in 1977. On April 11, Los Angeles had a 2–2 record. For the rest of the month, the Dodgers went 15–1, had a 7 1/2 game lead in the NL West, and the divisional race was as good as over. The Dodgers never had less than a 6 1/2 game lead for the remainder of the season. They eventually finished with a record of 98–64 and won the NL West by 10 games over the Reds. The Dodgers were headed to the NL Championship Series, where they were decided underdogs against the NL East's Philadelphia Phillies, who had won 101 games.

There was no love lost between the teams. Sutton started the trash-talking by saying that the Dodgers pitching staff was better than that of their counterparts in the city of brotherly love. He went further by saying Los Angeles "has more pitching depth, better defense, more guys capable of delivering offensively and a more consistent offense. I don't mean to take anything away from the Philadelphia offense, but as for big guns you're really only talking about Greg Luzinski and Mike Schmidt. They'll have to hit a lot of solo home runs to beat us. By contrast, we have a handful of guys who can break it open with one swing. I think we have an advantage in offense as well as in pitching. It's just awfully tough to stop us completely." Phillies manager Danny Ozark responded that Los Angeles was "not the toughest, because Cincinnati knocked the beans out of us. We haven't won a game in Cincinnati in, I think, nine games. We played .500 against the Dodgers this year. So if you ask me which I'd rather play against, I'll take the .500 club."

Considering the Phillies took Game One, 7–5, at Dodger Stadium, Ozark had every right to feel confident. But it did not last long. The Dodgers annihilated the Phillies, 7–1, the next day with Baker hitting a grand slam and Sutton pitching a complete game. Game Three was in Philly, and after scoring twice in the bottom of the eighth, the home team was sitting pretty with a 5–3 lead. Even more so in the top of the ninth with the Dodgers having nobody on and two out. It then fell apart. Vic Davalillo bunted his way on. Pinch-hitter Manny Mota doubled, and Davalillo scored on an error. Davey Lopes then singled home Mota, and the score was tied. Lopes was then picked off but reached second on a throwing error by pitcher Gene Garber. Bill Russell drove in Lopes, and the Dodgers had the lead. There was no coming back from that, and the Dodgers scored an improbable victory. And there was no coming back for the Phillies in the series. In Game Four, Tommy John pitched a complete game and Baker hit a two-run blast as the Dodgers won, 4–1. Los Angeles was headed to the fall classic. For the first time in fourteen years, it was a Dodgers-Yankees World Series.

THE 1977 WORLD SERIES

Yankees vs. Dodgers. Gullett vs. Sutton. Reggie vs. Reggie. A crowd of 56,668 watching the game at Yankee Stadium under the lights. The stage was set for a classic. But Gullett struggled in the first. Lopes led off with a walk. Russell then proceeded to hit a triple to deep left-center, scoring Lopes. After Smith walked, Russell scored on Cey's sacrifice fly. The Dodgers had an early 2–0 lead, but Sutton also had a rough first inning. After retiring the first two batters, he gave up consecutive singles to Munson, Jackson, and Chris Chambliss to cut the Dodgers' lead in half. Following that, though, both pitchers settled down. Gullett and Sutton got into a groove. That lasted until the sixth. With two out and Steve Garvey at first, Glenn Burke was at the plate. Burke hit one to right-center for a routine single. Garvey, who was off with the crack of the bat, rounded second, headed to third, and was waved home. Garvey was not exactly fleet of foot, the throw from center fielder Mickey Rivers was breathtakingly bad (I mean *bad*; go check it out on YouTube), and it was a close play, but he was called out. Garvey being thrown out at the plate hurt Los Angeles. And the Yankees took advantage. Willie Randolph led off for New York in the bottom of the inning. On a 2-2 count, he hit one over the left-field fence, and the game was tied. In the bottom of the eighth, Randolph was due to lead off again. Lasorda kept faith in Sutton. It was a mistake. Randolph walked, and Munson doubled to left. The Yankees had taken the lead, 3–2, and Gullett was looking to close it out in the ninth. It did not work out. Baker led off the inning with a single. With one out, Steve Yeager walked. Martin called to the pen and brought in Lyle. Pinch-hitter Lee Lacy singled, bringing home Baker with the tying run. Lyle remained in the game and was generally lights out from that point. So was Dodgers reliever Mike Garman, who threw three scoreless innings. The Yankees finally broke through in the bottom of the 12th. Lasorda brought in Rick Rhoden, who had appeared in 31 games in the regular season, none of them in relief. Indeed, he had only made one relief appearance over the past two seasons. And on October 11, 1977, it showed. Randolph led off with a double, and Lasorda elected to intentionally walk Munson. It set up the double play as well as bring to the plate Paul Blair, who had come in as a defensive replacement for Jackson in the ninth. Blair was never an offensive powerhouse but was considered a defensive specialist, winning eight Gold Gloves. On this occasion, it was his bat that drew all the headlines. On a 2-2 pitch, Blair singled to left. Randolph ran like his life depended on it, and the Yankees won the game, 4–3, in 12 innings. While they would rather the game not go into extra innings, it was a great opening win for New York and a demoralizing defeat for Los Angeles. But so-called momentum in baseball is often fleeting.

Martin sprang somewhat of a surprise by starting Catfish Hunter in Game Two. While still only thirty-one, Hunter was nearing the end of his illustrious career and had not pitched since September 10 due to injury. Martin's gamble did not pay off. The Dodgers lit up Hunter. Catfish only lasted 2 1/3 innings, giving up five runs with Cey, Steve Yeager, and Smith going deep. Garvey added another homer in the top off the ninth as the Dodgers roughed up the Yankees, 6–1, with Burt Hooton pitching a complete game while striking out eight. The big news following the game was not Los Angeles's leveling the Series, but rather the flare-up of the Jackson-Martin feud.

To put it mildly, Jackson could not believe that Martin handed Hunter the ball for Game Two considering Catfish's long layoff and declining fortunes on the mound. Jackson told reporters, "How could he pitch him? He hasn't pitched since September 10. How could he do anything? In a World Series, how do you make a decision like that on a guy like Hunter. It's like me sitting on the bench for a month and then being expected to get two hits. If you're gonna pitch the guy in the Series, then use him. Cat did his best, but . . . ah, the hell with it." Martin responded by not taking the high road, but by firing back: "If I'm going to back that ass . . . why doesn't he back me? . . . This isn't a one-way street. He has a lot of growing up to do. He's having enough trouble in the outfield without second-guessing the manager." Jackson tried to backtrack from his comments, but Martin was not buying it. The manager said that Jackson's comments would not harm New York's World Series chances because "Why should I pay attention to him? His teammates don't." Martin further added that if Jackson, who was struggling in the postseason, did not get a hit off the Dodgers' Game Three starter Tommy John, he would have to consider benching him. Asked to comment on the Jackson-Martin feud, Munson replied, "I do think it's unfortunate that at a time when we have a chance to win the championship, there's a guy out there trying to second-guess the manager." He added, "I used to know what was going on around here but I stopped mixing drinks a long time ago. I've got only five more games at the most to worry about all this crap." The Yankees were imploding, and after winning Game Two, surely all signs pointed to the Dodgers putting New York to the sword, right?

Once again, momentum was fleeting. In the top of the first at Dodger Stadium in front of 55,992, John was all kinds of awful. Rivers doubled to lead off proceedings. Then with one out, Munson doubled, allowing Rivers to score. Jackson singled (getting his lone hit of the night, but it was good enough for him to remain in the starting lineup), scoring Munson, and he reached second on an error by Baker. That error was important because it meant Jackson was in position to score on Lou Piniella's single. The Yankees led, 3–0, and Dodger Stadium was quiet. With Mike Torrez on the mound for New York, Los Angeles had opportunities to score in both the first and second. But they could not hit with runners in scoring position.

That changed in the third. With two out and runners at the corners, Baker was at the plate looking to atone for his error in the first. His sins were forgiven when on the sixth pitch of his at-bat he launched one to deep left. The three-run home run had tied the game. Momentum once again swung back to the Dodgers. This time it was even more fleeting. In the top of the fourth, the first two Yankees hitters reached via singles. Torrez bunted them over. And then a Rivers groundout scored Graig Nettles from third. New York had retaken the lead. With John still on the mound in the fifth, New York increased their lead. With one out, Jackson walked and Piniella singled, moving Jackson to second. Chambliss proceeded to hit a single to right. Jackson touched home plate, and New York led, 5–3, and that was the end of the scoring. New York had come to Los Angeles under a sea of controversy and walked away one step closer to a world championship. Dodgers fans were hoping for another momentum shift heading into Game Four.

It was not to be. After a pretty uneventful first, although the Dodgers once again failed to find a hit with a runner in scoring position, the game was blown open in the second. Jackson, who was heating up, led off the inning with a double. Piniella followed with an RBI single, and a double by Chambliss moved Piniella to third. Lasorda had seen enough and pulled starter Doug Rau and brought in Rick Rhoden. It did not stop the carnage. Nettles grounded out, but Piniella scored and Chambliss went to third. Bucky Dent then brought home Chambliss with a single. New York led, 3–0, and Los Angeles (the team, their fans, and the entire town) were in a state of shock. The Dodgers showed some signs of life in the third. Rhoden hit a ground-rule double, and Lopes homered to cut the margin to one. But Jackson hit a solo homer in the sixth, and with the Dodgers failing to get the crucial hit (they were 1-for-7 with runners in scoring position), New York won, 4–2, with Guidry pitching a four-hitter, striking out seven. The Bronx Bombers were one win away from reclaiming the mantle of the best team in baseball and piling on further misery to the Dodgers.

The celebration would have to wait a little longer. In Game Five, Sutton was decent for the Dodgers, pitching a complete game while giving up four runs. By contrast, Gullett was not, conceding six runs in just 4 1/3 innings. The Dodgers ended up winning, 10–4, with home runs from Steve Yeager and Smith. For New York, Munson went deep, as did Jackson in his last plate appearance of the day. While Gullett had a bad World Series, losing both of his starts, his fellow free-agent signing, Jackson, was turning his postseason around. New York and Steinbrenner in particular understood that a big free agent signing(s) could be the difference between climbing the summit and being left behind. Los Angeles owner Walter O'Malley was not interested in spending money on any big star. The main difference between the 1976 and 1977 Dodgers roster was that outfielder Bill Buckner was traded to the Cubs for another outfielder, Rick Monday. Monday only hit .230 with an OPS of .713 during the regular season. He appeared in four World Series games, hit .211 with a minuscule .549 OPS. While Smith and Baker had a very good World Series, the third outfield spot was a disaster for Los Angeles. Jackson in Dodger blue instead of pinstripes may well have resulted in title celebrations in Los Angeles. Instead, Jackson was about to go nuclear, become a Yankee legend, and forever be known as Mr. October.

In Game Six it was once again the Dodgers who took the lead. Mike Torrez got the first two Dodgers, but an error, a passed ball, and a walk put runners on first and second. And on an 0-2 count, Steve Garvey tripled the runners home. This was the fourth time in six games that Los Angeles opened the scoring. With Hooton, who was so good in Game Two, on the mound, the Dodgers had to be feeling great. That warm fuzzy feeling was not to last. In the bottom of the second, in front of 56,407 in the Bronx, Jackson walked on four pitches. This brought up Chris Chambliss, who was having a heck of a World Series, and this continued as he homered to right-center, and just like that the score was tied. But it did not take long for Los Angeles to retake the lead. In the top of the third, Smith hit a solo shot, and the Dodgers were in front, 3–2. Hooton made short work of New York in the bottom of the inning, and in the top of the fourth with one out, Monday and Yeager hit back-to-back singles. Monday made it to third, but Yeager pushed his luck, attempting to turn his single into a double. Right fielder Piniella made a nice throw and nailed the Dodgers catcher at second. Hooton struck out, and the threat was averted. It was to prove crucial. Munson led off the bottom of the inning with a single. This brought up Jackson, the man disliked by Martin and, at times, most of the locker room. After his walk in the second, Jackson decided to swing at the first pitch. Jackson made good contact, oh how he made good contact. A two-run homer, and New York had retaken the lead, 4–3. Lasorda had seen enough. Hooton was out, and Elias Sosa was on the mound. It did not help. New York added to their lead thanks to a Piniella sacrifice fly later in the inning. Jackson was not done. In the fifth, with a runner at first and two outs, he stepped to the plate. Considering his previous home run, maybe it would have been best to not throw Jackson anything near the strike zone. Sosa decided on doing the opposite. As for Jackson, he decided the best course of action was to swing away. It was the correct approach: another two-run homer to right. The fans at Yankee Stadium were going crazy. Two home runs in a World Series game are great; three home runs make a legend. In the bottom of the eighth, with Charlie Hough on the mound, up came Jackson with a deserved swagger in his step to open the inning. Once again, with two pitches resulting in two homers, the first pitch to Jackson should not have been anywhere near the strike zone. Hough did not get the memo. On the first pitch, Jackson once again swung away. And as soon as one heard the crack of the bat, one knew that Jackson was about to be in rarefied air. Babe Ruth had three-homer games in the World Series in 1926 and 1928. Three pitches, three home runs. And it was no longer Reggie Jackson rounding the basis, but Mr. October. New York ended up winning, 8–4. They were once again the New York F'n Yankees. World Series champions. Jackson told reporters, "I felt vindicated. . . . All that stuff I'd been through with Billy [Martin] none of it mattered anymore at the moment. I can't imagine ever feeling as good as I felt, taking that turn around the bases the third time." Jackson went on and said, "I felt like Superman. . . . Nothing can top this. Who's ever going to hit three home runs in a deciding World Series game? Babe Ruth, Hank Aaron, Joe DiMaggio? At least I was with them for one night." Lasorda told reporters, "We didn't hit like we were capable of hitting, but I don't want to alibi and take anything away from a great Yankee victory." It is true the Dodgers hitters could have performed better, but it was the pitching staff that was not up to par. Or more to the point, New York hitters were better than the Los Angeles pitchers. There was infighting all year in New York, the Bronx may well have been burning, but it did not matter. Perhaps 1978 would be a tranquil year for the men in pinstripes? Chambliss was not Nostradamus in this regard when he said, "I really doubt it. . . . We did it this year amidst controversy all season long. We'll just have to wait and see."

11

1978: MR. OCTOBER
STRIKES AGAIN

A NOTHER WORLD SERIES title for the Yankees and more heartbreak for the Dodgers. In 1981, Narcotics Anonymous released a guidebook with the following quote: "the definition of insanity is doing the same thing over and over and expecting different results." Yes; despite the common belief, Albert Einstein never uttered these words. After every World Series loss, the Dodgers front office was generally happy to go into the following year with a largely unchanged team. It worked in 1955, but for the other years insanity ran wild. There are two other quotes that perfectly capture the Dodgers: "Those who cannot remember the past are condemned to repeat it" and "History repeats itself, first as tragedy, second as farce." The Dodgers had already experienced back-to-back World Series losses to the Yankees while in Brooklyn. Would 1978 be the year the Dodgers do something different, learn from history, and prevent history from repeating itself? To quote *The Simpsons'* Nelson Muntz, "Ha Ha!"

THE YANKEES' 1978 SEASON

Of course, while history was repeating itself in a negative way for the Dodgers, the Yankees were loving the fact that history was seemingly in a loop where they were often baseball's most dominant team. However, to ascribe blind determinism to their success would be foolish in the extreme. Unlike the Dodgers, New York learned from history. Spending money on free agents played a large part in their 1977 triumph; as such, why deviate from that course of action?

New York already had one of the best closers in the game, the reigning Cy Young winner Sparky Lyle. But that was not enough for Steinbrenner. He went out and pursued Rich "Goose" Gossage. Gossage is now more known for his disparaging comments about players and the state of the game today. My personal "favorite" is his comments about Mariano Rivera: "I take exception to Mariano being called the best reliever ever. . . . But do what we did and we'll be able to compare apples to apples. I don't take anything away from Mariano; he's great. But what these guys do today is easy compared to what we did. It takes three guys to do what I did." Despite his inflated opinion of himself, Gossage was still a legendary pitcher. He is a member of the Hall of Fame and a nine-time All-Star. Gossage was a great reliever, but like so many relievers, he was a failed starter. Gossage was both a starter and a reliever in his first three seasons as a major leaguer with the White Sox but had little success. However, in 1975, he found his true calling as a closer.

He appeared in 62 games, was the last man on the mound in 49 of them, and led the AL in saves with 26. Considering this, it should have been a lock that Gossage would remain a closer. But a new manager took the helm, and Gossage was back being a mediocre starter the following year. In a piece of good fortune, Gossage was traded to the Pirates and reunited with the manager that made him a closer in Chicago, Chuck Tanner. Gossage had an outstanding season in Pittsburgh, saving 26 games with an ERA of 1.62. He wanted to remain a Pirate, was happy in Pittsburgh, but the team was seemingly not interested in keeping him, as they offered Gossage a contract for a lot lower than he thought he was worth. Leaving Pittsburgh, Gossage made one final stop at Three Rivers Stadium, emptied his locker, and said good-bye to Tanner. After that, Gossage noted he put his "bags in the car and just sat there and cried."

Gossage was headed for New York and the Yankees on a six-year, $3.6 million deal. As for Lyle, Nettles joked, "He went from Cy Young to sayonara." That was not entirely true, as Lyle still appeared in 59 games but only saved nine, and his ERA ballooned to 3.47. Gossage was the closer. Things did not go according to plan in April, as he did not record a save, was the losing pitcher in three of his first four appearances, and his first win did not occur until April 30. Even then, he picked up the win after blowing a save. Gossage, though, turned things around and ended up having a fine debut season with New York. He led the AL in saves (27) with an ERA of 2.01. Gossage was an All-Star and finished fifth in Cy Young voting. Signing a free agent once again paid dividends for New York. It was one of Gossage's teammates, a homegrown Yankee, who was the unanimous choice for the AL Cy Young Award.

Ron Guidry was drafted by the Yankees in the third round, pick 67, of the 1971 June amateur draft. While initially thought to be a starter, Guidry eventually was viewed as a reliever and made his major-league debut in 1975. While showing promise, Guidry could have been an Oriole. In June 1976, New York and Baltimore were working on a ten-player trade. It was because Guidry is a lefty that he was not traded. Then-Baltimore general manager Hank Peters told the *New York Times* in 1986 that "it wasn't that they were that high on Guidry. . . . He was left-handed and they didn't want to give up any more left-handed pitching." It was a wise decision by New York. In his third year in the majors, Guidry, to the surprise of many, made the team out of spring training, put it all together, and forced his way into the starting rotation before the month of April was over. Guidry had a mighty fine year including a couple of standout performances in the postseason. While 1977 was his breakout year, 1978 would be his career year. Guidry went 25–3 with a minuscule ERA of 1.74; he led the majors in wins and ERA (as a side note, Guidry also led the AL in ERA the following year despite his ERA ballooning to 2.78). Guidry was an All-Star, a Cy Young winner, and finished second in MVP voting (although based on WAR, he should have won the award. His WAR was 9.6. Jim Rice, who won the award, had a WAR of 7.6). While Guidry never reached those same heights again, he spent his entire career in pinstripes and was a four-time All-Star and five-time Gold Glove winner.

Considering that Guidry won 25 games and Gossage saved 27 games, one would assume that New York had it easy in the AL East. In reality, the Yankees were decidedly average for a majority of the first four months of the season. In April, they had a record of 10–9 and were 3 1/2 games out of first. A great month of May saw the team go 19–8, but the deficit was only cut by half a game. There was, though, no need for concern. There was a lot of baseball left. But in June the Yankees struggled to a 14–15 record, nine games out of first. And the shit hit the fan in July. On July 17, after an extra-inning loss to Kansas City, capping a horrible 2–12 run, New York was a mammoth 14 games behind the Boston Red Sox, who were 61–28.

There was also trouble brewing once again between Martin and Jackson. In the loss to the Royals, Martin put on the bunt sign in the bottom of the tenth with none out and Munson on first. A surprising choice perhaps considering that Jackson was at the plate. Jackson bunted the first pitch foul. As a result, Martin took off the bunt sign. Jackson ignored his manager and bunted. It went foul. Once again, Jackson tried to bunt. It was a failure, as instead he popped it up to the catcher. That bit of insubordination led to Martin, with Steinbrenner's support, suspending Jackson for five days. Martin told reporters that Jackson had "been working hard all year and didn't have a chip on his shoulder. We had talked the day before, and I had told him that I liked him no matter what he had heard and that I would give him a chance to play right field some."

New York won their next four games, and on July 23 against the White Sox in Chicago with Jackson back in uniform (but remaining on the bench) the Yankees won again, and the deficit was down to 10 games. Yet Martin was not happy, his health was seemingly in decline (and being reported on), he was perhaps drinking more than the recommended daily amount of alcohol, and he was greatly annoyed with Jackson talking about the incident. In Chicago, Jackson told reporters, "I had not been playing regularly and I wasn't swinging the bat very well. . . . I thought under the circumstances that bunting was the best thing I could do. . . . I didn't realize exactly what the consequences [of ignoring the manager] would be. I didn't consider it an act of defiance, and I don't feel I did anything wrong. I would even do it again if I didn't know what the consequences would be. For that reason, it would have been better if I had struck out swinging and avoided the hassle."

It would have been for the best if Jackson took the suspension on the chin. At the same time, despite his earlier conciliatory words, Martin did not like Jackson. Jackson's comments just riled up Martin more. And for all his positive qualities, Martin did not take slights well. When told of Jackson's comments, Martin fired back, telling reporters, "I'm saying [to Jackson] shut up. . . . We don't need none of your stuff. We're winning without you. We don't need you coming in and making all these comments. If he doesn't shut his mouth, he won't play and I don't care what George says. He can replace me right now if he doesn't like it." If Martin left it like that, his comments would have generated headlines, but most likely things would have blown over. Yet Martin was still fuming. Less than an hour later, he continued his tirade, saying Jackson and Steinbrenner "deserve each other. One's a born liar, the other's convicted." There is no doubt that Martin was calling Jackson a liar and Steinbrenner, who in 1974 pleaded guilty to election law violations and attempting to cover up such wrongdoing, a convict, a crook, a criminal. Reporters made sure to ask Martin whether his comments were on the record. Martin confirmed that they were.

Following such an outburst, Martin's time as New York manager was untenable. The following day, he announced his resignation. Martin told the assembled press, "I don't want to hurt this team's chances for the pennant with this undue publicity. The team has a shot at the pennant and I hope they win it. I owe it to my health and my mental well-being to resign. At this time I'm also sorry about these things that were written about George Steinbrenner. He does not deserve them nor did I say them. I've had my differences with George, but we've been able to resolve them." Soon after, Martin began crying almost uncontrollably and was helped out of the press conference. The recently fired manager of the White Sox, and a former Yankees pitching coach, Bob Lemon, was named as the new New York manager.

Soon Steinbrenner started to feel remorse and sadness that Martin was gone. Lemon was five days into his new role when on July 29 at Old-Timers' Day, Steinbrenner prepared a statement that was read by Bob Sheppard, the Yankees' public address announcer. Martin appeared on the field, and Sheppard told the crowd that in 1980 Martin would be back managing New York with Lemon the general manager. Everyone was shocked, the fans cheered, and as for Lemon, he was not told of the plan in advance. He had to be wondering what the hell he had gotten into.

Lemon, who began his playing career in the bigs with Cleveland in 1946, was a Hall of Fame pitcher. He spent 13 seasons in a Cleveland uniform, winning 207 games, was a seven-time All-Star, and was a member of the 1948 World Series-winning team. After retiring as a player, Lemon coached in the majors before becoming a minor-league manager. In 1970, he got his shot to lead a major-league club when he was appointed manager of the Royals. He lasted three seasons. He was named the 1971 AL Manager of the Year, but a fourth-place finish in 1972 ended his reign in Kansas City. It was not until 1977 that he got another chance to manage in the majors. Hired by the White Sox, Lemon turned the team around. In 1976, Chicago finished last in the AL West winning a paltry 64 games. In 1977, the team won 90 games, and Lemon was the Manager of the Year. However, the White Sox were mediocre the following year, and Lemon was fired in late June. Lucky for him, Martin uttered his infamous line, and Lemon was now in charge of New York.

Of course, when Lemon took over it was exceedingly unlikely that the Yankees' season would be anything other than an afterthought and a joke. But New York started playing consistent baseball, and the team enjoyed the way Lemon managed. Yet despite going 19–8 in August, the men in pinstripes were still 6 1/2 games out of first; the Red Sox were clear favorites to capture the division. However, the curse of the Bambino was still in full force at this time. In September, Boston posted a losing record, while New York went 22–8. As part of the Yankees' great month and the Red Sox's awful September, New York swept a four-game series in Boston. In the Boston Massacre, as it became known, New York won, 15–3, 13–2, 7–0, and 7–4. On October 1, the final day of the season, the Yankees led the division by one game. The Red Sox defeated the Blue Jays, but that would have been immaterial if New York won. The Yankees had won six straight, were riding high, and only had to defeat a Cleveland team that was firmly entrenched in fifth place in the AL East. And the game was at Yankee Stadium. Yet it was Cleveland who scored first, plating two in the first. Not to worry, New York tied the game in the bottom of the inning. But Catfish Hunter was a long way from his best, Cleveland scored four in the second, and ran away with the game, 9–2. A one-game playoff would decide the division winner. The game was held at Fenway Park because New York lost a coin toss. Appel notes that Steinbrenner berated a Yankee official because he called heads. Steinbrenner yelled, "You [expletive] idiot! Everyone knows it comes up tails seventy percent of the time!"

On a Monday afternoon, October 2, 1978, it was Guidry taking the mound for New York, while former Yankee Mike Torrez took the ball for Boston. Guidry was very good, but he allowed a solo shot to Carl Yastrzemski in the second and another run in the sixth. Torrez was even better, holding the Yankees scoreless through six. The seventh, however, was a bloodbath. In the top of the inning there were runners on first and second, with two out and Bucky Dent at the plate. Dent was not an offensive threat, let alone a power threat. Now in his sixth season, he had hit 22 home runs throughout his big-league career. But on this magical day in Boston, Dent fouled a ball off his foot and cracked his bat. He got another bat from Mickey Rivers. And on the very next pitch, Dent hit an improbable three-run shot; New York was in the lead. Oh, but they were not done. Rivers walked and stole second. Munson promptly doubled Rivers home to increase the lead. Jackson hit one out to begin the eighth, and it was party time on the Yankee bench. Boston came back to score a couple in the eighth. They made the game more interesting in the bottom of the ninth by putting runners on first and second with only one out. But Gossage got Rice to fly out, and Yastrzemski hit a lazy pop fly to third. New York won, 5–4, and were headed to the playoffs. Awaiting them were the Royals in the ALCS for the third straight year. And history repeated itself yet again.

New York easily took Game One, 7–1, while the men in pinstripes were never in the contest in Game Two, eventually losing, 10–4. Game Three was a back-and-forth affair. The Royals opened the scoring as George Brett led off the game with a home run. The Yankees tied it when Jackson led off the bottom of the second inning with a solo shot of his own. The Royals retook the lead when Brett hit another long ball in the third. But the Yankees then came back in the fourth thanks to an RBI single from Jackson, and Jackson later came around to score on an error. Brett was due to lead off the fifth, and considering he had taken Hunter deep in his previous two at-bats, surely it was time for Lemon to pull Hunter. Oh, no. Hunter stayed in the game, and Brett hit another homer, this one to tie the game, 3–3. Brett was dominating, but, for New York, Jackson was not doing too badly himself. And he put the Bronx Bombers back in front in the sixth with a sacrifice fly. Gossage came on to pitch in the seventh looking for a three-inning save. While he cut through the Royals in that inning, the eighth was not good at all. Kansas City scored twice and was now in the lead, 5–4. Gossage had blown the save opportunity, but he eventually picked up the win thanks to Munson. In the bottom of the eighth, with a runner on first and one out, the Yankees' captain was due up. As he waited for reliever Doug Bird to warm up, Munson chatted with Jackson, the on-deck hitter. Was Munson predicting a home run? Not quite, Jackson noted. "We were joking and he said, 'Bet I hit into a double play.' I said, 'Bet you don't.'" Jackson was right, Munson was wrong. On a 2-0 count, Munson made some beautiful contact. The ball kept on going for a two-run blast. New York led, 6–5, and this time Gossage took care of business, retiring the Royals in order in the ninth. In Game Four with Guidry on the mound, New York could already taste another World Series berth. But Brett led off the game with a triple and promptly scored when Hal McRae, the next batter, singled him home. Not the start Guidry and the Bronx Bombers were looking for. That would be the only run Guidry gave up in eight innings of work. Nettles tied the score in the second with a leadoff homer. And on the first pitch he saw in the sixth, Roy White hit one out himself. New York led, 2–1. Guidry opened the ninth looking for a complete game, but following a leadoff double, in came Gossage. Three batters up, three batters down. New York was AL champions and World Series bound. A truly remarkable effort considering their season was seemingly over only a few months back. Most other teams would have given up, but the 1978 New York Yankees, despite all the turmoil, would not roll over and die. They had too much pride for that. Now all they had to do was win it all again to cap off an astonishing season. As for Boston, Henry Hecht wrote in the *Philadelphia Inquirer* that "The Red Sox will live with the shame of 1978 for the rest of their lives. They blew it. It's that simple."

THE DODGERS' 1978 SEASON

Los Angeles had come so close once again to winning it all in 1977 but failed at the final hurdle. Not surprisingly, Lasorda talked up his team, stating, "This is a young team that has the ability to be better than it was last year . . . that can be more productive in each of the next several years. . . . The players know they can win. They know what it takes to reach the World

Series, and they want to do it again." Despite Lasorda's positivity, surely the Dodgers would learn from history and try to strengthen their squad, perhaps through a major trade or by going after a free agent or two. This was especially true considering that New York was a better team than in 1977 by adding free agents. Instead, Los Angeles decided on a different approach.

Los Angeles's "big" free agent signing was Terry Forster. Forster was an average starter for the Pirates and the White Sox. However, in 1974, he was the White Sox closer, and while he led the AL in saves, his 3.62 ERA was nothing to write home about. Maybe the Dodgers brass saw something in Forster or maybe they were lucky, as he became Los Angeles's closer and had a career year. Forster saved 22, and his ERA plummeted to 1.93. Forster worked out (at least for 1978; he never approached that level again for Los Angeles), but that was basically it for the Dodgers. The 1978 team was almost identical to the previous year's team.

A generous person would claim that the Dodgers hierarchy was confident that the team could win the World Series, as such a minor upgrade at closer was all that was needed. A skeptical person would claim that O'Malley was not willing to spend the money to sign top free agents because of the cost involved; profit was more important than winning a World Series. The skeptic would have had a point when in spring training the Dodgers announced that for away games the team would not have a 25-man traveling roster, but only 24. There is no universe where taking one less player on the road increases the chances of winning. It was done purely to save money. There was another incident that put other interests above a winning ballclub, namely, the trade of Glenn Burke to Oakland.

Burke was a utility outfielder who was an average player, but as he was only twenty-four and in his third major-league season, there was plenty of time for him to develop. In addition, he was incredibly popular in the clubhouse, a person whom almost all players liked. As a side note, Burke is widely credited with inventing the high-five. When Burke was traded, a number of Dodgers players could not believe it, and more than a few had tears in their eyes. In return for Burke, the Dodgers received Bill North, another outfielder. North, once a great player, was in the downside of his career. It was a perplexing trade, more so that it occurred in May. Neither the media nor the players could understand why the trade occurred, at least for baseball reasons. Looking back on the trade years later, Davey Lopes said, "You don't break up, disrupt a team going as well as it was going to make changes. I didn't feel it was going to make us a better ball club. Billy North was not going to make us, at that time, any better of a ballclub. Probably not the real reason why things happened." Dusty Baker added, "I think the Dodgers knew; I think that's why they traded Glenn."

It is almost certain that Los Angeles traded Burke because he was a homosexual. That Burke was gay did not bother his teammates. However, it allegedly bothered the Dodgers front office, especially as Burke was friends with another homosexual, who was also sometimes a cross-dresser, namely, Tommy Lasorda Jr., Lasorda's son. It is fair to say that Lasorda was not happy with his son's sexual orientation and that he was friends with Burke. Burke's time in Oakland did not go well; there, he was insulted for being gay, and he was out of baseball a couple of years later. He never got to fulfill his promise. Burke died in 1995 after a hard life; he was only forty-two. As I wrote in *The Dodgers*, "every year on April 20, the so-called National High Five Day, do not remember the Burke who invented the high-five, but the Burke who was persecuted because he was gay."

While the Dodgers clubhouse was united in bewilderment and sadness that Burke was traded, they were not exactly a unified, harmonious group of players in other aspects. Steve Garvey was on the surface the typical All-American great guy, a baseball heartthrob. To use a cliché, men wanted to be like him, and women wanted to marry him. Such an image rubbed some of his teammates the wrong way, perhaps none more so than Don Sutton. Sutton gave an interview with the *Washington Post* in which he praised Reggie Smith and decided to take a very public cheap shot at Garvey. Sutton said, "All you hear about on our team is Steve Garvey, the All-American boy. Well, the best player on this team for the last two years—and we all know it—is Reggie Smith. As Reggie goes, so goes us. . . . [but] Reggie doesn't go out and publicize himself. He doesn't smile at the right people or say the right things. He tells the truth, even if it sometimes alienates people. Reggie's not a facade or a Madison Avenue image. He's a real person." That Sutton would willingly go on the record to criticize Garvey as a person and when Los Angeles was in a tight race for the division crown was extraordinary. Garvey went to Lasorda and asked what he should do. Rather than speak of turning the cheek, Lasorda told Garvey that what he did was up to him, but, as recounted by Bill Plaschke in *I Live for This*, Lasorda said, "if it was me, and somebody said those things in the paper about me? The first time I saw him, I would deck him." Garvey took Lasorda's advice. Garvey confronted Sutton in the clubhouse later that day, and the two got into it. Both men landed some decent blows, which resulted in bruises and scratches, before teammates separated them. Sutton was fuming after the fight, although he was the one who caused the fracas by criticizing Garvey the person in public. Nevertheless, Sutton told Lasorda he planned to hold a press conference and throw more fuel on the fire by further bad-mouthing Garvey. Lasorda told Sutton that such an approach would not benefit Garvey, the Dodgers, or Sutton himself. Sutton eventually did hold a press conference and apologized for his behavior. Sutton told the assembled press that "For the last few days . . . I have thought of nothing else and I've tried over and over to figure out why this all had to happen. The only possible reason I can find is that my life isn't being lived according to what I know, as a human being and a Christian, to be right. If it were, then there would not have been an article in which I would offend any of my teammates." Thus, all was nice and rosy with the boys in blue. The fight did not lead to a massive winning streak nor did it lead to a collapse of monumental proportions. Instead, it was pretty much business as usual.

Business as usual meant that the Dodgers were in the NL West race from day one of the season. On May 1, Los Angeles was half a game out of first, a poor May only saw them 3 1/2 games back at the end of the month, and while June was looking to be a bad (six games back on June 27), the last few days were kind to the boys in blue, and they finished the month three games out of first. The Dodgers gained more ground in July (1 1/2 games back) and took the division lead on August 11. On August 20, the day of the infamous Garvey-Sutton fight, Los Angeles held a two-game lead. By the end of the month, their lead was exactly the same. September witnessed some great Dodgers baseball, and their lead ballooned to nine games; at that point, the team seemingly eased up on the pedal and made things interesting, but the division title was never truly in doubt. Los Angeles finished with a record of 95–67, 2 1/2 games ahead of Cincinnati. Awaiting them in the NL Championship Series were the Phillies, and history repeating itself once again.

Philadelphia manager Danny Ozark liked his team's chances heading into the NLCS. While every manager in a similar situation would say something like his team will win, but the opposition is tough and it should be a good series, Ozark decided on a different route. He said that the Phillies would beat the Dodgers, no surprise there, but he also predicted that they would sweep them. That was some bravado. Ozark was a coach for the Dodgers under Alston from 1965 to 1972 and perhaps had designs on managing in Los Angeles, and this explains why he made such an outlandish statement. Whatever the reason, Ozark's predication soon fell into the abyss.

In Game One, a high-scoring affair, Philadelphia took the lead in front of 63,460 rabid fans at Veteran Stadium through a Mike Schmidt sacrifice fly. But things soon fell apart for the Phillies. In the bottom of the third with one out, Lopes doubled, Bill Russell reached on an error, Smith drove in Lopes with an RBI single, and then on a 1-2 count Garvey homered. The Dodgers had a 4–1 lead. Los Angeles ended up winning, 9–5, with Garvey homering twice and Lopes and Yeager also hitting long balls. So much for Philadelphia sweeping the series. Game Two was more of a pitching duel. The Dodgers took the lead in the fourth on a Lopes solo shot to open the inning and added another two runs in the fifth. That was more than enough run support for Tommy John, who was magnificent, pitching a four-hit shutout. The Dodgers won, 4–0, as Lopes was a double away from the cycle, and it was the Phillies who were in danger of being swept. And the Dodgers were confident a sweep was on the cards because Sutton would be taking the mound in Game Three at Dodger Stadium. Sutton had never suffered a loss in the postseason, with Los Angeles posting a 5–2 record in those starts. However, in a sign of things to come, Sutton was not good at all, giving up seven runs in 5 2/3 innings as the Phillies defeated the Dodgers, 9–4. Game Four was tied at 4 after the regulation nine innings. Phillies reliever Tug McGraw made short work of the first two Dodgers in the bottom of the tenth. Cey then proceeded to walk on four straight balls. Baker went up hacking and on the first pitch he saw hit a routine flyball to Phillies Gold Glove center fielder Garry Maddox. The inning should have been over, but Maddox misplayed it for an error. Cey, now at second, scored two pitches later when Russell singled to center on a 1-0 count. The Dodgers won, 5–4. After the game, Maddox told the assembled press, "The ball was right in my glove. . . . Any kind of decision or factor was just how to hold my glove when I caught it. I ran after it and played it the way it was natural to me. It was not a tough play, just a routine line drive. It cost us a shot at being world champions. It's something I'll never forget the rest of my life. I'll just have to try not to let it get me down. I've had other crises in my life and this is another one." Whether history would have been different if Maddox had caught the ball will never be known; what is beyond a shadow of doubt was that the Dodgers were headed to another World Series and *another* meeting with the Yankees. As for Maddox, he would taste glory as a member of the 1980 Phillies world championship team.

THE 1978 WORLD SERIES

Somewhat surprisingly considering the Yankees were the defending champions and tended to dominate the Dodgers in the fall classic, Los Angeles was favored before the first World Series pitch was thrown. They had home field advantage. Moreover, New York had a number of injury concerns. Second baseman Willie Randolph's season was over due to a hamstring injury suffered in late September. Randolph's replacements at second for the duration of the World Series were rookie Brian Doyle, who had only 54 plate appearances all season, and Fred Stanley (regular season OPS of .606). Randolph was distraught he could not play, but that did not stop him from supporting Doyle. In 2015, Randolph told the *New York Daily News* that Doyle "was easy to root for. . . . He rooted for me. I just thought it was a great story—every World Series there's unsung heroes. I can't say I was surprised. He was always ready to play, never scared. He looked at it like his shot." While Doyle was ready to take his opportunity, all signs pointed to Dodgers success.

It certainly looked that way after Game One. In the bottom of the second, Baker led off with a solo shot off Ed Figueroa. With two outs and a runner at third, Lopes swung at the first pitch he saw. A smart approach, as his towering home run to left put Los Angeles up by three and knocked Figueroa out of the game. Lopes put the contest to bed in the fourth. With one out and runners on the corners, Lopes swung for the fences on a 1-0 count. The ball majestically flew into the center-left bleachers for a three-run blast, and the Dodgers led, 6–0. Tommy John was effective, and Los Angeles was never headed as they ended up winning, 11–5. Lopes told reporters that he was in the zone and when he feels like that, "I feel I can hit anyone at any time and anywhere. . . . Tonight, I was relaxed. I've probably never been more relaxed. I'm relaxed because I'm very confident that we're the best team until the Yankees prove otherwise." New York did not prove otherwise in Game Two.

The game pitted Burt Hooton against Catfish Hunter. Both pitchers performed well. It was not going to be a shootout like the previous game. New York opened the scoring in the third when with two out, and two men on, Jackson swung at the first pitch he saw, doubling home both runners. The Dodgers got one back in the fourth through a Ron Cey RBI single. Cey was the hero for Los Angeles in the sixth. There were two out and runners on the corners. On a 2-0 count, Hunter left one over the plate, and Cey did the rest. A three-run blast to left put the Dodgers up, 4–2. New York clawed one back through a Jackson RBI groundout an inning later. With Forster now on the mound, it seemed like the Dodgers would hold on. Yet Forster got into trouble in the ninth. With runners at first and second and one out and Munson and Jackson due up, Lasorda made a big call and brought in twenty-one-year-old rookie fire-brand Bob Welch. Welch would end up playing in the majors for 17 seasons, be a part of two World Series teams, and win a Cy Young award. But that was all to come. Lasorda brought in Welch to blow away the final two Yankees with heat. He did not make his debut with the Dodgers until June 20, appeared in 23 games, and had a minuscule ERA of 2.02. His last appearance was in Game One of the NLCS against the Phillies one week prior. Welch was well rested and ready. On an 0-1 count, Munson hit a bullet to right, but straight at Smith. Two out. It was now Welch vs. Jackson, Mr. October himself. There was no finesse involved. It was just heat after heat. And Jackson swinging and fouling pitches off. After an eight-pitch battle, the count was 3-2. Jackson was made for these moments. He was ready. Welch threw another fastball, and Mr. October would go down in flames. Strike three. The ballgame was over. Los Angeles took the contest, 4–3, was riding high, and led the Fall Classic, 2–0. Jackson was irate heading to the dugout and smashed his bat against the wall. While some in the media tried to make something of Jackson's show of anger, and arguably Martin would have done so too, Lemon was having none of it. He said, "The guy was hyped up. The kid just struck him out to win a World Series game. Hell, I didn't expect him to walk into the dugout and set his bat and helmet down gently and say, 'Gee, fellows, I'm sorry I struck out.' Reggie was hot and we should have gotten out of his way." Reggie had lost the battle, but the war was a long way from being over. Especially with the Series headed to New York and the cauldron of Yankee Stadium for three games.

Indeed, Game Three belonged almost entirely to New York. Los Angeles had their chances, but just as in past World Series games, they did not take advantage of them. It began in the top of the first. The second batter up, Russell, reached on a single, but he was soon erased attempting to steal. In the bottom of the inning, Mickey Rivers also reached first on a single, but he too was gunned down trying to steal second. Not to worry, as following the caught stealing, Roy White homered down the right-field line. New York extended their lead in the second through some small ball. The first two hitters reached, followed by a groundout moving the runners over, and another groundout plated a run. Sutton did not have his best stuff, but then again neither did

Guidry. A two-out RBI single by Russell in the third cut the margin by one. Yet once again, Los Angeles could not get the big hit. In both the fifth and the sixth, the Dodgers left the bases loaded. And they paid the price. New York put the game out of reach in the seventh. With runners at the corners and only one out, Munson singled on an 0-2 count, plating one. Lasorda had seen enough, pulling Sutton and bringing in Lance Rautzhan to face Jackson. Of course, Jackson swung at the first pitch. He singled to left to extend New York's lead, while Munson moved to third. Damned if you do, damned if you don't, but no way should Rautzhan have thrown anything near the strike zone on the first pitch. Piniella then swung at the first pitch he saw. He grounded out, but it was good enough for Munson to score. New York led, 5–1, and that was all, folks. Guidry pitched a complete game, but he gave up eight hits and seven walks. How Los Angeles only scored once is amazing, but on more than one occasion, Guidry was bailed out by some show-stopping defense by Nettles at third base.

Game Four would end up being the turning point of the Series, and it was Mr. October right in the center of controversy. Ed Figueroa was on the mound for New York, Tommy John for Los Angeles. Both teams had opportunities early, but the game remained scoreless heading to the top of the fifth. With runners at first and second and two out, on a 1-0 count, Smith powered one to deep right field. A three-run home run. Los Angeles was seemingly as good as home. Except they were not. In the bottom of the sixth, John got into some trouble. Jackson singled home a run. This brought up Piniella. On a 1-0 count, he hit one straight to Russell at short. Russell stepped on second for the out and threw to first. An easy double play. The inning was over. Except the double play never occurred. Russell's throw to first never reached its intended destination. The ball caromed off of Jackson's hip and scooted away, allowing a run to score. The Dodgers were shocked the umpire did not call interference on Jackson. They were certain that he deliberately stuck out his hip. Whatever the truth, the deficit was cut by one. Forster was brought into the game in the eighth looking for a two-inning save, but he could not get the job done. New York tied the game through a Munson double. And they won it in the 10th. Welch was on the mound throwing heat. With a man on first and two out, he faced a rematch with Jackson. Jackson won this battle with single to right, moving the runner over. Piniella then completed the comeback. On an 0-1 count he singled to center for the walk-off victory. Welch went from hero to zero, while Jackson was either a hero or a villain, depending on whom you asked. In *Becoming Mr. October*, Jackson claimed that the throw was headed straight for a place where no man wants to be hit, thus "I moved just a little. I could've just hit the dirt. I could've jumped all the way to one side or another. But I thought, *I'm in my right-of-way. I'm in the baseline. I'm going to be out anyway, so why not just stand there and play stupid?* I thought, *I'm out anyway, so it's not so bad if I stay here and let it hit me.*" After the game, Russell said, "Reggie saw the ball coming. . . . He moved right into it. That's interference." I watched and rewatched the play over and over, and I honestly did not know whether Jackson did anything wrong. There was some movement toward the ball, but it was not pronounced, and the throw was close enough to him that even in this era of instant replay (and for sure the Dodgers would have challenged the call), I doubt the call would have been overturned.

Professional athletes are usually not rattled by a single play. While the Yankees tied the World Series up with that victory, there was still plenty of baseball left. The Dodgers players could have moved on mentally, but they did not. That play doomed their World Series. It messed with their minds. Looking back at the play, Cey said, "The interference issue with Reggie Jackson was the one that pulled the rug right out from under us and that's still my biggest nightmare in baseball. . . . If the call is made properly and if they huddled together like they should have, we would have walked off the field with a 3–0 lead [*sic*: the score would have been 3–1]. We end up losing that game. The next day we were flat, deflated. And so I feel legitimately that '78 was the one that got away and it's still hard to talk about." The Dodgers were lost in their own minds.

Nevertheless, they opened Game Five by scoring in the first and the third to open up a 2–0 lead. The play involving Jackson's hip was seemingly long forgotten. Or was it? A tiny bit of Yankee pressure, and the Dodgers wilted. In the bottom of the third, New York played a bit of small ball. Hooton walked Dent on four pitches to open the inning, Rivers followed with a single. Dent was brought home by a White single. Rivers and White then pulled off a double steal, and both then scored on Munson's single, with Munson reaching third on the throw and an error. Jackson struck out, but Munson scored on Piniella's single. Hooton was out of the game, and New York led, 4–2. But the Yankees were not done; they added three in the fourth, four in the seventh, and another one in the eighth to destroy and demoralize the Dodgers, 12–2. New York rookie Jim Beattie pitched his first complete game in the majors, striking out eight as the Yankees took a 3–2 lead.

DODGERS VS. YANKEES

The Series moved back to Los Angeles, but the Dodgers were done. The New York cauldron was just too hot for the Dodgers players to handle. The Bronx was burning once again, and the Dodgers melted. After Game Five, Russell shouted at some reporters, "Any of you guys from the [*New York*] *Post*? . . . Guys from the *Post* are no good—just like this town." Smith said, "This city . . . is filthy and so are its people." Lopes added, "They ought to drop a bomb on this park [Yankee Stadium]. . . . Everything is bad about it . . . the dimensions, the fans . . . the fans are the most vulgar I've ever seen." Oh, yes, the Dodgers were lost in their own minds, while Yankees were riding high.

And while it would have been nice to win the World Series in New York, the Yankees had the pleasure of humiliating the Dodgers in Los Angeles. Sutton took the ball for the home side, while Hunter did likewise for the visitors. Once again, it was Los Angeles that opened the scoring. Lopes started the bottom of the first with a home run. But just like in the previous game, a tiny bit of Yankees pressure and the Dodgers folded. In the top of the second, with two on and one out, Doyle, who was having a heck of a Series, doubled home a run. Dent followed that with a two-run single. While Los Angles clawed one back in the third, it was false hope. New York scored twice in the sixth, and to cap off a great night for New York, Jackson (who else?) hit a two-run homer in the seventh. Mr. October had another awesome World Series. Jackson's home run ended the scoring, Sutton lost his third postseason game, Hunter pitched a strong seven innings, and for the 27th Dodger out, Gossage got Cey to pop it up to Munson. New York won, 7–2. The Yankees had done it once again. Their season looked to be over when Martin quit, but they staged an improbable comeback just to make the postseason, they lost the first two games in the World Series, but they never quit. The 1978 season was a special one for New York, and it was utter humiliation and despair for Los Angeles. The 1978 World Series truly captured the domination the Yankees had over the Dodgers; nothing else comes close. New York got stronger under the pressure; Los Angeles wilted.

Gossage recalls that "when we won the World Series in LA, it was very subdued in the clubhouse. You would never believe we had won the World Series. We were so exhausted. . . . [What] we went through . . . everybody was just worn out, mentally and physically, from chasing down the Red Sox and all the pressure we played under for so long. It was the first time I won, and I remember thinking these celebrations were supposed to be louder." The celebrations may have been subdued, but the Yankees were atop the baseball throne, while the Dodgers were once again wondering what could have been. History had repeated itself.

12

1981: FERNANDOMANIA

ANOTHER WORLD SERIES loss to the Yankees led to a funk for the 1979 Dodgers. While the offense was one of the best in the league, the pitching staff was mediocre. Sutton had a down year, Rau was injured for the second half, and in a potential case of the Dodgers front office caring more about money than on-field success, John was lost to the Yankees before the season got underway. John's agent noted that "We repeatedly attempted to sit down with the Dodgers last winter. . . . We tried to say, 'Hey, Tommy's two-year contract is up this year, he can become a free agent when the season ends, he wants to sign here again, let's get a new contract out of the way so it's off everyone's mind. Nothing. April. May. June. They didn't really sit down with us until July. . . . Now, of course, what we want isn't what we wanted four or five months ago." Los Angeles finished the season with a record of 79–83 and in third place in the NL West. The season will always be remembered, however, for the death of Walter O'Malley. He died of cancer on August

9. O'Malley was a visionary in moving the Dodgers west, and at the same time he was a businessman first and foremost. He knew the wealth a team in Los Angeles could bring.

The 1980 Dodgers were vastly improved. It was largely the same team as in the previous season (Los Angeles did sign a couple of free agents, starting pitcher Dave Goltz and reliever Don Stanhouse, but to say they underperformed would be a vast understatement), but a lack of injuries and the rise of some youngsters (outfielder Pedro Guerrero in particular) kept the Dodgers in contention all season. Los Angeles was vying with Houston for the NL West crown. With three games left in the season, the Astros led by three games, but their final series for the year would match them with the Dodgers in sunny California. The Dodgers won all three games to set up a one-game playoff for the division title at Dodger Stadium, but with Goltz on the mound and everything to play for, the Astros obliterated the Dodgers, 7–1, to win the NL West. So close, but in the end nothing to show for the season.

As for New York, considering they just went back-to-back, there was seemingly no reason why the team could not three-peat. However, ten days after the 1978 World Series began came a horror stretch for the Yankees. On that day, Lemon's son, Jerry, died in a car crash. That put a black cloud over the season and, combined with injuries, the Yankees were only 34–31 when Steinbrenner acted and replaced Lemon with Martin. Unlike the previous year, there would be no miraculous comeback. Instead, 1979 would be remembered for one of the darkest days in Yankees history.

Since he made his major-league debut, Munson had never been confined to the disabled list. As a catcher, this was even more remarkable. Of course, that also meant his body was aching and he was often downright tired. Munson thought about one day playing for Cleveland to be closer to home. Quite simply, he missed his wife and family. To that end, during 1978 spring training, Munson began flying lessons. Steinbrenner, however, included a "no flying" clause in his contract. That clause was removed in 1979, as Steinbrenner thought allowing Munson to fly home to see his family would dispel any notion the catcher had about leaving the Yankees. On an offday on August 2, Munson was trying out his new purchase, a Cessna Citation jet. He was practicing takeoffs and landings. There were two other people on board. After a few successful attempts, Munson made a series of errors. The plane made a crash landing with Munson breaking his neck. Munson managed to ask his passengers whether they were okay. However, a fire broke out, and his fellow passengers were unable to rescue Munson and were forced to flee as smoke and fire engulfed the cockpit. Munson was thirty-two years old. Baseball did not matter much to the Yankees players for the rest of the season. Nettles noted, "When Thurman got killed, you know, we just lost all—the whole season was just kind of lost. . . . We just realized we couldn't do it and, you know, it demoralized a lot of us." New York finished the season with a record of 89–71, fourth in the AL East; not that it mattered in the slightest.

New York would start the new decade with a new manager. Martin was fired after he got into a fight with a marshmallow salesman after the season. Martin noted that "the marshmallow man I hit was saying bad things about New York and the Yankees." Martin was out, and into the hot seat was Dick Howser. Howser was a former major-league player (including two seasons with New York) and was the Yankees' third-base coach from 1969 until 1978. In 1978, he managed New York for one game (a loss) before Bob Lemon took over. That was his only major-league managerial experience prior to landing the gig. The 1980 Yankees were a very good team, winning 103 games and the AL East. However, in the ALCS, the Royals swept the Bronx Bombers. Just like the 1980 Dodgers, New York's season was one of promise, but the team ended up on the outside looking in.

THE DODGERS' 1981 SEASON

After losing John to the Yankees via free agency the previous season, the 1981 campaign began without Sutton. He signed with the Astros, a division rival. Los Angeles lost two top-of-the-rotation starting pitchers in two years to their rivals, their foray into free agency in 1980 was a bust due to targeting the wrong players, yet other teams (in particular the Yankees) benefited greatly from signing superstar players. Thus, one would assume the Dodgers would learn from the previous year and go out and do their best (i.e. spend, spend, spend) to sign a free agent superstar or two. Instead, Los Angeles management did very little to improve; just a minor change here and there. Yet they ended up lucky, very lucky indeed, in large part due to the emergence of Fernandomania and a midseason work stoppage.

In 1978, Fernando Valenzuela was seventeen years old when he was discovered by a Dodger scout, Mike Brito, playing pro ball in Mexico. Britto pleaded with Dodgers management to sign Valenzuela. Yet Dodgers GM Al Campanis was not impressed due to Valenzuela not having an athlete's body, being under six feet tall, and not having a cannon for an arm. However, Brito was not deterred and the following year convinced Campanis to go down to Mexico and see Valenzuela in action. Campanis was awed, but by this stage, the Yankees were also interested in Valenzuela. Yet for once it was the Dodgers who were willing to part with more money, and as a result Valenzuela became a Dodger.

While management was impressed with Valenzuela, they thought he needed another pitch in his arsenal. Bobby Castillo was the one who taught Valenzuela his soon-to-be-famous screwball. Castillo told the *Los Angeles Times*, "He didn't speak English and I didn't speak Spanish that well . . . but we did communicate. He caught on quickly. It was like it was meant for him." Valenzuela, though, said he was not a natural at all. "The first half [in 1980], it wasn't going that well. . . . I said, 'I don't want to throw it anymore. I want to go back to what I do.' They told me, 'No. We don't care about your record. We don't care how many games you win. We want you to keep practicing it.' By the second half, it was a lot better. By then, I had good rotation on it and good control." And the rest is history.

Valenzuela made his major-league debut for the Dodgers on September 15 in relief. While he gave up two runs, they were not earned. He eventually appeared in 10 games, pitching 17 2/3 innings, and gave up zero earned runs. In a big what-if, maybe if he were brought up earlier, the Dodgers would have won the NL West and not the Astros. Valenzuela was projected to be Los Angeles's fourth or fifth starter in 1981, but a rash of injuries and a good showing in spring training resulted in Valenzuela being Los Angeles's Opening Day starter. The Dodgers beat the Astros, 2–0, with Valenzuela pitching a five-hit shutout. He was great, and it was the start of an outrageous run. Valenzuela won his first eight starts, conceding only four runs. There were five shutouts, seven complete games, and the only time he did not pitch the entire game was one where the Dodgers won in 10 innings (Valenzuela pitched nine innings). Just mind-blowing. Of course, whether a rookie should have been as overworked as Valenzuela was is another story. Valenzuela ended the season with a record of 13–7 with an ERA of 2.48, led the league in starts (25), innings pitched (191 2/3), complete games (11), shutouts (8), and strikeouts (180). He was an All-Star, Rookie of the Year, Silver Slugger, finished fifth in MVP voting, and won the Cy Young Award. Amusingly, Valenzuela was unaware of who Cy Young was. He stated, "I do not know who he was, but a trophy carries his name, so he must be someone very special to baseball." Valenzuela was someone living the dream, and he was humbled by the adoration of the fans: "Having all the people from the Hispanic community, and really all the communities in Los Angeles, that gave me such a lift. . . . Knowing that the people are there waiting to see what could happen next, that's one of the things that I always enjoyed. People didn't expect anything, but to be able to see the emotion and the excitement when I had a great game, that's all I could ever ask for."

Largely because of Valenzuela, Los Angeles went streaking early in the season. They were 14–4 in April and 19–10 in May and led the NL West by 5 1/2 games. The team cooled off considerably from there, and on June 11, their lead had been cut to a half-game. Los Angeles was a good ballclub, but the Reds and Astros were arguably better. But something truly fortuitous happened to Los Angeles. There was a players' strike.

On June 12, the players struck over free agency. An agreement was not reached until August, with play resuming on the 10th of the month. MLB in their infinite wisdom decided that all teams leading their divisions on June 12 were automatically granted a place in the postseason. The first-half division winners would play the team that finished first in their division in the second half. Thus, the Dodgers were headed to the playoffs. That was fortunate because in the second half of the season, Los Angeles was decidedly average and ended up with a record of 27–26, fourth in the NL West. The Astros ended up winning the second-half NL West crown by 1 1/2 games over the Reds. As such, even though Cincinnati over both halves of the season not only had the best record in the NL West, not only the best record in the NL, but the best record in baseball, they did not make the playoffs. This is still a sore spot for Reds' fans today. Instead of the best team in baseball being in the NL West Division Series, it was a matchup between Los Angeles and Houston.

The *Washington Post* was less than enthused about the series, noting that the "Dodger-Astro series really is a showdown between two decimated teams. . . . The Dodgers are in worse shape. Their long-running, stand-pat infield finally has fallen apart from ceaseless use. Shortstop Bill Russell, nursing three injuries, returned to the lineup on Sunday. Dave Lopes will try to play for the first time in weeks in the playoff opener. Ron Cey still hasn't taken batting practice after suffering a broken forearm. He might be back by the league championship series. Once-great Reggie Smith now is a pinch hitter." As for Houston, one former Dodger would have been salivating at the chance to play against his old team, but Don Sutton suffered a season-ending injury ironically enough pitching against Los Angeles the last weekend of the regular season. Sutton was at the plate and squared up to bunt when a fastball from Jerry Reuss smashed into his kneecap. And with one pitch, Sutton would be a spectator for the rest of the season. Not surprisingly, Reuss denied deliberately trying to hit Sutton. Sutton gave Reuss the benefit of the doubt but did note that the pitch "was way inside, I had no chance."

After the first two games of the NLDS, it seemed that Houston would not miss the services of Sutton. The Astros won Game One, 3–1, thanks to a walk-off two-run homer from Alan Ashby. There were more walk-off heroics for Houston in Game Two. Heading into the bottom of the 11th, neither team had troubled the scorer. But with the bases loaded and two out, Denny Walling singled in the winning run. Two walk-off losses in a row would doom all but the most mentally tough teams. And while the 1981 Dodgers may not have been the best team in franchise history, they did have a never-say-die attitude. With the next three games in Los Angeles, the home team was hoping for an epic comeback. Aiding their cause was the fact that the Astros seemingly did not like playing in Los Angeles; they lost 11 of their last 13 at Dodger Stadium (although one of their wins was the one-game playoff the previous season to clinch the NL West crown). And where there is life, there is hope. In Game Three, the Dodgers scored three in the first through a Baker RBI double and a Garvey two-run home run and were never headed, winning, 6–1. Game Four was an outstanding pitching duel between Valenzuela and Vern Ruhle. Ruhle was superb, conceding only two runs on four hits across eight innings. Unfortunately for Houston, Valenzuela was better. He pitched a complete game, allowing four hits but crucially only conceding one run. The NLDS was tied. Taking the mound for Houston in the decider was future Hall of Famer Nolan Ryan, while thirty-two-year-old Jerry Reuss took the ball for Los Angeles. Both pitchers were on their game, although both teams squandered opportunities, and the game remained scoreless heading into the sixth. It was then that the Dodger bats, who were having an awful series, got hot. They scored three runs in the inning, knocking Ryan out of the game. Los Angeles would add another run in the seventh thanks to a Garvey triple. Houston was shocked, Los Angeles was jubilant, and Reuss was magnificent, pitching a five-hit shutout as the Dodgers won, 4–0.

Up next were the Montreal Expos in the NLCS. The Expos were in their first and, as history would show, only postseason in Montreal's history. After overcoming the Phillies in five games in the other NLDS and having home-field advantage, the Expos and the entire city of Montreal were salivating over a potential World Series appearance.

However, it was Los Angeles who dominated Game One. Home runs from Pedro Guerrero and Mike Scioscia, as well as a magnificent pitching performance from Hooton, saw the Dodgers easily take the opener, 5–1. With Valenzuela scheduled to start Game Two, Montreal was under enormous pressure. But Valenzuela did not have his best stuff, although he only conceded three runs in six innings of work. Yet the Dodger bats once again hibernated, mustering only five hits and only drawing two walks across nine innings. Ray Burris pitched a five-hitter as Montreal leveled the series with a 3–0 victory. Back in Montreal, it was the Expos riding high, while Lasorda was fuming. His anger was toward a newspaper columnist who claimed that the Dodgers were at a distinct disadvantage because they would be playing in Montreal's artcic conditions. Rick Monday recounted to author Jonah Keri what Lasorda did next: "'I don't want anyone wearing their jackets!' Tommy told us. So, we're introduced, we don't have our jackets, we're on the third-base line and they proceed to introduce all but two people even in attendance for the game. They introduced everybody, and all the while the boys from Hollywood are standing there, shivering. And we're thinking, 'Whose great idea is this?! It's cold!'" Although the Dodgers took a 1–0 lead in Game Three, a horrible bottom of the sixth ruined their chances. With two on and two out, Larry Parrish swung at the first pitch from Jerry Reuss and singled to left field, bringing home the tying run. Jerry White followed with a home run, and, with the Dodger hitters looking like they all had an extra shot of Nyquil to combat the cold, Montreal took Game Three, 4–1. Los Angeles was staring down the proverbial barrel. Montreal only had to take one of the two remaining games at home to secure their first-ever trip to the World Series. The Dodgers opened the scoring in Game Four in the third on Baker's RBI double, but Montreal tied the game in the bottom of the fourth. The game remained deadlocked until the top of the eighth. It then fell apart for Montreal. With a runner on first and one out, Garvey swung at the first pitch (a good approach; just ask Mr. October) and belted a two-run homer. There was further carnage in the top of the ninth as the Dodgers added four more runs and ran out winners, 7–1.

It would come down to a deciding fifth game on October 19. But because of arctic conditions, the game was postponed until the following day. The weather was still horrid when the teams took the field on what later was to be dubbed "Blue

Monday." Montreal opened the scoring in the first, and the party was seemingly just getting started for the Expos, but the Dodgers were the ultimate party poopers. They tied the score up with a Valenzuela groundout in the fifth. Ray Burris pitched magnificently for the Expos through eight but was pulled for a pinch-hitter in the bottom of the inning. In the ninth, the Expos did not turn to one of their relievers, but rather a starter, Steve Rogers. Rogers had not pitched in relief in three years. Years later, he told Keri that Montreal "sent me down to warm up in a spot I wasn't necessarily expecting. I was fine physically, but my adrenaline was pumping too hard. I didn't control it and I was overthrowing the sinker. Mechanically, I lost the angle. I just took the bad mechanics from the bullpen out to the mound. I was going to have a throw day on either the second or third day [after winning Game Three], so I mean, I could have thrown five innings if they needed it. Physically and mentally at least, I was fine." Rogers retired the first two Dodgers. This brought up Rick Monday. On a 3-1 count, Monday made some nice contact. The ball just kept on going until it cleared the center-field fence. The Dodgers were in the lead. Valenzuela was looking for a complete game, but with two outs in the ninth, he lost his command and walked two batters. Lasorda pulled him and brought in Bob Welch. Jerry White swung at the first pitch and grounded out. Los Angeles was World Series bound. As for the Expos, they would never appear in the postseason again, and to say some of their players were bitter is a huge understatement. Outfielder Tim Raines remarked to Keri that "We probably had the best team in baseball. No, we did have the best team in baseball that year. We'd have kicked the Yankees' ass that year. If the Dodgers beat them, we'd have probably swept them. We had the team." The Expos may have been *the* team, they may have been better than the Dodgers, but all that mattered was that Los Angeles did not wilt under the pressure. And because of that, they were heading to the World Series.

THE YANKEES' 1981 SEASON

After the Yankees were swept by the Royals in the first round of playoffs in 1980, one knew that there would be changes. There was one player that Steinbrenner wanted above all others—outfielder Dave Winfield. Winfield had spent a wonderful eight years in a Padres uniform, never gracing the minor leagues with his presence. Steinbrenner thought Winfield in pinstripes would be magical. Winfield recounted that "he wanted me at any cost, and it resulted in an incredible courtship, with George at his most charming. Flowers, Broadway shows, dinner at the 21 Club, chauffeured limousines. Even telegrams in the middle of the night . . . 'We want you in New York.'"

Winfield signed a ten-year deal with New York that included cost-of-living increases. Almost as soon as the ink was dry, Steinbrenner started to regret the deal. Steinbrenner seemingly never considered how much the cost-of-living increases would add up to. The contract was renegotiated in New York's favor, and a buyout after eight years was now included even before Winfield put on the pinstripes. To paraphrase Van Halen, the relationship turned tragic just like magic often does. Nevertheless, Winfield had a very good season. He led the team in hits, doubles, RBIs, OBP, and OPS. However, for as good as Winfield was as a Yankee, Steinbrenner never got over the fact he was unable to grasp the complexity of Winfield's contract. Murray Chass, writing in the *New York Times* in 2001, noted "Steinbrenner, who did so much to make Winfield's life miserable in the eight-plus years he played for the Yankees, never appreciated the type of player he had. All he did was look at Winfield's hitting statistics. When they lacked lusty numbers, he criticized Winfield. Unlike players and managers from other teams, Steinbrenner never understood the contributions Winfield made with his outfield defense and his base running." Considering his time as a Yankee was not the most pleasant, and even though Steinbrenner did try to make amends for his actions, it was not surprising that when Winfield was elected to the Hall of Fame, he wanted to go in as a San Diego Padre.

Despite Steinbrenner's misgivings and even self-sabotage (he paid a gambler $40,000 to try to find dirt on Winfield), New York was a better team with Dave Winfield. Just like they were with another Dave: Dave Righetti. Righetti was drafted 10th by the Texas Rangers in January 1977. The Rangers also drafted Dave's brother, Steve. Dave was the star, while Steve was drafted in the sixth round. A member of the Rangers told Dave that "if you don't sign this contract, I'm not going to sign your brother. The only way he's going to get a shot is with a package deal." Dave duly signed. Righetti had big-league potential from the get-go; as such, it was somewhat of a surprise that he was included in a November 1978 ten-man trade between the Rangers and the Yankees. Righetti excelled in the minors, and he was a late-season call-up in 1979, appearing in three games. Nineteen eighty was not his best year, as he stayed in the minors and struggled somewhat. However, a strong start in 1981 saw his promotion to pinstripes in late May. He excelled with New

York, winning his first four games (he was credited with three wins), while only conceding six runs. He finished the season with a record of 8–4 and an ERA of 2.05 on the way to being named Rookie of the Year. Righetti never reached those same heights as a starter, although he pitched a no-hitter in 1983. He was then converted to a closer and enjoyed 16 years in the majors, twice being named an All-Star. Following his retirement as a player, Righetti eventually became a pitching coach with the Giants from 2000 until 2017.

Calling up Righetti when they did may have meant the difference between making the playoffs and missing out altogether. On May 23, the day of his first start, New York was two games out of first. By June 11, he had made four starts, and, as noted above, the Yankees won all four games. They had a two-game lead in the division. Of course, there was the players' strike, and, as with Los Angeles, because New York led their division, they were granted an automatic playoff spot. And that was very fortunate because the Yankees were mediocre in the second half of the season; they finished sixth with a record of 25–26. But none of that mattered. New York was heading to the playoffs, although with a recently installed manager.

Following the relative success of the 1980 Yankees, manager Dick Howser had every right to be satisfied. But, like New York managers before and after him, he was not happy with Steinbrenner's constant interference. Steinbrenner also was not happy that Howser used to hang up on him and was embarrassed that the Royals had swept the Yankees in the playoffs. Thus, Howser jumped before he was pushed (or may well have been pushed), and in was Gene Michael. Michael played 10 years in the majors, including stints with both the Yankees and Dodgers.

Following the end of his playing days, he became a coach with the Yankees and was their Triple-A manager in 1979 and GM in 1980. With Michael in charge, New York had a winning record and was heading to the playoffs, but he was getting annoyed at Steinbrenner's interference as well as the boss's criticism of his performance. Michael had had enough and told Steinbrenner to stop interfering or fire him. On September 6, Steinbrenner fired him. And back in the hot seat was Lemon. New York had a losing record under Lemon (11–14), but it did not matter. The Yankees were heading to the ALDS to face the Milwaukee Brewers.

The Brewers had a decent first half, finishing third in the AL East. They were even better in the second half, winning the division by 1 1/2 games. Considering how New York played in the second half, and that there was a managerial change, the Brewers were the team with momentum. However, as we have seen, momentum is fleeting. In Game One in Milwaukee, the Brewers held a two-run lead heading into the fourth. The Yankee bats then got hot, and they scored four runs in the fourth, eventually hanging on for a 5–3 victory. Piniella hit a solo homer in the fourth, and Jackson added a two-run blast in the ninth as the Yankees won Game Two, 3–0. Righetti pitched six scoreless innings, and Gossage pitched 2 2/3 innings for the save. The series then headed to New York, but even though the Yankees had home-field advantage and "momentum," it was the Brewers' turn to win two in a row. They beat the Yankees, 5–3, in Game Three, with all their runs coming in the seventh and eighth. New York starting pitcher Tommy John was left in too long. He gave up two runs in the seventh, but rather than being pulled, he was allowed to start the eighth, where he promptly gave up a home run to the leadoff hitter. Not smart managing. In Game Four, Milwaukee won a pitchers' duel, 2–1, as New York was an inglorious 0-for-7 with runners in scoring position. Thus, it came down to Game Five. Milwaukee had a two-run lead heading into the fourth, only for the lead to evaporate as New York added a four-spot thanks to back-to-back homers by Jackson and Oscar Gamble. The Yankees wound up winning, 7–3. Up next, the Oakland Athletics, managed by Billy Martin, in the ALCS.

While the Yankees struggled to overcome the Brewers in the ALDS, the Athletics swept the Royals. The A's also had a better regular-season record and home-field advantage in the ALCS. All signs pointed to the Athletics advancing to the World Series. It did not quite work out that way. In Game One, New York scored three runs in the first as Nettles cleared the bases with a double. That ended the Yankees' scoring for the day, but it was more than enough, as John was solid through six, only conceding a run. Ron Davis and Gossage combined for three scoreless innings in relief, with the latter picking up the save as New York won, 3–1. In Game Two, New York once again opened the scoring in the bottom of the first, this time through a Jackson RBI groundout. Oakland tied the game in the third before adding two more runs in the fourth. Though once again, their half of the fourth would prove kind to New York. No, they did not add a four-spot; this time, they scored seven runs. RBI singles by Randolph and Larry Milbourne, a two-run double by Winfield, and a three-run homer by Piniella doomed Oakland. New York wound up winning, 13–3, in a massacre. The series then headed to Oakland, and Game Three was a pitchers' duel. Righetti was great for New York, going six scoreless innings. It was the Yankees who opened the scoring in the sixth, thanks to a home run from an unlikely source, Willie Randolph. The second baseman, never a power threat, only hit two homers all season, but on October 15, 1981, his home run put New York in the lead. New York clung to a one-run lead until the ninth. In the top of the inning, just like in Game One, Nettles smacked a bases-clearing double. New York led, 4–0, and Gossage made relatively short work of the Athletics in the bottom of the inning. Oakland was shell-shocked, while New York was in party mode as the Yankees were heading to yet another World Series. On a side note, October 15 was a great day for the Yankees, but a horrible day for the rest of the world. It was at Game Three in Oakland that "The Wave" first appeared. Krazy George Henderson, a professional cheerleader, was the man behind it. And the world was slightly worse off from that point forward.

THE 1981 WORLD SERIES

New York had home-field advantage for the fall classic and was facing the Dodgers, who, as we have seen, almost always lost the Big One. The Yankees had just swept the Athletics, while Los Angeles had a very tough series against the Expos. One advantage in the Dodgers' favor was that Reggie Jackson, Mr. October himself, was battling a calf injury and would miss the first three games of the Series.

Jerry Reuss was handed the ball for the Dodgers in Game One, while Guidry took the mound for the Yankees. And the game was effectively over after one inning. Guidry had no trouble getting through the first inning. This was not the case for Reuss. With a runner on first and two out, Piniella hit a ground-rule double. Up to the plate stepped thirty-five-year-old Bob Watson. In his second year in pinstripes, the veteran first baseman had a season to forget, hitting .212 with an OPS of .701. However, on this night in the Bronx, Watson relived his glory days by just clearing the fence for a three-run-blast. New York added another run in the third via a Piniella RBI single and another one in the fourth when Winfield drew a bases-loaded walk. Los Angeles came back with a Yeager solo shot in the fifth and two runs in the eighth, but it was a dead cat bounce. Guidry picked up the win and Gossage the save as New York took the opener, 5–3. It was a great start for New York, while Los Angeles players may well have been getting flashbacks to their horrid times at Yankee Stadium during the 1977 and 1978 World Series.

Game Two did not help in that regard. Burt Hooton tossed six innings of one-run ball for the Dodgers, the lone run coming from a Larry Milbourne RBI double. As good as Hooton was, John was even better. While pitching the Yankees to a win was undoubtedly at the forefront of his mind, that Los Angeles's management did not seemingly wanted to keep him around added extra motivation for John to do well. And that he did. John went seven innings, striking out four while only allowing three hits. Gossage pitched the final two innings for the save as New York won, 3–0. Los Angeles only had four hits and one walk for the game. Their bats were just not just cold, but totally iced over. Rather than trying to work the count, Dodgers hitters swung early and often. It was a horrible approach. But as horrible as they were, John and Gossage were superb. On a night where hits were at a premium (New York only managed six), the Yankees, as was often the case in World Series games against the Dodgers, pitched, hit, and fielded better. New York took the first two games of the fall classic, and Los Angeles's only hope was if the warmer climate of sunny California would result in the thawing of their bats.

Eager to keep the Dodgers' bats ice cold was Righetti. His opposite number, fellow rookie Valenzuela, was hoping to keep Los Angeles in the Series. Fernando walked two in the first, but a double play got him out of the inning. As mediocre as Valenzuela was in the first, Righetti was downright awful in the bottom of the frame. Lopes doubled to lead off the inning, and Russell bunted for a single, moving Lopes to third. Righetti came back to get the next two hitters. He then battled Cey. After seven pitches, the count was 2-2. Number eight would be lucky for Cey and the Dodgers. A towering home run to left field put Los Angeles up by three. However, as average as Valenzuela was in the first, he was worse in the second and third. Watson opened the second inning with a leadoff homer, and Rick Cerone followed with a double. Cerone later scored on a single by Milbourne. In the third, with a man on first, Cerone did even better, launching a ball into the stands on a 1-0 count. All of a sudden New York had a 4–3 lead. Yet, rather than pull Valenzuela, which was the obvious move, Lasorda kept faith in him. While Valenzuela later noted that he convinced Lasorda to keep him out there, the Dodgers manager had a different, and perhaps revisionist, recollection. He told ESPN baseball writer Tony Jackson that "everybody thought I was going to take him out. . . . A lot of people wanted me to take him out. But I knew him. He loved to pitch out of jams. He used to pitch like he didn't know we had a bullpen. He didn't like to come out of games. A lot of guys, when they get in trouble, they're looking down there for help. But not him."

While Lasorda kept Valenzuela in, Lemon quickly pulled Righetti after the first two Dodgers reached in the third. George Frazier was brought in and got the Yankees out of the inning unscathed. New York clung to their one-run lead until the bottom of the fifth. The first two Dodgers reached, but rather than pulling Frazier, Lemon kept the faith. It was misplaced. Pedro Guerrero doubled, tying the game. Following an intentional walk to load the bases with none out, Frazier was pulled. Rudy May came in and induced a double play, but the runner from third scored. The Dodgers had the lead. New York's best chance to tie the game came in the eighth. The first two Yankees reached base, but Lasorda once again stayed with Valenzuela. He was rewarded when pinch-hitter Bobby Murcer tried to bunt. Rather than advancing the runners, he hit into a pop-fly double play. Randolph then grounded out on a 3-1 count to end the inning. New York went quietly in the ninth. The Dodgers won, 5–4, with Valenzuela somehow picking up the win in a complete game where he gave up nine hits and seven walks. He was helped by New York's pitiful 1-for-10 with runners in scoring position. The Dodgers were not much better, going 3-for-13, but it was enough.

Following the top of the third in Game Four, Los Angeles was seemingly once again down and out. Starter Bob Welch could not record an out. The Yankees opened the game by going triple, double, walk, and single. Welch was out, and Dave Goltz was in. Somehow, despite all the early carnage, New York only scored two runs in the inning. Not to worry, they added a run through a Randolph solo shot in the second, and another run in the third, but they did leave the bases loaded. Still, New York had a comfortable 4–0 lead. It was a little less comfortable following the bottom half of the inning as Los Angeles scored twice through some small ball. New York once again left the bases loaded in the fourth. Keep doing this, and the baseball gods get angry. And they took their revenge as Cey cut the margin to one in the fifth with an RBI single. The gods were seemingly appeased when the Yankees added two more in the top of the sixth for a three-run lead. Yet they were about to reap their vengeance on New York and make Los Angeles smile. In the bottom of the inning with one out, Mike Scioscia walked. Up came pinch-hitter Jay Johnstone. Johnstone only hit .205 for the year, collecting all of 17 hits. Yet on October 24, 1981, he was a Dodger legend, smashing a 1-2 pitch to right-center to cut the margin to one. The Dodgers, though, were not yet done. Lopes reached on a two-base error by Jackson (Mr. October was back in the lineup and was having a great day with the bat, but not the glove). Lopes promptly stole third and was brought home on Russell's RBI single. The game was tied at 6. The seventh would bring the Dodgers more joy. With George Frazier on the mound, they started the inning by going single, double, and intentional walk to load the bases with no one out. Frazier was then out of the game and having a fall classic to forget. The Dodgers then appeased the gods by not leaving the bases loaded. A Yeager sacrifice fly and a Lopes RBI single saw the home team lead by two. Mr. October kept New York in the contest by belting a solo shot in the eighth, but he was not given another opportunity to bat as Los Angeles barely held on, winning a true roller coaster of a game, 8–7. The World Series was tied at two wins apiece.

Game Five was more of a traditional baseball contest: low scoring with hits few and far between. Guidry was on the mound for the visitors and Reuss for the home side. It was New York that opened the scoring. Jackson led off the second inning with a ground-rule double. He moved to third following an error by Lopes that put Watson on first. Lopes had a horrible day with the glove. He may have been channeling Dem Bums of a bygone era, as he had three errors for the game (and six for the entire fall classic). Piniella singled Jackson home, and New York had the lead. A double-play ball and a groundout would end the inning. The Yankees clung onto the lead until the seventh. Guidry was great, only giving up two hits and two walks and was in cruise control. But a crash was about to occur. With one out, and the Dodgers' chances of staging a comeback dwindling, Guerrero belted an 0-1 pitch for a solo shot to tie the game. If one is good, two is better; at least from the Dodgers' perspective. Yeager now stepped to the plate. And on a 1-2 pitch, he hit a solo shot of his own. Los Angeles took the lead. And that ended the scoring for the day. The Dodgers won, 2–1. Reuss pitched a gem, giving up only five hits and three walks, while striking out six on the way to a complete game. Los Angeles was only one win away from World Series glory, but they would have to do it in Yankee Stadium.

And it seemed they would have to do so without Cey. In the eighth inning of Game Five, Gossage threw a ball up and in to the third baseman. Cey could not get out of way of the pitch in time, with the ball smashing into his helmet. Gossage was understandably shaken up over the pitch. He told the *New York Times*, "Nobody wants to hurt anybody. . . . You want to win at every expense. But not that expense." Luckily, Cey only had a concussion. He should not have played in Game Six, but concussion protocol not being the same back then as it is today, he was declared fit. And he took his place in the Dodgers' lineup.

While Cey escaped the beaning with a concussion, there was another injury, but not to a player. Following Game Five, Steinbrenner held a hastily arranged press conference during the wee hours of the morning. The Yankees boss told the assembled media that he got into a brawl with two Dodgers fans in an elevator at the Hyatt-Wilshire Hotel in Los Angeles. As a result of the fight, Steinbrenner broke his thumb, and it was in a cast. He claimed, "I was coming down the elevator to have dinner. . . . There were two people, one in the elevator and one holding the door. One had a beer in his hand. Then he said some things about New York City and the people who live there. The next thing I knew he hit me. I'm getting too old for that. I don't condone that sort of thing. I get tired once in a while of people knocking New York. The fight was started not by me." He further added that "there are two guys in this town looking for their teeth and two guys who will probably sue me." Certainly an amazing story, but like many, a story not necessarily grounded in reality. Steinbrenner claimed that the two men were in their twenties, but the Yankees boss was such a fighting machine, he got the better of them. Also, the two men have never been arrested or even identified. Maybe, just maybe, instead of a knock-em-down brawl in an elevator, Steinbrenner broke his thumb hitting a wall or something like that in anger over the Yankees dropping three straight. Whatever happened that night, Steinbrenner took the truth with him to the grave.

Trying to keep New York in the World Series was John, while Hooton was trying to lead Los Angeles to October glory in front of a hostile crowd in Game Six. Steinbrenner must have been pleased when the Yankees opened the scoring in the third through a Randolph solo shot. Yet Los Angeles came right back in the top of the fourth with Yeager driving a run home on an RBI single. And it all fell apart for the Yankees in the bottom of the inning. With a runner on second and two out, the Dodgers elected to intentionally walk Milbourne to bring up the pitcher's spot. Lemon decided to pinch hit for John. Pinch-hitter Bobby Murcer just missed hitting one out, inning over. To say that John was irate about being pulled so early was an understatement; he screamed at Lemon in the dugout. Lemon then decided to bring in George Frazier, who was having a rough World Series and was already charged with two losses. It would soon be three. Lopes led off with a single and moved to second on a sacrifice bunt. Frazier got Garvey to fly out for the second out. This brought up Cey, still feeling the effects of the concussion suffered in Game Five. Concussion or not, Cey swung at the first pitch and singled to center, scoring Lopes and giving the Dodgers the lead. Baker followed with a single of his own, moving Cey to third. They both scored on Guerrero's triple, making it 4–1. The Dodgers were riding high. Los Angeles added four more runs in the sixth, and a solo shot by Guerrero in the eighth was the cherry on top as Los Angeles defeated New York, 9–2. The Los Angeles Dodgers were World Series champions. As Russell told *Sports Illustrated*, "It was a silent feeling that this might be our last chance [for the famed Dodgers infield of Garvey, Lopes, Russell, and Cey]. We didn't mention it, but it was there. I'm glad it was against the Yankees. Not that we felt we owed them one, but it was just nice. Of course, we're too old to win it. We're over the hill. We've only been doing it for eight years. I think we dispelled any doubts."

Rather than just simply congratulate the Dodgers, Steinbrenner issued an apology for the Yankees' World Series performance. He wrote, "I want to sincerely apologize to the people of New York and to the fans of the New York Yankees everywhere for the performance of the Yankee team in the World Series. I also want to assure you that we will be at work immediately to prepare for 1982. I want also to extend my congratulations to Peter O'Malley and the Dodger organization—and to my friend, Tom Lasorda, who managed a superb season, playoffs and a brilliant World Series." The apology did not sit well with many players from both teams. Dodgers players thought Steinbrenner should have just simply congratulated them. As for the Yankees, Jackson chimed in by saying, "I guess you'll be reading a lot of propaganda from George in the next few days. I mean, we made it to the World Series. Are we supposed to do time because we lost?" Indeed, the Yankees were only a few short years past going back-to back. They had nothing to apologize for, and another World Series title was surely just right around the corner, right? As for the Dodgers, they could savor the moment. They were a good team, but a long way from a great one. However, the playoffs are often random, and Los Angeles got hot at the right time and refused to give in when they were seemingly down and out in all three of their playoff series. To defeat New York in Yankee Stadium must have been extrasweet for those players and Lasorda, who suffered through the back-to-back losses in 1977 and 1978. Little did anyone know that it would be a long time before there was another Dodgers-Yankees game; and as of this writing, October 28, 1981 was the last time the two teams would play each other in the World Series.

13

INTERLEAGUE PLAY AND SOME CONCLUDING THOUGHTS

FOLLOWING THEIR WORLD Series triumph, Los Angeles had a few more opportunities to go to the fall classic during the 1980s. However, in both 1983 and 1985, the Dodgers lost in the NLCS. They would have to wait until 1988 for the next World Series berth. Their World Series victory over the Oakland Athletics that year will always be remembered for Orel Hershiser's dominant pitching performance and Kirk Gibson's walk-off homer in Game One. Every Dodgers fan can still recall Vin Scully's call of the home run; "High fly ball into right field, she is gone! In a year that has been so improbable, the impossible has happened." One reason why the home run is so memorable is that it was the highlight of the Dodgers' last World Series victory to date. The storied Los Angeles Dodgers did not even make it back to the World Series until 2017, when they lost in seven games to the Houston Astros. In light of the Astros' sign-stealing scandal, all Dodger fans, players, and the organization as a whole cannot help but think they were cheated out of a World Series title. Nevertheless, in the great Dodger tradition, they followed up a World Series loss with another World Series loss, this time in 2018, to the Red Sox, who are also under investigation for cheating during the regular season

While Los Angeles had a fairly successful 1980s, the Yankees never once made it to the playoffs after the World Series loss and were often total afterthoughts in the AL East. Indeed, New York did not appear in the playoffs until 1995, when they lost to the Mariners in five in the ALDS. That was, however, just a very small taste of what was to come. Three World Series victories in four years ended the 1990s on a fantastic note. The new millennium would also prove kind: two World Series triumphs, four World Series appearances, and making the playoffs in every year of the 2000s except in 2008. The 2010s would not be as good to the proud franchise. No World Series appearances, with the closest coming in 2017, when they lost in seven in the ALCS to the Astros. The closest we have come to another Dodgers-Yankees World Series matchup was in 2017. Considering Los Angeles lost to the Astros, it was not only the Yankees wishing that they made it to the fall classic.

While there has yet to be a Dodgers-Yankees World Series game since 1981, beginning in the new millennium, there have been a number of interleague games between the two teams. Interleague play was introduced by MLB in 1997, yet in their infinite wisdom, the first time New York was matched up against Los Angeles was not until 2004.

2004: THREE-GAME SERIES AT DODGER STADIUM

One could argue that the most logical venue for the first interleague meeting between New York and Los Angles would be Yankee Stadium, the sight of so many of their great battles. Instead, MLB decided to send the Yankees to California. I could wax lyrically about how both teams and their respective fans were riding on every pitch, the electricity so thick you could cut it with a knife, and so on. And while it was cool that the Yankees were playing the Dodgers, the reality is it was just another regular season game; the series was just three out of 162. On June 18, Dodgers starter Jeff Weaver threw the first competitive pitch between the two teams since 1981. The Yankees opened the scoring in the third by plating three, but the Dodgers leveled it in the fourth through a run-scoring wild pitch and a two-run single from current Dodgers manager Dave Roberts. Los Angeles would eventually take the opener, 6–3. In the second game, New York scored four in the first with the big blow being a three-run shot by Hideki Matsui on an 0-2 pitch off his fellow countryman Hideo Nomo. While Nomo homered himself in the fifth, New York was never headed, winning, 6–2. The final game of the series was the most interesting and nerve-racking. The Dodgers scored four times in the second including a leadoff homer from Shawn Green. New York rallied with back-to-back home runs from Matsui and Miguel Cairo at the start of the third inning. Matsui further cut the lead in the seventh through an RBI triple, but the Dodgers came straight back in the bottom of the inning courtesy of a Roberts RBI double. Los Angeles's All-Star closer Eric Gagne faced the heart of the Yankee order in the ninth. Jason Giambi opened proceedings with a solo shot to cut the lead to one. Gagne made short work of Gary Shef-field and Jorge Posada. Up stepped Matsui. After a seven-pitch battle, Gagne struck him out. Los Angeles won the game, 5–4, and took the series. The next matchup between the two teams would not take place for another six years.

2010: THE BROXTON GAME

The Yankees returned to Dodger Stadium for a three-game series in June 2010. Once again, MLB thought it was better to send the Yankees to sunny California rather than the Dodgers back to New York. Adding a tiny bit of spice to the series is that Los Angeles was now managed by Joe Torre, who had led the Yankees to six pennants and four world championships.

The first game was a tight affair with Manny Ramirez opening the scoring in the bottom of the first with an RBI single, but New York tied it up in the second with a Posada single driving in Alex Rodriguez, who opened the inning with a double. A-Rod would later homer in the sixth as New York took the opener, 2–1. CC Sabathia only gave up four hits in eight innings while picking up the win, and Mariano Rivera stuck out the side in the ninth, earning the save.

The second game saw the Yankees jump out to an early lead thanks to a three-run blast from Mark Teixeira in the first. However, Los Angeles scored two in the bottom of the inning. And while New York scored another in the third, their lead was not to last. The Dodgers plated three in the bottom of the inning to take the lead. They piled on more runs in the fourth and the seventh and cruised to an easy 9–4 victory. Considering the score and that he was hardly underworked, Dodgers closer

Jonathan Broxton was brought in to record the final four outs. And this leads us to what has become known as Broxton Game.

The third game was broadcast live on ESPN on *Sunday Night Baseball*. The Dodgers led, 6–2, heading into the top of the ninth. Even though it was not a save situation, and he was overworked, Torre brought in Broxton. It was Broxton's fourth appearance in five days. To say that Broxton had nothing in the tank is a vast understatement. While he retired the first batter, it then became brutal. When all was said and done, Broxton got all three outs, but not before allowing four runs to score and throwing 48 pitches. It was just cruel. The Yankees ended up winning it in 10 innings, 8–6, on Robinson Cano's two-run homer off George Sherrill. While the final score was 8–6, to this day all that is remembered is that Torre left Broxton out on the mound to wither and die. Torre must have had his reasons for keeping Broxton on the mound, but whatever they were, the reality is that Broxton was never the same again. He quickly went from an elite closer to a good-to-average reliever.

2013: THE DODGERS RETURN TO NEW YORK

Finally, in 2013, the Dodgers returned to New York to play the Yankees. But the baseball gods were still angry at MLB for waiting so long to schedule an interleague meeting between the two teams. The first game scheduled on June 18 was rained out. As such, there was a doubleheader scheduled for the next day. The Dodgers' manager was former Yankee great Don Mattingly, while taking the mound for the Yankees in the first game was former Dodger Hiroki Kuroda. And Kuroda was brilliant, going 6 2/3 innings while only giving up one run. New York won,

6–4, with Ichiro Suzuki going 3-for-4, scoring twice, driving in three, and hitting a solo shot, to boot. In the second game of the doubleheader, the Dodgers scored twice in the first and were never headed, winning, 6–0. Yasiel Puig homered, while the Yankees could only muster three hits.

For the first time in interleague play between the two teams, there was a series in each city. On July 30, New York headed to Los Angeles. Both starting pitchers, Zack Greinke for the Dodgers and Andy Pettitte for the Yankees, gave up two runs apiece in seven innings. The score was deadlocked going into the bottom of the ninth. With Mark Ellis at the plate and two out, Andre Ethier stole second. That was to prove decisive, as on a 3-2 count, Ellis singled to center, scoring Ethier. It was the most dramatic Dodgers victory against the Yankees since 1981, albeit on a much smaller scale. Not be outdone, New York had their own theatrical victory the following night. The game was scoreless heading to the ninth. Clayton Kershaw was superb for the Dodgers, while Kuroda was equally strong for New York. Mattingly replaced Kershaw for the ninth, and that was all she wrote. Derek Jeter led off the inning with a walk. With two out, the Dodgers intentionally walked Ichiro. Paco Rodriguez then came in, and it was a dumpster fire. Lyle Overbay singled, scoring a run. Then both Ichiro and Overbay scored on an error by second baseman Mark Ellis. Rivera made short work of Los Angeles in the bottom of the inning as New York won, 3–0, and split the four games in two cities between the teams.

2016: BACK TO YANKEE STADIUM

Shockingly, MLB realized that bringing the Dodgers to New York was a good idea. Thus, the Dodgers were back where it all began to play a three-game series against the Yankees. The first game was a blowout as Los Angeles piled on the runs early, winning, 8–2, getting home runs from Yasiel Puig and Justin Turner. While the Dodgers bats were nuclear, the next day they were ice cold. Los Angeles only managed five hits and went 0-for-5 with runners in scoring position. New York was not much better, collecting eight hits while failing to get a hit with a runner in scoring position in two tries. But New York had some power; Jacoby Ellsbury and Didi Gregorius hit back-to-back solo shots in the seventh, while Gary Sanchez led off the eighth with a solo shot of his own as the Yankees won, 3–0. In the final game of the three-game set, both teams' bats were no longer ice cold; they were totally frozen. New York only had three hits, while the Dodgers had four. New York was 0-for-6 with runners in scoring position, the Dodgers were 1-for-6. Neither team bothered to trouble the scorer until the top of the ninth. Corey Seager reached on an error to open the inning, stole second, and was brought home on Turner's RBI double. With two out, Turner scored on another error. Kenley Jansen picked up the save, and Los Angeles took the game, 2–0, and won the series.

2019: WHAT COULD HAVE BEEN

Three years later, the Yankees were back to Dodger Stadium for a three-game series. However, unlike almost all interleague games, this series took on extra importance, as both Los Angeles and New York were running away with their respective division titles and had the two best records in baseball; as such, there was more than one article touting this as a potential World Series matchup. The first game was a rout. New York opened the scoring in the third through home runs by Aaron Judge and Gary Sanchez. Los Angeles got one back in the bottom of the inning, but Didi Gregorius blasted a grand slam in the top of the fifth, and the game was effectively over. For good measure, Gregorius hit a solo shot in the ninth as the Yankees destroyed the Dodgers, 10–2. Los Angeles's offense was equally bad in the second game, once again only managing two runs. A two-run blast from Justin Turner in the fourth did the damage. Yet New York hitters were worse. Aaron Judge homered for their only run an inning later. Jansen picked up the save by striking out Sanchez with the bases loaded to send the home crowd happy (although there were a lot of Yankees fans present). In the third game of the series, the Dodgers offense was even worse, managing only one run on five hits. New York were better in that they picked up eight hits; three were home runs. The Yankees won, 5–1. Before the game, Judge promised an elderly fan that he would homer. And Judge did exactly that. In the sixth inning, Judge destroyed a hanging Kershaw curveball for a solo shot.

SOME CONCLUDING THOUGHTS

In the preface, I posed the following questions: Were the Yankees so much better than the Dodgers? Were the Dodgers "chokers" when it mattered most? Or was it simply the case that the baseball gods were actually malevolent and favored the team that would be later known to its detractors as the Evil Empire over the boys in blue? As we have seen throughout the book, the New York Yankees were favored by the baseball gods, lied, cheated, and stole World Series crowns from the Dodgers, whether the Brooklyn or Los Angeles team, and were basically undeserving of all the titles when they beat the Dodgers. I did write the preceding sentence with a smile on my face. The reality is that the Yankees were not favored by the baseball gods or any other mythical beings. Nor did they cheat, although whether Reggie Jackson's use of his hip in the 1978 fall classic could go into the cheating category is open to debate. The men in pinstripes were simply that much better than the boys in blue when it mattered most. Their starting pitchers usually went deeper into games, and their bats got the crucial hits when it mattered most; as we have seen, the Dodgers' inability to hit with runners in scoring position became almost a running joke in a number of World Series games. In addition to what was happening on the field, Yankees managers often got the best of their Dodger counterparts. All these things combined put New York at a great advantage. These things can account for why the Yankees beat the Dodgers again and again. By contrast, the Dodgers were triumphant when they had great starting pitching from the likes of Johnny Podres, Sandy Koufax, and Don Drysdale, or almost the entire 1981 pitching staff. In 1981, they also greatly benefited from Lasorda outmanaging Lemon.

There was another reason why the Yankees had a better record in the World Series: George Steinbrenner. With the advent of free agency, the Yankees' owner realized that spending money to acquire the top free agents greatly increased the chances a team would not only make the postseason, but win it all. This lesson has seemingly been forgotten today by most. While the Yankees spent big in both 1977 and 1978 to acquire Reggie Jackson amongst others, the Dodgers' foray in free agency was a disaster. If you are going to spend money on free agents, you should first ensure that they be good. And while not every free agent signing worked, Dave Winfield in the 1981 World Series being a prime example, it may well have been the difference between two additional World Series titles in New York instead of Los Angeles. Spending money paid off for the Dodgers in 1981: they outbid the Yankees for the services of Fernando Valenzuela. He was instrumental in not only getting Los Angeles to the postseason (without his hot start, it would have been the Reds and not the Dodgers in the NLDS), but in making the World Series and winning it all. Spending money on quality players pays off.

All these things combined added up to why the Yankees defeated the Dodgers in eight of the eleven World Series matchups. In the end, the Yankees were just that damn good.

ACKNOWLEDGMENTS

THANK YOU TO everyone at Sports Publishing. A special shout-out to my editor, Jason Katzman, who has been a joy to work with. Likewise, copy editor Ken Samelson and proofreader Bob Mitchell for making the manuscript readable.

The only other people I would like to thank are my wife, Su Lan, and our daughter, Valentina. Writing a book is often a very lonely experience. However, knowing that they are in my life always makes me smile and brings me joy. This book would not have been possible without them. My wife and daughter provide me with the inspiration to write. As such, I dedicate the book to them.

BIBLIOGRAPHICAL NOTES

BOTH THIS BOOK and I owe a debt of gratitude to *Baseball Reference* (baseball-reference.com). The people behind it are the true custodians of the game, and I cannot thank them enough. Quite simply, they made my job much easier than it would have otherwise been. Likewise, the *New York Times* and *Los Angeles Times* archives were invaluable. That their archives are available on the Internet saved me hundreds of hours of research. I must make mention of *Sports Illustrated*. It was through them that I realized how powerful the written word could be. The tremendous Society for American Baseball Research Baseball Biography Project (https://sabr.org/bioproject) is a treasure trove of information. The biographies of thousands of players, owners, and officials is breathtaking in scope. From Hank Aaron to Bob Zuk, everyone of note in the baseball world is covered. Arguably the best in an amazing collection is David Krell's entry on Joe Pepitone (sabr.org/bioproj/person/99cb58c9#_ednref9). It is a brilliant piece of writing. As soon as you finish this book, go read Pepitone's biography.

There is a long, fine tradition of books on the history of the New York Yankees. Two of the best are Marty Appel's *Pinstripe Empire: The New York Yankees from Before the Babe to After the Boss* (Bloomsbury USA, 2012) and *New York Times Story of the Yankees: 382 Articles, Profiles and Essays from 1903 to Present* (Black Dog & Leventhal, 2012). Roger Kahn's *The Era, 1947-1957: When the Yankees, the Giants, and the Dodgers Ruled the World* (Diversion Books, 2014) is a wonderful book looking at the Yankees' domination of that time period. Another book looking at that time period is David Fischer's *The New York Yankees of the 1950s: Mantle, Stengel, Berra, and a Decade of Dominance* (Lyons Press, 2019). For a great overview of the Yankees and the very tumultuous 1977 season and of New York in general, one should read Jonathan Mahler's *Ladies and Gentlemen, the Bronx Is Burning: 1977, Baseball, Politics, and the Battle for the Soul of a City* (Picador, 2006).

One could list hundreds of autobiographies and biographies on Yankees legends. Three in the top tier are Marty Appel, *Casey Stengel: Baseball's Greatest Character* (Doubleday, 2017); Jane Leavy, *The Last Boy: Mickey Mantle and the End of America's Childhood* (Harper, 2010); and Bill Pennington, *Billy Martin: Baseball's Flawed Genius* (Houghton Mifflin Harcourt, 2015). Of course, every baseball fan should read *Ball Four: The Final Pitch* (Turner, 2014) by Jim Bouton. Bouton's tell-all book is still a classic today.

Glenn Stout and Richard A. Johnson's history of the Dodgers, *The Dodgers: 120 Years of Dodger Baseball* (Houghton Mifflin Harcourt, 2004), is a fountain of information. For those seeking an oral history of the Los Angeles Dodgers up to 2001, Steve Delsohn has you covered in *True Blue: The Dramatic History of the Los Angeles Dodgers, Told by the Men Who Lived It* (Harper Perennial, 2002). Likewise, Peter Golenbock's *Bums: An Oral History of the Brooklyn Dodgers* (Dover Publications, 2010) is a superb oral history of Dem Bums. And I would be remiss if I did not mention my recently updated book on the Dodgers covering the team's time in Los Angeles, *The Dodgers: 60 Years in Los Angeles* (Sports Publishing, 2020).

Peter Jensen Brown's "The Grim Reality of the 'Trolley Dodgers'" (esnpc.blogspot.com/2014/04/the-grim-reality-of-trolley -dodgers.html) is simply a superb article on how the Dodgers got their nickname. In an equally fascinating article, John Thorn explains the origins of the 1927 Yankees getting the moniker Murderers' Row ("Why Were They Called Murderers' Row?"; (1927-the-diary-of-myles-thomas.espn.com/why-were-they -called-murderers-row-47cfd21c3be4).

Michael Leahy's book on the 1960s Dodgers, *The Last Innocents: The Collision of the Turbulent Sixties and the Los Angeles Dodgers* (Harper, 2016), is a captivating study on when Los Angeles could have ruled the baseball world and how it all fell apart. Michael Fallon's *Dodgerland: Decadent Los Angeles and the 1977–78 Dodgers* (University of Nebraska Press, 2016) is a great book on two Dodgers teams that came oh-so-close. In a similar vein, Jason Turbow has written a very good book on the 1981 Dodgers, *They Bled Blue: Fernandomania, Strike-Season Mayhem, and the Weirdest Championship Baseball Had Ever Seen: The 1981 Los Angeles Dodgers* (Houghton Mifflin Harcourt, 2019).